The Gallup Survey of Britain

THE GALLUP SURVEY OF BRITAIN

Gordon Heald and Robert J. Wybrow

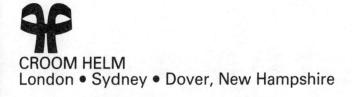

CROOM HELM
London • Sydney • Dover, New Hampshire

© 1986 Gallup
Croom Helm Ltd, Provident House, Burrell Row,
Beckenham, Kent BR3 1AT
Croom Helm Australia Pty Ltd, Suite 4, 6th Floor,
64-76 Kippax Street, Surry Hills, NSW 2010, Australia

British Library Cataloguing in Publication Data

Heald, Gordon
    The Gallup Survey of Britain
    1. Public opinion — Great Britain —
    History — 20th century
    I. Title   II. Wybrow, Robert J.
    303.3′8′0941   HN400.P8

    ISBN 0-7099-3846-2

Croom Helm, 51 Washington Street, Dover,
New Hampshire 03820, USA

Library of Congress Cataloging in Publication Data

The gallup survey of Britain, 1985.

    Includes index.
    1. Public opinion—Great Britain.   2. Great Britain—
politics and government—public opinion.   I. Heald,
Gordon. II. Wybrow, Robert. III. Gallup International, inc.
HN400.Z9P84   1986   303.3′8′0941   86-6327
ISBN 0-7099-3846-2

Typeset in 10pt Times Roman by Leaper & Gard Ltd, Bristol, England
Printed and bound in Great Britain
by Billing & Sons Limited, Worcester.

Contents

Foreword

For more than twenty-five years Gallup has appeared regularly in the *Daily Telegraph* and the *Sunday Telegraph*, and before that for almost as long in the *News Chronicle* until its demise. Despite monthly publication of its main political barometer questions and another dozen or more polls throughout the year, this is only the tip of the iceberg as far as the extensive file of data collected by Gallup is concerned. This volume of The Gallup Survey attempts to pull together these published findings plus the mass of questions that are not otherwise published except in Gallup's own monthly publication, the Gallup Political Index. The vast bulk of the earlier material covering 1937-1975 is also available in two bound volumes, providing the source for some of the long-term trends discussed in this book.

As far as possible, we have attempted to give the reader the actual wording of the questions asked and as much detail on the data as space permits, to enable readers to make their own judgements about the results. It should be borne in mind that, with a few specified exceptions, the material is based on nationally representative samples of approximately 1000 adults aged 18 and over. Analyses are available for all the questions by voting intention, sex, age, and socio-economic class, and we have tried to incorporate in the body of the text any significant differences in the replies across these groups. Where such analyses have not been given, but a reader is interested in them, we would be pleased to supply copies for a notional cost to cover the xeroxing.

We must also thank the more than one hundred thousand members of the British public who gave their time and views to Gallup interviewers throughout 1985. Without them none of this would have been possible. Finally our thanks to the four secretaries, Jean, Jo, Anne-Marie, and Julia, who persevered with the authors' scrawls on top of all the other work being done at the time.

Gordon Heald and Robert Wybrow   January 1986

1 The Year Begins

Despite George Orwell's horrific forecast about life in 1984, the year passed without the gloom and doom penned thirty-six years earlier. Not that the public took the completely opposite view. In a study conducted in December 1983 on the subject of Orwell's book and certain of its ideas, Gallup asked people to say how likely they thought it was that certain losses of freedom would take place or if these had already begun to occur. Majorities of the public thought that in Britain 'there is no real privacy because the government can learn anything it wants about you', that 'people are asked to make sacrifices, but government officials themselves live in luxury'. Fifty-nine per cent said that such things were already happening, while a further 57 per cent thought that 'the government uses false words and statistics to hide bad news about the economy and quality of life'. Almost two in five saw Britain as a place where 'poor people think their only chance of getting ahead in life is by winning a lottery'. Other material, contained in later chapters of this book, will shed more light on the public's views on poverty in contemporary Britain.

So four of the losses of freedom seen by Orwell were accepted as already happening by a substantial section of the British public. Yet some of his other pronouncements were less widely accepted. The idea that 'the country is ruled by a dictator' ('Big Sister', perhaps, rather than 'Big Brother') was agreed with by 16 per cent of the public, and 11 per cent thought that 'the government urges people to surrender freedom in order to gain greater security'. Fewer than one in ten accepted that 'the government urges citizens to hate people in other countries', 'the government says the only way we can have peace is by waging war', 'anybody who criticises the government is severely punished' or that 'the government hopes that someday all children will be produced by artificial insemination'. On these last four items, majorities of the public felt it was unlikely that such things would ever happen in Britain.

In the real world, in December 1984, the rush for British Telecom shares resulted in the issue being four times over subscribed. The following day, thousands were either killed or injured when a toxic gas leaked from an underground storage tank near Bhopal, India — and the British Goverment decided to oppose a European Commission directive to reduce sulphur dioxide and nitrogen oxide emissions from power stations in Britain. Later that month, an independent inspector recommended the development of Stansted as London's third airport and that a fifth terminal be built at Heathrow. Less than a week before Christmas 1984 the pound fell to a new low against the dollar of $1.1663, and then, in January, even further still to $1.1185, though confounding statements made by certain pundits concerning a par rate during 1985. In mid-January, for the first time since 1981, and against the Government's tenets on the subject of market forces, the Bank of England imposed a minimum lending rate of 12 per cent. By the end of the month British banks had raised their lending rates to 14 per cent, compared with an inflation rate of 4.6 per cent in December. Meanwhile, unemployment rose to a new high of more than 3.3 million, or almost 14 per cent of the workforce.

Politically, the Conservatives began the year six points ahead of Labour, continuing a run of good figures through the winter. Yet Mrs Thatcher's personal popularity was on the decline, close to its low since the 1983 election, and nine points down on her standing in January 1984. Mr Kinnock and Mr Steel were also in the popularity doldrums. Only that of Dr Owen remained significantly above his low point, though even his had slid seven points since the conference season.

Unemployment continued to dominate the public's list of the most urgent problems facing the country, as it had done for some time. In January the public could not decide which party was most capable of dealing with the problem, though two in three thought the Conservatives would win the next election. This was also thought to be the party with the best policies, the best leaders and — in Mrs Thatcher — the best prime minister: an auspicious start for the government as it moved towards the mid-term period.

The End-of-Year Poll

For almost 30 years Gallup has conducted a December poll on the public's view of the coming year. This has also been carried out in many of the major countries of the world where Gallup-affiliated companies operate. According to the public's predictions, 1985

Table 1.1: Prospects for the Coming Year

Q. *So far as you are concerned, do you think that 19— (next year) will be better or worse than 19— (this year)?*

	Better	Worse	Index
1957	39	6	+33
1958	35	7	+28
1959	46	6	+40
1960	40	14	+26
1961	38	18	+20
1962	34	30	+ 4
1963	54	7	+47
1964	39	24	+15
1965	42	21	+21
1966	27	38	−11
1967	22	48	−26
1968	22	41	−19
1969	40	17	+23
1970	27	42	−15
1971	42	28	+14
1972	39	31	+ 8
1973	25	46	−21
1974	14	64	−50
1975	31	35	− 4
1976	21	48	−27
1977	53	18	+35
1978	28	36	− 8
1979	16	66	−50
1980	20	58	−38
1981	30	40	−10
1982	39	28	+11
1983	36	34	+ 2
1984	37	33	+ 4

Note: The year indicated relates to the year in which the questions were asked. The results therefore relate to prospects in the coming year.

can be summarised as being a year that was expected to be no better nor worse overall than 1984 had been.

Although the proportion by which the optimists outnumbered the pessimists was small, one has to go back to the early 1960s to find a period of three consecutive 'optimistic' years, in marked contrast to the pessimism evident from the mid-1970s onwards.

Comparisons can also be made across a number of other countries in a slightly earlier poll. In Greece, Brazil, Argentina, the United States, Australia and South Korea, for example, majorities thought that 1985 would be better than 1984. Majorities in West

Germany, Austria, Finland and Norway, on the other hand, felt that 1985 would be a worse year.

Other questions asked in the end-of-year poll related to the economy, namely economic difficulty or prosperity, full employment or rising unemployment, an increase or decrease in industrial disputes, a rise or fall in prices and increases or cuts in taxation. Twenty years or so ago, the prices question had a meaning, but with the advent of the rise in oil prices and the inflation which became worldwide, price rises became so locked into the economic system that the question was no longer useful as in earlier years. For this reason it does not figure in the following table:

Table 1.2: The Economy in the Coming Year

Q. *Which of these do you think is likely to be true of 19—
   (next year)?*
   *A year of economic prosperity or a year of economic
   difficulty?*
   *A year of full employment or a year of rising
   unemployment?*
   *A year of strikes and industrial disputes or a year of
   industrial peace?*
   A year when taxes will rise or a year when taxes will fall?

	Economic difficulty	Rising unemployment	Strikes	Rising taxes
1957	NA	37	48	38
1958	NA	61	38	25
1959	NA	36	46	23
1960	51	61	52	55
1961	51	41	45	56
1962	43	66	31	33
1963	20	22	40	48
1964	51	22	34	75
1965	40	29	55	68
1966	65	69	53	60
1967	63	58	60	82
1968	71	62	69	73
1969	39	42	64	57
1970	60	61	70	40
1971	52	63	56	35
1972	54	49	64	57
1973	67	35	77	66
1974	85	80	80	78
1975	73	74	53	65
1976	77	69	47	74

1977	36	38	65	19
1978	52	51	65	46
1979	77	72	72	40
1980	74	77	47	67
1981	72	72	62	68
1982	55	62	37	28
1983	53	52	55	65
1984	53	60	48	35

The public, therefore, took a relatively pessimistic view of 1985 as far as the economic situation was concerned, except on the subject of taxation. Almost as many (31 per cent) expected taxes to fall during the year as expected them to rise (35 per cent). As for strikes — the so-called 'British disease' — these are by no means confined to this country alone. Majorities in, for example, Denmark, France, the Netherlands, Spain, Bolivia, Colombia, Peru, Uruguay and the Philippines plus a majority of whites in South Africa thought that 1985 would see more industrial unrest.

Prospects for the world as a whole were also thought to be less than promising. Two in five (42 per cent) of the British public felt that 1985 would be a troubled year, with much international discord. One in four (23 per cent) thought it would be a peaceful year more or less free of international disputes, while 35 per cent were undecided. This was an improvement on the previous six years, slightly above the average (20 per cent) for the 1970s, but below the average (28 per cent) for the 1960s.

In 30 countries, people were also asked how they rated the chances of a world war breaking out within the next decade. Judging by the proportions saying it was a worse than 50-50 chance, the public were reasonably optimistic. Yet there were exceptions to this view: Peru, for instance, topped the table, with 66 per cent of its general public putting the chances of a war at six in ten or worse. The proportions, on the same dimension, were as follows: 43 per cent in Colombia, 41 per cent in Bolivia, 33 per cent in Mexico and 28 per cent in the United States. This compared with an average throughout the EEC of only 13 per cent rating the chances of another world war at worse than 50-50.

Changes were also noted in these countries' views of the superpowers, the United States, Russia and China. Since 1957 Gallup has asked people whether American power in the world would increase or decline, posing a similar question about Russia; and in 1965, China was added to the suite of questions. During this period, with two exceptions, a plurality each year has expected the three countries' power in the world to increase. The notable exceptions were in 1973 and in 1974, the closing years of the war in Vietnam, when more people thought that America's power in the world would decline than saw it increasing. In the 1980s, however, the position has been reversed. Two in five (42 per cent), for example, thought American power in the world would increase in 1985, almost four times the number thinking it would decline. This compared with 38 per cent expecting an increase in China's power throughout the world, and 24 per cent — the lowest in almost 30 years — expecting Russia's power to increase.

New Year Resolutions

Little appears to have changed in almost 40 years as far as the British attitude towards New Year resolutions is concerned. In 1947, 26 per cent had made a resolution, and in 1985 23 per cent had done so. Perhaps surprisingly, there was not a gender gap on this question, but there was an age difference in the latest results: whereas 28 per cent of the under-35s had made a resolution, the proportion dropped to only 13 per cent among those aged 65 and over.

What is more, the most frequently mentioned resolution has not changed since 1947. Then, top of the list was cutting down on smoking, mentioned by 17 per cent, compared with 22 per cent in the 1985 study. In second place for 1985 was slimming or dieting — hardly a problem in the post-war years — mentioned by 21 per cent. Smoking topped the list among men (32 per cent), while women put dieting (33 per cent) at the top of theirs. We appear to have become slightly stronger-willed since the war, with 70 per cent of us claiming to have kept our resolutions compared with 62 per cent in 1947.

2 Domestic Politics

The Fortunes of the Parties in 1985

Appendix D gives details of the most closely watched Gallup statistics, the proportions who said how they would vote if an election were to be held 'tomorrow'. The pattern can be summarised very simply: overall, party support fluctuated quite sharply, more so than in 1984. The following table shows the average for each of the parties over the years and the monthly highs and lows in 1984 and 1985.

While the Conservatives were ahead of Labour in 1984, with the Alliance in a poor third place, it is obvious that the situation in 1985 became much more of a 'three-horse race'. The Conservatives had lost on average eight points, while the Alliance made gains of eight points. The volatility in support for the Conservatives and for the Alliance was significantly higher in 1985 than it had been the previous year. Alternatively, the degree of volatility in Labour's share remained very similar.

As has already been mentioned, the Conservatives began 1985 where they had been for most of 1984: in the lead, with a six-point advantage over Labour, and 13½-point advantage over the Liberal/SDP Alliance. They were still ahead in February, but both Labour and the Alliance were close behind. Mr Lawson's Budget was not well received, putting Labour into the lead, and the county

Table 2.1: Party Fortunes in 1984 and 1985

Q. If there were a general election tomorrow, which party would you support?

| | 1984 | | | 1985 | | |
	Average	High	Low	Average	High	Low
Conservative	40	44½	36	32	39	24
Labour	35½	39	30½	35	40	29½
Liberal/SDP	22½	27½	19½	30½	39	25½

elections pushed the Conservatives into third place. The Alliance's victory at Brecon and Radnor in July brought them more media publicity, helping to keep the Conservatives in third place; and in August, at 24 per cent, the Conservatives were only one point above their all-time post-war low. Yet from then on support for the Conservatives improved, and battle was joined between Labour and the Alliance to see who would take the lead. Labour was ahead in August, the Alliance took over in September, and Labour regained the lead in October. In December, all three parties were within half a point of one another — the closest they had ever been.

These figures, however, are those published in the *Daily Telegraph*, based on approximately 1,000 people who are usually interviewed around the second week in the month. Detailed analyses on a sample of this size are not particularly productive, and the figures will be especially susceptible to short-term effects, such as the Budget in the March figures and the SDP Conference in September. Because Gallup is polling most weeks of the year it is able to generate large samples of electors within a relatively short period of time: on average, around 8,000 in a month. This enables quite detailed demographic analyses of the data to be performed and gives the capability of looking at shifts in voting patterns by type of constituency. The following table shows the best and worst months overall for each of the parties compared with a similar cumulative sample in July 1983, which, as shown, was very similar to the actual election results of the previous month.

It is obvious that even in their best month, January, the Conservatives still fell short of their share of the votes at the 1983 general election, and at their worst were almost twenty points adrift. Labour, on the other hand, were consistently above their disastrous 1983 level, though not by much in September. The Alliance's peak and nadir straddled their 1983 performance, but their September share was significantly better than what they had achieved in the election.

Let us first look in detail at the Conservatives. In none of the groups itemised in Table 2.2 did they achieve their 1983 share of votes. Overall, they held on to 86 per cent of their 1983 support in their best month, January. Their loss was greatest among young adults, aged 18–34, and in trade-union households, where they only retained 80 per cent of their 1983 support. At their low point,

Table 2.2: The Ups and Downs of the Parties in 1985

| | Conservative | | | Labour | | | Alliance | | |
	July 1983	High Jan	Low Aug	July 1983	High April	Low Sept	July 1983	High Sept	Low April
Nation	44.0	37.7	26.9	27.7	38.5	31.4	26.9	38.1	25.7
Men	43.5	37.0	25.9	30.0	39.2	32.5	24.9	36.8	24.4
Women	44.4	38.3	28.0	25.6	37.8	30.3	28.9	39.3	27.0
18–24	42.5	34.1	24.2	27.6	44.7	37.7	27.9	34.2	20.6
25–34	43.2	35.3	27.1	27.3	38.1	32.9	28.1	38.2	28.3
18–34	42.9	34.7	25.7	27.5	41.3	35.2	28.0	36.3	24.6
35–44	45.7	39.8	25.1	22.5	34.7	29.6	30.3	40.7	27.5
45–64	43.4	37.9	28.2	29.1	37.8	29.5	26.1	38.4	27.0
65+	45.3	41.4	28.9	30.9	38.1	29.0	23.1	38.3	23.9
AB	60.9	52.7	40.8	10.9	18.2	14.9	27.7	40.7	29.9
C1	54.5	46.4	33.3	14.9	26.5	22.0	29.5	41.3	29.5
ABC1	57.2	49.1	36.5	13.3	23.0	18.9	28.7	41.1	29.7
C2	40.3	34.0	21.7	31.3	43.2	35.5	26.7	37.4	24.5
DE	30.8	26.3	19.8	42.6	54.0	43.8	24.9	34.8	21.8
C2DE	35.8	30.2	20.8	36.7	48.5	39.6	25.8	36.1	23.2
Home owners	53.2	44.8	33.0	18.8	28.9	23.8	27.3	40.4	28.4
Council tenants	25.0	21.9	15.1	46.1	58.3	48.5	26.3	32.7	19.9
Trade-union households	35.2	27.9	17.3	32.8	45.2	39.2	30.5	39.5	27.6
Unemployed persons	25.5	22.8	17.7	47.9	58.0	45.5	23.7	34.0	20.7

Comparison	June result	July poll
Conservative	43.5	44.0
Labour	28.3	27.7
Alliance	26.0	26.9

in August, they were down to 61 per cent of their 1983 share. The 18–24 age group, in particular, were deserting the Conservatives at this time, along with C2s (the market research industry's classification for skilled manual workers) and people in trade-union households. Labour, on the other hand, in their worst month, September, were still 13 per cent up on their election support and 39 per cent in their best month, April. Even this improvement, however, would not be enough to give Labour the seats it needed to form a majority government. We shall therefore concentrate on this 'best option' level. In contrast to the Conservatives, where the decline in support had been relatively uniform between men and women, Labour's increased support among women (a rise of 48 per cent) was significantly higher than it had been among men (a rise of 31 per cent). Though where support for the Conservatives had shown the greatest decline — among young adults — Labour did much better than average; among the under 25s they attained 162 per cent of the 1983 support, compared with 123 per cent among those aged 65 and over. Paradoxically, Labour's best improvement in the social classes came in the non-manual group, where it is less likely to do any good: among this middle-class group, Labour's share improved by 73 per cent compared to 38 per cent among the skilled manual worker's group. Similarly, Labour did better among homeowners (a rise of 54 per cent) than among council tenants, its traditional supporters, where it achieved a mere 26 per cent improvement. And although its share of support among trade-union households and the unemployed had increased, this was only an average improvement among the former group and a below-average one among the latter.

The Alliance had a problem similar to Labour's in terms of its best result in 1985: 38 per cent support was not really enough to put it into power with an absolute majority, though it would, of course, pick up substantially more seats than it had in 1983. Overall, the Alliance's share in September, its best month, corresponded to an index of 142 compared with the July 1983 figures. Thus, they were doing just slightly better than Labour. In contrast to both the Conservatives and Labour, the Alliance did better among men (up to 48 per cent) than it did among women (up by 36 per cent). The age pattern shows a fairly static level of support, but comparisons with 1983 show an above-average improvement among people aged 65 or over of 66 per cent. Analysis by social class revealed no significant improvements above the norm, though the improvement among home-owners was slightly above average and the improvement among council tenants below average.

These, then, were just some of the findings from the detailed monthly analyses, amounting to over a hundred pages of computer printout consisting in the main of demographic tabulations but including a number of analyses by constituency type. In order to illustrate some of the shifts in party support since 1983, it may be useful to look at the details in May, when Labour had 34.0 per cent over the month as a whole, the Alliance had 32.2 per cent, and the Conservatives 31.8 per cent — all three levels being very similar to the 1985 average. Politically, the country could be said to be 'Two Nations' after the 1983 election, with the Conservatives dominating the southern half of the country and Labour ahead in the northern half. In May, the Conservatives were barely ahead of the Alliance in the south, and Labour had pulled even further ahead in the north.

In the Conservative-held seats where Labour had been in second

Table 2.3: The 'Two Nations'

Q. If there were a general election tomorrow, which party would you support?

	South/Midlands		Wales/North/Scotland	
	June 1983	May 1985	June 1983	May 1985
Conservatives	49.4	37.1	35.1	24.1
Labour	22.6	27.2	36.4	43.9
Alliance	27.2	35.0	24.3	28.2
Other	0.8	0.7	4.1	3.8

place in 1983 — 13 per cent behind — the positions had been partially reversed by May. Labour had gone into a five-point lead over the Conservatives, with the Alliance a close third. In the Conservative-held seats where the Alliance had come second in 1983, the Conservatives' share had fallen from 54 per cent to 36 per cent, just one per cent ahead of the Alliance (35 per cent) with Labour at 27 per cent. In the third major grouping of seats — Labour-held with the Conservatives as runners-up — the former's share of the votes remained static at 46 per cent, while the Conservatives' had dropped from 31 per cent to 24 per cent and that of the Alliance had risen seven points to 28 per cent. An entirely separate group that was also analysed were seats where the Alliance had come second in 1983 with 30 per cent or more of the votes. In these seats in 1983, the Conservatives were the major party with 51 per cent, ahead of the Alliance with 33 per cent and Labour, poorly placed with 14 per cent. In May, the figures were 36 per cent, 36 per cent and 27 per cent respectively. Thus support for the Alliance had remained fairly static in these seats, while that for the Conservatives had fallen by 15 per cent and Labour had gained 13 per cent.

Finally, with an eye on the next election, Gallup had been following Labour's performance in its target seats: the chosen seats that it must win to stand any chance of regaining power and where special efforts would be made to this end. The following table shows the position in these seats in the 1983 general election compared with a cumulated analysis of 28,159 interviews conducted across the country from September to November.

Table 2.4: Labour's Target Seats

Q. *If there were a general election tomorrow, which party would you support?*

	June 1983	Sept-Nov 1985	Difference
Conservatives	41.9	30.7	−11.2
Labour	32.0	36.5	+ 4.5
Alliance	24.4	30.9	+ 6.5
Other	1.8	2.1	+ 0.3

Although Labour had increased their share in these seats by 4.5 per cent, the Alliance had done even better, increasing their share by 6.5 per cent. This is in contrast to the national situation for the same period, where support for Labour had gone up by 5.9 per cent and that for the Alliance by 5.7 per cent. Thus Labour were doing slightly worse in their target seats in the autumn than they were nationally, while the Alliance was doing slightly better.

Closeness to Party

In addition to the standard questions on how people would vote if there were a general election 'tomorrow', Gallup also asks people to recall how they voted in the 1983 general election, and how close — if at all — they feel to any of the three main party groupings. Logically, the replies to the first of these two questions should be very similar to the 1983 results after certain alterations in the electorate — the inclusion of new voters, or deaths — have been taken into account and some allowance has been made for memory distortion due to the passage of time. What actually occurs is distantly removed from this logic, as the following table shows:

Table 2.5: Voting Recall in the 1983 General Election

Q. Were you able to go and vote in the general election in June 1983, or were you prevented? If voted: *For which party did you vote? (Quarterly averages. Figures are share of votes for the three main parties to enable comparison with the 1983 result.)*

	Conservative	Labour	Alliance
1983 result	43.5	28.3	26.0
1983 Q3	44.5	29.0	25.0
Q4	45.7	32.5	20.0
1984 Q1	44.8	34.9	18.7
Q2	43.7	35.5	19.2
Q3	43.4	36.1	18.2
Q4	45.3	33.7	19.2
1985 Q1	44.6	35.4	18.3
Q2	43.5	36.6	18.0
Q3	41.7	37.3	19.0
Q4	44.0	36.3	18.2

It is fairly obvious that at least three quite distinct patterns emerge from the above figures. The first is the consistently similar 'recall' to the 1983 share of votes for the Conservative Party, exceeded in the last quarter of 1983 by two points and being two points down in the third quarter of 1985. This is in marked contrast to the substantial shifts of support in the 'election tomorrow' question, though the two sets of figures, when charted, show similar peaks and troughs. The figures for Labour, on the other hand, take on a completely different pattern, bearing no relationship to the 1983 results with the exception of the first few months following the election. From then on the recall figures follow very closely the pattern of replies to the standard voting question, as though the person questioned were undergoing some form of internal rationalisation process. The results for the Alliance form yet another different pattern. By the end of 1983, recall of voting for the Liberals or the SDP had fallen to 20 per cent and failed to do better than that over the next two years, tending to wobble around the 18 or 19 per cent mark — well below their 1983 share. While this static position emerged, their level of support in the 'tomorrow' question went from almost 30 per cent in the summer of 1983 to less than 20 per cent in the following winter, and then slowly recovered to almost 40 per cent in the summer of 1985. Thus we have three quite distinct phenomena. Traditional theories suggested that voting recall tended to move in sequence with current voting intentions — and God help anyone who obtained 'inaccurate' recall data and tried to correct for it! Perhaps this is an instance of the way in which the Alliance has broken the political mould, and new theories will now have to be propounded.

One line of thought is related to the second question Gallup now asks, which had previously been discontinued. There is no doubt that Alliance supporters tend to have a looser attachment to their party than do either Conservatives or Labourites. This is illustrated by the following table showing the replies for August 1982 (when the question was discontinued) compared with September 1985 (when it was reinstated).

Table 2.6: Party Affinity

Q. *Do you consider yourself to be close to any particular party?* If yes: *Do you feel yourself to be very close to this party, fairly close or merely a sympathiser?*

	August 1982			September 1985		
	Con	Lab	Lib/SDP	Con	Lab	Lib/SDP
Very close	10.6	13.2	5.6	7.7	9.8	3.0
Fairly close	26.0	25.4	15.2	20.0	21.0	9.4
Merely a sympathiser	22.1	20.0	19.0	17.7	17.8	15.2
Not close to any party	40.5	40.0	59.3	54.0	50.9	71.5

Thus in both the 1982 and 1985 studies, the proportion saying they were close to a party was slightly higher among Labour supporters than among Conservatives, and in the case of Alliance supporters significantly lower still. There had also been a significant increase for each of the three party groups in the proportion saying they were not close to any party. There is, however, yet another comparison that can be made between the 1982 and 1985 results. Taking the proportions saying they were either 'very close' or 'fairly close' to a party, Labour had held on to 80 per cent (30.8 as a percentage of 38.6) of their supporters, while the Conservatives had held on to 75 per cent and the Alliance on to only 60 per cent.

The Election Winners

Although there were significant variations in the public's voting intentions over the two-and-a-half years since the 1983 general election, the public always opted for the Conservatives as the winners of the next election. As can be seen from columns 11 and 12 of Appendix D, only in August 1985 did Labour succeed in closing the gap between themselves and the Conservatives; otherwise the Conservatives were ahead by up to 50 per cent.

Table 2.7: The Next Election

Q. Irrespective of how you yourself will vote, who do you think will win the next general election? (Quarterly averages)

		Conservative	Labour
1983:	Q1	63	16
	Q2	74	12
	Q3	56	13
	Q4	50	27
1984:	Q1	56	27
	Q2	50	30
	Q3	49	31
	Q4	66	17
1985:	Q1	60	21
	Q2	48	28
	Q3	37	28
	Q4	44	26

The public have had a pretty good track record so far in forecasting who would win the elections, starting with Labour in 1945. In 1970, they — in company with most of the polls — thought Labour would win again, but they got it wrong.

They were back on course in February 1974, getting the subsequent election result correct in October, at the 1979 election and finally in 1983. One word of warning, however: from the end of 1979, through 1980, 1981 and the early part of 1982, Labour was the public's choice as winner of the next election — almost three years after the 1979 election. And yet just over a year later, the Conservatives romped home in the 1983 general election.

The Best Party

In addition to the standard question on voting in a 'general election tomorrow', Gallup asked a number of others on where the parties stood in public esteem. For example, after saying what they thought was the most urgent problem facing the country, people would be asked which party was best able to tackle that problem. As the following table shows, Labour and the Conservatives were within a few points of each other in January and February, with the Alliance adrift in third place. From March through the rest of the year, Labour went into a significant lead over the Conservatives, to be approached only once, by the Alliance, in September. (This was almost certainly an 'artificial' figure for the Liberals and the SDP brought about by the timing of their party conferences.)

Table 2.8: The Best Party for Problem-Solving

Q. Which party do you think can best handle that problem (the most urgent problem facing the country)?

	Conservative	Labour	Alliance
January	26	28	16
February	24	27	15
March	22	36	15
April	22	33	13
May	20	33	17
June	25	32	17
July	19	35	19
August	15	36	18
September	19	25	22
October	23	31	15
November	24	30	15
December	23	30	17

Thus, throughout the year, Labour were on average ten points ahead of the Conservatives on this question — before the one in three 'undecided' were excluded — compared with a lead of a little over three points in voting support terms. Labour's historical image of being the best party to handle the problem of unemployment was not paying off for them in electoral popularity, despite the public's obvious concern about the lack of jobs.

On the wider issues of general policies and leadership, the Conservatives were well placed for most of the year, particularly on the latter. As will be seen later, it was the Alliance who presented more of a threat to the Conservatives on the question of leadership.

Table 2.9: The Party with the Best Policies

Q. *Taking everything into account, which party has the best policies?*

	Conservative	Labour	Alliance
January	34	27	20
February	36	25	22
March	29	33	21
April	32	30	20
May	30	27	27
June	32	28	23
July	27	31	23
August	25	34	25
September	28	23	29
October	28	31	21
November	32	28	19
December	31	26	24

The Conservatives were in the lead for seven months of the year, Labour was ahead in four months, and the Alliance once — in September. For the Conservatives, the year was one of decline until August, when only one in four of the general public thought that they had the best policies overall. September saw a modest improvement, which was maintained for the remainder of the year. Labour's fortunes fluctuated just as much, peaking at 33 per cent in March, falling back, then peaking again in August at 34 per cent, only to fall eleven points in a month in the run-up to the party conferences.

Mention has already been made elsewhere of the public's lack of enthusiasm for Labour's leaders over the last few years, although Mr Kinnock did considerably better than Mr Foot had done. Yet despite this improvement, an average of only 22 per cent of the public throughout 1985 thought that Labour had the best leaders. This compared with 39 per cent for the Conservatives and 26 per cent for the Alliance.

As can be seen, the Conservatives led on this question for most of the year, with the exceptions of July and September when the Alliance moved ahead by a narrow, insignificant single point. However, this did serve to emphasise the Alliance's need for media exposure, as the July improvement was a function of the Alliance's success in the Brecon and Radnor by-election, while September's

Table 2.10: The Party with the Best Leaders

Q. Taking everything into account, which party has the best leaders?

	Conservative	Labour	Alliance
January	45	20	22
February	43	18	25
March	41	22	23
April	44	23	20
May	39	19	28
June	41	22	25
July	32	22	33
August	33	23	31
September	34	17	35
October	37	26	21
November	39	26	23
December	42	22	23

reflected the good conference performance by Dr David Owen in particular.

Labour, however, did slightly better on a question about the party leaders and their prime ministerial potential. Yet the Conservatives, in the form of Mrs Thatcher, still tended to dominate the replies to the question:

Table 2.11: The Best Prime Minister

Q. Who would make the best prime minister: Mrs Thatcher, Mr Kinnock, Mr Steel or Dr Owen?

	Thatcher	Kinnock	Steel	Owen
January	35	22	16	17
February	33	20	17	19
March	32	25	18	16
April	34	23	15	19
May	32	22	18	18
June	34	22	21	15
July	27	24	21	19
August	25	25	22	16
September	27	18	19	24
October	30	29	16	14
November	31	27	15	16
December	33	24	17	15

Mrs Thatcher, perhaps with the incumbent's built-in advantage, topped the table every month, though Mr Kinnock tied with her in August. Mrs Thatcher's lead over Mr Kinnock on this question was eight points, and he in turn was ahead of the two Alliance leaders for most of the year. However, if the scores for David Steel and David Owen are combined, their average throughout the year was 35 compared to 31 for Mrs Thatcher and 23 for Mr Kinnock.

In December, an additional six specific dimensions were added:

Table 2.12: The Best Leader

Q. Thinking of these four party leaders, which one do you think would be the one ...?

	Thatcher	Kinnock	Steel	Owen
Most able to unite the nation	27	23	14	15
Most likely to get things done	44	25	12	9
Most likely to improve Britain's standing abroad	42	19	9	12
With most concern for all groups in society	15	34	19	17
Who would get the most out of a team	34	23	14	13
Most in touch with ordinary people's problems	11	42	17	14

As can be seen, Mrs Thatcher had a substantial advantage in three of the items, plus a less significant one in a fourth, but did poorly in the two dealing with the 'common touch' items — a long-standing criticism. In sharp contrast with the nine in ten Conservatives thinking Mrs Thatcher would be the best for getting things done and for Britain's standing abroad, less than one in two (47 per cent) thought she had most concern for all groups in society, while even fewer (35 per cent) saw her as being most in touch. Among Labour supporters, the lowest mention for Mr Kinnock (53 per cent) came on the item of Britain's standing abroad.

Gallup also asks every month — and has done so since 1984 — a battery of questions asking people which party they thought had the best policies to deal with eight items. The following table shows the 1985 quarterly averages for each of these items, with comparisons for June 1983:

Table 2.13: The Best Party on Issues

Q. Which party do you think has the best policies to deal with:

	June 1983	Q1 1985	Q2 1985	Q3 1985	Q4 1985
a) Inflation and prices					
Conservative	53	44	42	37	42
Labour	19	24	25	25	24
Alliance	13	11	13	15	13
b) Unemployment					
Conservative	32	18	17	15	18
Labour	32	42	43	41	40
Alliance	19	15	16	20	16
c) Britain's defence					
Conservative	53	48	46	43	46
Labour	17	22	23	21	21
Alliance	17	11	12	15	12
d) Common Market					
Conservative	47	39	39	34	38
Labour	21	23	25	23	21
Alliance	16	11	12	13	11
e) Strikes and industrial disputes					
Conservative	47	37	43	37	42
Labour	25	33	30	30	29
Alliance	14	12	12	14	11
f) National Health Service					
Conservative	28	17	16	15	16
Labour	38	51	50	49	48
Alliance	18	14	14	18	15
g) Education and Schools					
Conservative	36	24	23	20	22
Labour	31	42	42	40	39
Alliance	18	14	17	20	17
h) Law and Order					
Conservative	48	50	45	42	45
Labour	19	21	23	21	21
Alliance	13	9	10	13	11

The table shows the Conservatives dominating five of the issues in 1983: inflation, defence, the Common Market, strikes, and law and order. On the other hand, Labour was ahead on the National Health Service, while there was little dividing the two main parties on the remaining items. Throughout 1985, the Conservatives continued to be in the lead on inflation, the Common Market, and law and order. On the issues of strikes and industrial disputes, they were still the public's top party in the spring of 1984; but as the miners' strike showed no sign of being resolved Labour went into the lead for four months, from June to September. By October 1984 the Conservatives were back ahead of Labour and retained that position throughout 1985. Labour held onto its advantage as the party with the best policies to handle the National Health Service, and by the early part of 1984 was also thought to be the best party to handle the problem of unemployment and education. One can also see a gradual improvement for the Alliance throughout 1985 on all the issues, so that by the third quarter they were ahead of the Conservatives on unemployment and the National Health Service.

The Left–Right Scale

In September, people were asked to place themselves, as well as the four parties, on a left–right scale. The replies, compared with those of November 1980, are shown in the following table:

Table 2.14: Left–Right Scale — Self-Perception

Q. In political matters, people talk of 'the left' and 'the right'. How would you place your views on this scale?

	Public		Conservatives		Labour	
	Nov 1980	Sept 1985	Nov 1980	Sept 1985	Nov 1980	Sept 1985
Far/substantially left	5	5	1	0	8	11
Moderately/slightly left	22	23	4	6	37	35
All left	27	28	5	6	45	46
Middle-of-the-road	9	11	5	7	8	12
Moderately/slightly right	39	37	60	57	21	18
Far/substantially right	9	7	20	16	3	5
All right	48	44	80	73	24	23
Don't know	17	17	10	14	22	20

Thus, over the five-year period, little had changed for the public as a whole or for supporters of either the Conservative or Labour parties. There were still definite differences between Conservatives and Labour supporters. Conservative views were more clear-cut:

they saw themselves in the main as right-wing. On the other hand, Labour supporters' rating of themselves spread across the whole left–right spectrum. Further, the number of 'don't knows' among Labour supporters was around double that among Conservatives.

Table 2.15: Unity Index

Q. Do you think that the ... Party is united or divided at the present time? (Index is percentage 'united' minus percentage 'divided'.)

	1983		1984		1985	
	Con	Lab	Con	Lab	Con	Lab
January	+49	−70	+45	−33	+11	−60
February	+41	−70	+23	−26	+10	−63
March	+59	−75	+22	−16	+ 6	−46
April	+55	−54	+16	−27	+ 8	−48
May	+55	−58	+28	−27	− 1	−44
June	+59	−65	+19	−31	− 6	−42
July	+56	−76	0	−22	− 2	−52
August	+59	−84	+13	−40	− 8	−49
September	+56	−85	+21	−32	+ 8	−52
October	+36	−27	+48	−55	+18	−49
November	+37	−23	+45	−52	+20	−51
December	+27	−19	+ 5	−64	+29	−61

Table 2.16: The Favoured Parties

Q. Regardless of your personal opinion, do you think that most people in Britain are holding a favourable opinion of the ... Party, or don't you think so? (Figures show percentage saying 'yes'.)

		Lab	Con	SDP	Lib
1983					
	January	23	49	24	28
	February	25	50	19	27
	March	18	47	44	42
	April	27	47	25	31
	May	25	58	20	30
	June	17	62	36	38
	July	16	68	34	44
	August	13	62	38	42
	September	14	67	38	38
	October	29	59	32	38
	November	28	54	25	34
	December	33	50	27	30

1984

January	28	57	23	29
February	31	53	24	30
March	37	46	30	34
April	33	47	26	32
May	34	44	34	38
June	33	39	31	33
July	36	36	35	33
August	32	37	31	33
September	30	40	29	30
October	25	52	30	28
November	23	54	29	28
December	20	44	31	31

1985

January	23	46	36	36
February	21	41	34	31
March	32	34	31	32
April	33	34	31	32
May	29	29	49	46
June	33	30	44	44
July	30	25	49	48
August	35	20	47	44
September	28	28	47	43
October	36	29	41	39
November	33	33	39	37
December	29	32	45	42

The Conservative Party

As in 1984, the Conservatives went into 1985 with a lead over both Labour and the Alliance, although in 1984 the advantage had been slimmer. January 1985 saw the Conservatives six points ahead of Labour and $13\frac{1}{2}$ points ahead of the Alliance compared with three and a half and 22 points respectively a year earlier. But as has been mentioned elsewhere, this lead was soon reversed. In contrast to the Labour Party, the Conservatives have tended to project an image of unity over the years; though even this image was badly dented in 1985. For the first time in the last three years, the unity index (Table 2.15) went negative and remained so for four consecutive months throughout the summer, before reversing to positive scores. This was matched by a decline in the proportion of the public who saw the party as being 'popular' (Table 2.16).

The table shows almost one in two of the public in January thinking that the party was popular, ten points above the two Alliance parties and with twice the number of points for Labour.

They were still ahead in February, but by March — with Nigel Lawson's unpopular Budget — all four parties were perceived as being equal in popularity. The decline continued, so that in August only 20 per cent of the public thought the Conservatives were a popular party; but then a modest revival occurred towards the end of the year.

Throughout the year, Gallup were also asking an image battery of statements about the Conservative Party, dating back to shortly after the 1983 general election. The results to this series show strong, stable and negative attitudes as well as a number of changing ones (Table 2.17).

The two strongest attitudes of the nine tested dealt with the leadership of the party and with its policies on social services expenditure. One of Mrs Thatcher's most enduring characteristics has been the strength of her personality, but even here the public's perception of the party as having strong leadership was on the decline. For instance, in 1983 the average of those saying 'the Conservatives provide strong leadership' was 81 per cent, dropping to 76 per cent in 1984 and to 74 per cent in 1985. On the other hand, despite the protestations of government ministers that there were no cutbacks in the social services and that in fact more was being spent in this area, an increasingly large proportion of the public felt that the Conservatives were involved in unacceptable cutbacks in the social services. From an average of 77 per cent in both 1983 and 1984, the average rose to 82 per cent in 1985.

In fact, on all the items, with the possible exception of one, the shift in opinion was in a negative direction. The exception concerned the statement 'The Conservatives are the only party that can control the unions.' Over the three years as a whole, the figures have averaged around the low 40 per cent mark, rising in the short term to 49 per cent in the winter of 1983/84, falling back to 38 per cent in the summer of 1984 when the miners' dispute appeared insoluble, and then increasing again once the dispute was ended. On the other hand, the remaining statements all showed shifts in the annual averages in a range of eight to ten points — either increases or decreases, but always unfavourable to the government. More people, for example, took the view that 'Causing unemployment to rise is not an acceptable way to deal with inflation', while fewer agreed that 'The Conservative Party has kept its election promises.'

In December, Gallup asked three questions about each of the

Table 2.17: Image of the Conservative Party

Q. Now let's turn to the Conservative Party. Please tell me whether you agree or disagree with these things:

	Aug 1983	Oct 1983	Nov 1983	Jan 1984	May 1984	Aug 1984	Sept 1984	Jan 1985	Apr 1985	Aug 1985	Sept 1985
The Conservatives are too rigid and inflexible	65	64	71	64	70	71	71	76	73	78	71
The Conservatives are the only party that can control the unions	46	44	49	49	40	38	38	41	49	43	42
The Conservatives provide strong leadership	85	79	80	80	78	74	70	79	77	73	66
The Conservatives don't care what hardships their policies cause	58	57	58	59	59	63	60	64	65	70	66
The Conservative Party has kept its election promises	35	30	33	30	29	29	28	25	25	21	20
The Conservatives have failed to solve Britain's most important problems	63	59	64	63	64	67	66	74	71	75	67
The Conservatives look after the interests of the rich, not of ordinary people	59	61	57	61	65	63	64	64	66	74	71
The Conservatives want to cut back too much on health, education and other services	75	78	78	78	75	75	79	82	81	85	80
Causing unemployment to rise is not an acceptable way of dealing with inflation	69	67	67	68	73	70	71	77	73	77	77

three parties: their tendency to extremism, their impartiality and their policies. In summary, the Conservative Party was seen as an extreme party, looking after one class only, but with clear policies. One in two (52 per cent) of the public thought the Conservative Party was an extreme party, while 30 per cent thought it was a moderate party. Although a majority (59 per cent) of Conservatives saw their party as moderate, 28 per cent thought it was extreme. Similarly, two in three (69 per cent) of the general public thought the party was good for one class only, and 22 per cent thought it was good for all clasees. Again, a majority (62 per cent) of Conservatives thought their party was good for all classes, but a substantial minority (27 per cent) were critical. On the other hand, two in three (65 per cent) of the general public — including 90 per cent of Conservatives — thought the party had clear policies — in contrast to the other two parties. Just over one in five (22 per cent) thought the Conservative Party had vague policies.

Media Impact

The apparent volatility of public opinion as measured by the polls is partly a function of sampling fluctuations but even more a function of people changing or adapting their points of view as they receive more information from a variety of sources, the most important of which is the media, television in particular. Gallup had experimented in the past with the idea of what events could change peoples' attitudes, and it returned to the topic in late March. Quite simply, people were asked whether they had seen or heard anything over the previous seven days that had made them feel more favourably or less favourably inclined towards the Conservative Party. In the first survey, 9 per cent said something had happened to make them feel more favourably towards the Conservatives, while 31 per cent said they had become less favourably inclined towards them. As it happened, the Budget dominated the replies given by both groups of people regardless of whether they had become more favourably or less favourably inclined towards the party.

The questions were continued throughout April and the first half of May. The proportion saying they had become more favourably inclined towards the Conservatives ranged between 3 and 7 per cent over the period in question, while the proportion becoming less favourably inclined started at around one in three and fell to a little under one in four. At the end of March, general policies, the Budget, unemployment and price increases, were the four main reasons given for having a less favourable attitude towards the Conservatives. In early April Mrs Thatcher began an eleven-day tour of Asia, and her remarks while on the trip dominated the list of reasons given in mid-April, to be replaced by the government's social security policy at the end of the month and early May.

Mrs Thatcher

In 1985 Mrs Thatcher celebrated ten years as leader of the Conservative Party and, at the end of the party's annual conference in Blackpool, her sixtieth birthday. In December 1981, when support for both the Conservative and Labour Parties fell to a post-war low point and support for the Alliance reached 50½ per cent, Mrs Thatcher's personal popularity stood at 25 per cent, making her the least popular prime minister since the war. Within six months, however, the public's rating of her had doubled following the Falklands War. Her personal popularity was somewhat on the wane in 1985, after peaking at 50 per cent in October 1984. The proportion satisfied with Mrs Thatcher's performance as prime minister began the year at 40 per cent — a ten-point drop since the previous October — and continued to decline to a low point in August of 30 per cent, itself the lowest since the Falklands War. Table 2.18 shows comparisons with her predecessors for the last forty years.

Table 2.18: Prime Ministers' Popularity 1945–1985

Q. Are you satisfied or dissatisfied with ... as prime minister?

	High	Low	Average
Government:			
1945–51 Labour			
Attlee (Aug 1945–Sept 1951)	66	37	47
1951–55 Conservative			
Churchill (Dec 1951–Jan 1956)	56	48	52
Eden (April/May 1955)	73	71	72
1955–59 Conservative			
Eden (July 1955 –Dec 1956)	70	41	55
Macmillan (Feb 1957–Aug 1959)	67	30	50
1959–64 Conservative			
Macmillan (Feb1960–Oct 1963)	79	35	52
Home (Nov 1963–Sept 1964)	48	42	45

Table 2.18 continued

1964–66 Labour Wilson (Nov 1964–Feb 1966)	66	48	59
1966–70 Labour Wilson (Apr1966–June 1970)	69	27	41
1970–74 Conservative Heath (Sept 1970–Feb 1974)	45	31	37

1974–79 Labour
  Wilson (Apr 1974–Mar 1976)
  Callaghan (Apr 1976–Apr 1979)
	53
	59
		40
		33
			46
			46

1979–83 Conservative Thatcher (June 1979–June 1983)	52	25	39
1983— Conservative Thatcher (July 1983–Dec 1985)	53	30	42

But that was only one measure of the public's attitude towards Mrs Thatcher. In July 1975, people were shown a list of twelve statements and asked to say which of them they felt was true of the four party leaders. The replies concerning Mrs Thatcher are compared in the following table with those concerning her predecessor, Edward Heath, in April 1968 and the then prime minister, Harold Wilson:

Table 2.19: Mrs Thatcher's Image

Q. Which of these statements would you say are true of Mrs Thatcher?

	Thatcher	Heath	Wilson
She shows no sympathy for ordinary people	58	16	22
You can't trust what she says	40	13	48
I wouldn't want to have her as a friend	36	13	20
I don't find her interesting on TV	24	27	20
She doesn't stand for the party's traditional policies	19	9	26
Newspaper stories about her are dull	15	19	14
She doesn't seem to have any real friends	14	8	15

She doesn't give a clear lead to her party	13	27	23
She never says anything of importance	11	16	12
She doesn't seem a big enough woman for the job	9	30	26
She never does anything of importance	9	21	15
She doesn't seem to be particularly clever	7	12	13
None of these	20	18	14

As can be seen, the public held differing images of the three leaders. 'Lack of sympathy' topped the list for Mrs Thatcher, followed by 'untrustworthy' and 'not a person people would want as a friend'. For Edward Heath, the top three were to do with a dull, 'little man' personality, while lack of trust was what dominated the public's view of Harold Wilson 17 years ago.

The image of Mrs Thatcher as being unsympathetic is mirrored in the replies to a much more detailed image study conducted periodically since 1977. The figures in the following table are the proportions agreeing with each of the statements. One other statement, 'I prefer Mr Heath', asked from October 1977 to April 1981, has been deleted from the table.

Table 2.20: Mrs Thatcher's Image

Q. Here are some things people have said about Mrs Thatcher. For each of them, would you tell me whether you agree or disagree?

	Oct 1977	April 1978	April 1979	April 1981	May 1983	July 1984	Jan 1985	Positive/ negative shifts
She is a strong personality	84	80	79	91	94	95	95	+11
She speaks her mind	83	82	81	85	90	89	91	+ 8
She is a good speaker	81	74	75	80	83	83	83	+ 2

Table 2.20 continued

She's trying hard at her job	91	90	93	81	86	81	82	− 9
She's not in touch with the working class/ordinary people	54	56	52	73	63	73	74	−20
She thinks a lot of herself	59	62	54	67	68	72	73	−14
She divides the country	31	40	37	70	60	67	71	−40
She knows what she is talking about	70	67	75	55	66	63	65	− 5
She is a snob, talks down to people	40	43	37	50	52	58	57	−17
Her ideas are destructive, not constructive	23	30	25	57	42	47	50	−27
She talks a lot but doesn't do much	47	51	39	53	42	47	49	− 2
She knows about the problems of the cost of living	64	63	73	44	49	43	43	−21
She has good or new ideas	55	53	58	41	48	40	40	−15
It's time we had a woman in power	37	32	36	32	39	39	40	+ 3
She doesn't come over well	43	45	46	49	35	44	39	− 4
She is too critical of Russia	32	29	28	45	37	41	39	− 7
She's catty/bitchy	32	37	29	34	37	35	37	− 5
I don't like women leaders	28	31	29	21	17	19	16	+12

The final column, headed 'Positive/negative shifts', is simply the difference between the October 1977 study and the January 1985 repeat, where a plus sign indicates an increase in agreement with a positive statement or a decline in agreement with a negative statement and a minus sign indicates the reverse.

Of interest are not only the shifts in attitudes over the eight-year period but their effect on the ranking of the statements. The biggest shift, for example — of forty points in a negative direction — on Mrs Thatcher's divisiveness pushed that attribute from close to the bottom of the list to seventh place. First, however, what about the significant positive shifts? Almost everbody agreed with the concept that Mrs Thatcher was a strong personality and that she spoke her mind. Similarly, the proportion disliking women leaders had declined by twelve points. Those were the only three statements out of eighteen tested, where significant shifts had occurred in a positive direction.

Mention has been made already of the sharp increase in the proportion of the general public agreeing with the statement that Mrs Thatcher divides the country: up from 31 per cent in 1977 to 71 per cent in 1985. A slightly less severe shift was the doubling of the proportion saying that Mrs Thatcher's ideas were destructive, not constructive. This was closely followed by perhaps two related statements: an increase in the number of those agreeing that Mrs Thatcher was out of touch and a decline in the number of those thinking she knew about the problems of the cost of living. Finally, there was a growing picture of Mrs Thatcher as a self-opinionated snob. Nevertheless, the top four statements receiving the highest agreement were all positive and, on balance, showed little sign of weakening.

In September and again in October, to try to measure the impact of the party conference, Gallup asked another image question:

Table 2.21: Mrs Thatcher, her Personality and Policies

Q. Which of these statements comes closest to your view of Mrs Thatcher?

| | General public | | Conservatives | |
	Sept	Oct	Sept	Oct
I like Mrs Thatcher and I like her policies	21	22	65	66
I like Mrs Thatcher but I dislike her policies	20	19	14	14
I dislike Mrs Thatcher but I like her policies	8	10	13	14
I dislike Mrs Thatcher and I dislike her policies	46	45	4	4
None of these	4	3	5	2

Table 2.21 continued

Summary:				
Like personality	41	41	79	80
Dislike personality	54	55	17	18
Like policies	29	32	78	80
Dislike policies	66	64	18	18

In contrast to the Labour Party Conference, at which Mr Kinnock's success as a speaker appears to have raised his standing among the general public, the Conservative Party Conference had no effect on the public's attitude towards Mrs Thatcher's personality or policies. Neither did it appear to have any impact on the views of the party faithful.

In early November, as part of a study mentioned elsewhere on prime ministerial qualities, people were asked which of 14 qualities applied to Mrs Thatcher. The top two qualities attributed to Mrs Thatcher were based on her determination and her dislike of compromise. In the following table, the first column shows the percentage of the general public who said it was very important that a prime minister should possess the quality, while the third column is a combination of the first two, that is 'thought the quality was very important' and 'thought Mrs Thatcher had it'.

Table 2.22: Mrs Thatcher's qualities

Q. Which, if any, of these do you think applies to Mrs Thatcher?

	'Very important' quality	Mrs Thatcher has:	'Very important' and Mrs Thatcher has:
The country's interests above party advantage	79	19	16
A clear view and purpose for the future of this country	78	27	22
Understanding of ordinary people	74	12	8
Ability for handling economic and financial affairs	72	17	13

A team of first-rate men and women as ministers or potential ministers behind her	72	14	11
Ability to handle problems at home	67	13	10
The respect and loyalty of her colleagues in Parliament	63	18	13
Ability to handle foreign affairs	62	21	15
Respect of leaders of other countries	49	23	13
Determination to pursue policies, even when they are unpopular	49	52	28
Skill developed from long experience in politics	45	24	12
Sincerely held principles and views which she will not compromise	42	43	17
Ability as speaker on TV	36	29	12
Background of a happy family life	26	15	5

Thus, the two qualities on which Mrs Thatcher scored highest were those ranking tenth and twelfth in importance respectively. Mrs Thatcher, it would appear, excelled in at least two characteristics to which the public gave a relatively low priority. Among Conservatives, these two qualities, plus 'a clear view and purpose', were the top three they attributed to Mrs Thatcher, though they were not necessarily the top three in importance. Again among Conservatives, the item on which Mrs Thatcher scored lowest, as she did with the public at large, was 'understanding of ordinary people' — mentioned by 22 per cent and 12 per cent respectively. Among her political opponents, the top three qualities they thought applied to Mrs Thatcher were: 'determination', 'sincerely held principles', and 'ability as speaker on TV'.

Finally, in December people were asked which of eight qualities applied to Mrs Thatcher:

Table 2.23: Mrs Thatcher's Qualities

Q. Which of the qualities on this card would you say Mrs Thatcher has:

	General public	Con	Lab	Lib/SDP
Tough	77	84	71	79
Determined	73	89	56	76
Sticks to principles	64	83	48	63
Decisive	51	71	31	52
Shrewd	51	63	41	49
Caring	13	34	2	5
Listens to reason	12	28	5	3
Likeable as a person	9	20	3	4
None of these; don't know	5	1	7	4

Thus Mrs Thatcher scored highly on the 'tough, resolute, principled' dimensions — substantially higher than did the other three party leaders — but she did significantly less well, even among her own party's supporters, on the subject of her potential for dealing with other people.

The 'Thatcherism' Scale

As part of its 1983 general election study for BBC Television, carried out in co-operation with Professor Ivor Crewe of the University of Essex, Gallup asked a set of five questions designed to measure acceptance of the basic philosophies espoused by Mrs Thatcher. The questions were repeated in October 1984 and yet again in September 1985. The trend over the three studies shows a gradual rejection of the ideas which had helped them win the 1983 election.

Comparisons with June 1983 show reversals of the figures on the first and third items, a shift away from 'Thatcherism' on the second and fourth, while the fifth already had a majority disagreeing with the idea of not compromising with the rest of the world. Among Conservatives, 10 per cent fewer believed in sticking to one's

Table 2.24: 'Thatcherism' Scale

	June 1983	Oct 1984	Sept 1985
Q. When dealing with political opponents, which is better: sticking firmly to one's beliefs or trying to meet them half-way?			
Sticking to beliefs	50	39	39
Meeting them half-way	38	51	52
Neither; both; don't know	12	11	9
Q. When government make decisions about the economy, which is better: to involve major interests like trade unions and business, or to keep them at arm's length?			
Involve interests	60	65	69
Keep at arm's length	28	23	22
Neither; both; don't know	12	12	9
Q. In difficult economic times, which is better: for the government to be caring, or for the government to be tough?			
Caring	34	45	50
Tough	46	37	36
Neither; both; don't know	20	18	14
Q. It is sometimes said that no government of any party can in fact do much to create economic prosperity, that is up to people themselves. Do you agree or disagree?			
Agree	48	42	41
Disagree	37	44	43
Don't know	15	14	16
Q. In its relations with the rest of the world, which is better: for Britain to stick resolutely to its own position, or for Britain to meet other countries half-way?			
Stick to own position	30	34	30
Meet them half way	60	54	60
Neither; both; don't know	10	12	10

beliefs when dealing with political opponents, 5 per cent fewer wanted a tough policy in difficult economic times, and 6 per cent fewer wanted major interests kept at arm's length when decisions were being made about the nation's economy. On the final two items, there has not been much of a shift in attitudes since 1983. Conservatives, therefore, still support the ideas in the main, though a majority of them in both 1983 and 1985 wanted a more flexible approach when dealing with other countries.

The Consequences of a Conservative Victory

In May, almost two years after the 1983 general election, people were asked about the effect of another Conservative victory on a number of items. For instance, majorities expected there to be greater encouragement for small businesses, a reduction in the power of the unions, and less government help for the nationalised industries. Compared with 1983, more people foresaw increased government control over people's lives, more control over income and more direct taxation. The results in full were as follows:

Table 2.25: Consequences of a Conservative Victory

Q. If the Conservative Party won the next general election, do you think there would be more or less ..., or wouldn't things change?

| | May 1983 | | | | May 1985 | | | |
	More	Less	No change	Don't know	More	Less	No change	Don't know
Encouragement for small businesses	64	12	15	8	58	14	18	10
Law and order	51	8	33	8	48	8	34	11
Unemployment	51	17	25	7	45	16	27	12
Industrial disputes	42	24	27	8	42	25	22	11
Inflation	37	29	28	6	35	26	28	10
Control of incomes	35	13	38	13	41	15	27	17
Government control over people's lives	30	18	40	13	41	14	31	14
Direct taxation, for example income tax	28	16	44	11	35	21	33	11

Government help for the nationalised industries	15	46	26	12	14	57	16	13
Personal freedom	14	19	56	10	14	30	42	14
Immigrants	9	33	45	13	11	37	36	16
Union power	7	62	23	8	7	67	18	9

As can be seen, the biggest shifts were on government control over people's lives, taxation, government help for the nationalised industries and personal freedom.

The Left–Right Scale

Table 2.26: Left–Right Scale — the Conservative Party

Q. *Whereabouts on this scale would you place the Conservative Party?*

	1983				Oct	1984			1985	
	Jan	June	Sept	Sept/Oct	Oct	May	Sept	Sept	Sept	Sept
Far left	2	3	4	2	2	2	3	2	3	3
Substantially left	1	1	2	1	2	1	1	1	1	2
Moderately left	2	1	2	3	2	1	2	2	1	2
Slightly left	2	2	1	1	2	2	2	1	2	1
All left	7	7	9	7	8	6	8	6	7	8
Middle of the road	1	2	2	2	2	2	0	1	2	1
Slightly right	4	5	4	4	6	5	4	6	6	5
Moderately right	20	21	17	16	17	18	16	15	15	14
Substantially right	28	29	25	29	27	27	25	27	26	24
Far right	19	19	21	22	18	22	23	21	25	26
All right	71	74	67	71	68	72	68	69	72	69
Don't know	21	17	23	21	22	20	24	24	20	22

Around 70 per cent of the general public correctly identified the Conservative Party as a party of the right in politics, though for another one in five the concept of left–right is meaningless in so far as it concerns the Conservatives. Looking back over the past three years, the proportion placing it as 'far right' or 'substantially right' shows little significant change, ranging between 45 per cent and 51 per cent. The main shift has occurred in this grouping, with an increase in the more extreme answer 'far right'. The movement is slight, though consistent, averaging 20 per cent in 1983, 22 per cent in 1984, and 26 per cent in 1985.

In September, Conservatives were asked which was stronger: their liking of the party or their dislike of Labour. Just over one in three (38 per cent) said that positive reasons were stronger, while slightly more (46 per cent) said that negative reasons were more important. Little had changed since June 1983, when the results had been 40 per cent and 48 per cent respectively.

A Less Concerned, Less Responsible Party

Throughout 1985, one in two of the general public saw the Conservative Party as becoming less concerned for people's interests and around one in three thought that the party was becoming less responsible in its approach to the important issues facing the country.

Among Conservatives in September, 28 per cent said the party was becoming more concerned for the interests of people like themselves, but 14 per cent said they were becoming less concerned. In all other sections of the public, critics outnumbered supporters by at least three to one, with the 35–44 age group and the poorest group being particularly critical.

Table 2.27: The Conservative Party Less Concerned

Q. Do you think the Conservative Party is becoming more concerned for the interests of people like yourself, less concerned, or is there no change?

	Feb/Mar	June	Sept
More concerned	11	12	11
Less concerned	50	51	49
No change	35	35	37
Don't know	4	2	3

The general public were less critical of the Conservative Party's handling of the important issues facing the country, though the critics outnumbered the supporters by around two to one.

Table 2.28: The Conservative Party Less Responsible

Q. Do you think the Conservative Party is becoming more responsible in its approach to the important issues facing the country, less responsible, or is there no change?

	Feb/Mar	June	Sept
More responsible	19	19	17
Less responsible	37	36	36
No change	38	41	42
Don't know	6	3	4

Two in five Conservatives saw their party as becoming more responsible, while only 9 per cent thought they were becoming less responsible. The position was reversed among all the other groups analysed; and again it was the 35–44 age group and the poorest group which contained the largest proportion of critics.

The Government's Problems

Another question periodically asked by Gallup, particularly in their pre-conference study, deals with the public's approval or otherwise of the government's handling of certain major policy areas. For example, majorities — and quite substantial majorities in some cases — disapproved of the government's handling of full employment, the health service, education, pensions, the cost of living and prices, housing, strikes, the economy, immigration and defence — in all, eleven of the 14 items. The following table, however, is shown in the form of an index, where a plus indicates more approving than disapproving and a minus indicates the opposite.

As can be seen, all but three issues showed a negative shift in the index between September 1984 and a year later. The exceptions were roads, the health service and strikes, the last-named improvement almost certainly being a reflection of the government's handling of the miners' dispute.

This is confirmed by the replies to another question. In June 1984, when the miners' strike was in its early days, 14 per cent of the public agreed with the statement that 'The government now has the unions firmly under control' and 78 per cent disagreed.

Table 2.29: Approval Index

Q. In general, would you say you approve or disapprove of the way the government is handling ...?

	Sept 1984	June 1985	Sept 1985
Law and order	+ 7	+ 2	− 1
Defence and armaments	+ 4	− 3	−12
Common Market	− 2	+ 9	− 6
Immigration	−10	− 8	−27
Housing	−10	−26	−32
Economic and financial affairs generally	−12	−16	−20
Roads	−25	−28	−21
Cost of living and prices	−25	−26	−29
Taxation	−28	−24	−32
Strikes and labour relations	−29	− 3	−19
Old age pensions	−36	−35	−42
Education	−37	−36	−48
Full employment	−55	−62	−63
National Health Service	−60	−51	−54

The following March, after the NUM had voted to abandon the strike, the proportion agreeing had trebled to 42 per cent, not far short of the number of those disagreeing, 45 per cent. Agreement, however, fell to 38 per cent in June and to 34 per cent in July before recovering to 46 per cent in November.

The public remained unconcerned about the likelihood of the government being overthrown by revolution sometime in the next ten years. In September 1984, 12 per cent thought that it was at least quite likely, compared with 10 per cent in November 1985. One in four thought such an event not very likely and 61 per cent thought that it was not at all likely.

Another question Gallup has regularly asked since 1945 measures the public's general attitude towards the government.

Appendix D shows the monthly figures for 1984 and 1985, while the following table averages out the figures for the last three years:

Table 2.30: Approval of the Government's Record

Q. Do you approve or disapprove of the government's record to date? (Quarterly averages for proportions approving.)

	1983	1984	1985
Quarter 1	41	41	31
Quarter 2	42	38	30
Quarter 3	46	35	27
Quarter 4	40	39	31

After their victory in the June 1983 general election, approval of the government peaked in the third quarter at 46 per cent: the highest quarterly average for any government since the beginning of 1966, when majorities of the public approved of the government. Approval declined through 1984, though it recovered slightly in the fourth quarter before dropping twelve points in 1985. The increase in the final quarter of 1985 reflected an upward movement in support for the Conservatives from 27 per cent to 33 per cent in voting intentions.

In December, to test the efficacy of government policies — whatever the political hue of that government — people were asked whether any government could deal with various problems. In every case — including on the issue of a reduction in unemployment — majorities thought that much could be done, despite Government protestations to the contrary.

It is perhaps unnecessary to state that majorities of Labour supporters — ranging from around two in three upwards — felt that a government could do quite a bit to solve the problems. This view, however, was also held by majorities of Conservatives on each of the eight issues. On the other hand, Alliance supporters did not agree with the other two parties' supporters on prices and strikes in particular; for example, one in two Alliance supporters thought there was very little any government could do to keep prices down, and slightly fewer thought little could be done to prevent strikes.

Table 2.31: Something Can Be Done

Q. Some people say that British governments nowadays — of whatever party — can actually do little to change things. Others say they can do quite a bit. Do you think that British governments nowadays can do very little, or quite a bit...?

	Very little	Quite a bit	Don't know
To keep prices down	38	58	5
To prevent strikes	37	56	8
To reduce unemployment	36	59	5
To control wage and salary increases	32	60	8
To reduce taxes	31	61	8
To reduce crime	29	65	6
To improve the general standard of living	28	65	6
To improve health and social services	16	81	4

The Labour Party

Labour began the year six points behind the Conservatives in Gallup's standard voting question, but this at least was an improvement on their level of support just two months earlier, when the gap had been 14 points. Almost inevitably, Labour entered 1985 as a divided party in the public perception: an image they had projected for a number of years and which was to stay with them throughout the year. In January, three-quarters of the public said Labour was a divided party, while only 16 per cent thought they were united. As can be seen in Table 2.15, their unity index was never better than −42 in 1985 — that is, 42 per cent more said Labour was divided than said she was united — and never better than −16 since the 1983 general election.

This image of disunity can be seen in the following table, which also shows other long-standing image problems for Labour: extremism, poor leadership, and a potentially dangerous one in its policy on nuclear weapons.

Looking back to late 1983, when Neil Kinnock took over from Michael Foot as Labour's leader, a number of distinct image changes are noticeable. Although a majority of the public held to the view of Labour as a party that had become too extreme, the percentage

Table 2.32: Image of the Labour Party

Q. I am going to read out some things people are saying about the Labour Party. Could you tell me for each whether you agree or disagree?
(Figures show percentage agreeing.)

	Aug 1983	Oct 1983	Nov 1983	Jan 1984	May 1984	Aug 1984	Sept 1984	Jan 1985	Apr 1985	Aug 1985	Sept 1985
Labour has become too extreme	71	71	60	62	58	62	56	65	57	59	59
Labour is the only party that can turn out the present government	29	31	55	55	49	52	50	41	53	39	30
Labour Party leadership is poor now	91	87	37	45	48	58	57	65	59	62	63
Labour would bring in real, thorough-going changes	59	57	64	62	62	64	60	58	64	65	59
Labour is too split and divided	86	84	59	61	60	63	68	75	67	70	72
Labour is the only party that looks after ordinary working people and their families	36	34	43	44	44	44	39	41	47	44	36
It's not very clear today what a vote for Labour means these days	74	73	64	67	65	62	64	72	64	67	63
Labour's policy of getting rid of all our nuclear weapons would be dangerous	75	74	69	69	71	65	62	70	67	65	62
The economy will be in a worse state under Labour	58	56	48	47	46	44	43	46	45	42	49

dropped from somewhere in the seventies to the sixties or even lower. There was an even bigger improvement on one important dimension: 'Labour is the only party that can turn out the present government': from around 30 per cent, following the Alliance's partial success in the 1983 general election, the proportion accepting this view jumped to 55 per cent but then declined as the Alliance made a comeback. Similarly, the proportion agreeing with the idea that 'Labour Party leadership is poor now' dropped dramatically with the election of Mr Kinnock, but was accepted by a majority of the public within a year. Labour's policy on nuclear weapons — which probably contributed to their failure in 1983 — remained a problem issue through 1984 and 1985, though possibly a diminishing one. In 1983, for example, the average proportion agreeing with the statement 'Labour's policy of getting rid of all our nuclear weapons would be dangerous' was around 73 per cent, dropped to 67 per cent in 1984, and in 1985 averaged 66 per cent — still an unacceptably high level from Labour's point of view.

As part of another attitude battery, people have been asked periodically whether they agreed or disagreed with the statement that 'Labour is starting to pull itself together and regain its strength.' In June 1984, 56 per cent of the public agreed with this statement, but the proportion dropped to 45 per cent of the public in March 1985; even so, 80 per cent of Labour supporters held the same view. In June, and again in July, the proportion among the general public rose to 51 per cent, and then to 58 per cent in November.

The climate of opinion for Labour in 1985 was not particularly good. On the dimension of party unity, for example, the party did not do well; neither did it do so in the public's perception of the party as being 'popular'. Table 2.16 shows that the proportion thinking that most people in Britain held a favourable opinion of Labour fell in the early summer of 1983, during and immediately after the general election, to just 13 per cent. With Neil Kinnock as leader, the figure rose to a high of 37 per cent in March 1984; yet this was still significantly below the best figure for both the Conservatives and the two Alliance parties.

Three other questions were asked about the Labour Party in December. The first of these dealt with one of Labour's bugbears: extremism. The general public was almost evenly divided on whether or not Labour was an extreme party (39 per cent) or a moderate one (40 per cent) — in contrast to the public's view of an extreme Conservative Party. The public was also evenly split on the subject of Labour's favouritism: 45 per cent thought it was good for one class only, while 43 per cent thought it was good for all classes. The third of the questions highlighted one of Labour's continuing problems. Almost one in two (48 per cent) of the public — including 20 per cent of Labour supporters — thought Labour had vague policies. Just over one in three (38 per cent) of the public thought they had clear policies.

Mr Kinnock

The public's initial rating of Mr Kinnock in October 1983 was in sharp contrast to its rating of Mr Foot in the final months of his leadership of the Labour Party. In September 1983, only 9 per cent thought that Mr Foot was proving a good leader; but by then it had long been realised that his term was over. A month later, 58 per cent thought that Mr Kinnock would prove to be a good leader; but these early hopes evaporated and his personal rating fell in 1984 to 35 per cent in October. The beginning of 1985 saw his image in no better shape, dropping to 31 per cent approval in February and then, after a slight improvement, further still to 29 per cent in September. However, his performance at the party conference, where he was seen to be particularly critical of the local council leaders in Liverpool, helped to boost his popularity to 50 per cent, at the same time putting his party into a six-point lead over the Conservatives. Table 2.33 shows the comparisons for his predecessors over the last 30 years:

Table 2.33: Opposition Leaders' Popularity 1955-1985

Q. Do you think ... is or is not proving a good leader of the ... Party?

Government		High	Low	Average
1955-59	Conservative:			
	Gaitskell (May 1956-Aug 1959)	53	32	43
1959-64	Conservative:			
	Gaitskell (Feb 1960-Jan 1963)	57	35	47
	Wilson (Mar 1963-Sept 1964)	67	44	59
1964-66	Labour:			
	Home (Nov 1964-July 1965)	41	32	37
	Heath (Aug 1965-Feb 1966)	51	40	47
1966-70	Labour:			
	Heath (Apr 1966-June 1970)	46	24	33

Table 2.33 continued

1970–74	Conservative:			
	Wilson (Sept 1970–Feb 1974)	66	37	49
1974–79	Labour:			
	Heath (Apr 1974–Jan 1975)	38	29	33
	Thatcher (Feb 1975–Apr 1979)	64	31	41
1979–83	Conservative:			
	Callaghan (June 1979–Oct 1980)	63	46	53
	Foot (Nov 1980–June 1983)	38	14	21
1983—	Conservative:			
	Foot (July 1983–Sept 1983)	11	9	10
	Kinnock (Oct 1983–Dec 1985)	58	29	40

In July, Gallup repeated a personality image question asked first about Mr Kinnock in September 1984. As can be seen from the following table, not much had changed over the ten months between the two studies:

Table 2.34: Mr Kinnock's Image

Q. Which of these statements would you say are true of Mr Kinnock?

	Sept 1984	July 1985
He doesn't give a clear lead to his party	29	30
He doesn't seem to be a big enough man for the job.	29	28
I don't find him interesting on television	26	20
You can't trust what he says	25	23
I wouldn't want to have him as a friend	21	16
He never says anything of importance	20	19
Newspaper stories about him are dull	19	16
He never does anything of importance	19	16
He doesn't seem to be particularly clever	18	14
He doesn't stand for the party's traditional policies	14	11
He doesn't seem to have any real friends	8	5
He shows no sympathy for ordinary people	7	4
None of these; don't know	34	33

Among Labour supporters, the main criticisms were that he doesn't give a clear lead to Labour (16 per cent), that newspaper stories about him were dull (15 per cent), and that he doesn't appear a big enough man for the job (14 per cent).

In September, in the week before the party conference, and then again in late October when the conference season was over, Gallup asked another question to measure Neil Kinnock's popularity.

Table 2.35: Mr Kinnock, His Personality and Policies

Q. Which of these statements comes closest to your views of Mr Kinnock?

	General public		Labour supporters	
	Sept	Oct	Sept	Oct
I like Mr Kinnock and I like his policies	27	34	65	73
I like Mr Kinnock but I dislike his policies	31	29	12	9
I dislike Mr Kinnock but I like his policies	7	9	8	11
I dislike Mr Kinnock and I dislike his policies	25	21	6	5
None of these	11	6	9	2
Summary:				
Like personality	58	63	77	82
Dislike personality	32	30	14	16
Like policies	34	43	73	84
Dislike policies	56	50	18	14

The increase in Mr Kinnock's overall rating after the conference, already mentioned, can be seen to be more a reflection of his policies than his personality — both for the general public and for Labour supporters.

In comparison with its image of Mrs Thatcher, the public image of Mr Kinnock was less well-defined. For example, in the November study mentioned elsewhere, Mrs Thatcher obtained a grand total of 327 per cent across the 14 attributes, while Mr Kinnock scored 236, as can be seen below. In the following table, the first column shows the percentage of the general public who said it was very important that a prime minister had the quality; the second shows the percentage thinking Mr Kinnock had the quality; and the third column is a combination of the first two, that is thought the quality was very important and thought it applied to Mr Kinnock.

Table 2.36: Mr Kinnock's Qualities

Q. Which, if any, of these do you think applies to Mr Kinnock?

	'Very important' quality	Mr Kinnock has:	'Very important' and Mr Kinnock has:
The country's interests above party advantages	79	19	16
A clear view and purpose for the future of this country	78	20	17
Understanding of ordinary people	74	45	35
Ability to handle economic and financial affairs	72	11	9
A team of first-rate men and women as ministers or potential ministers behind him	72	8	6
Ability to handle problems at home	67	14	11
The respect and loyalty of his colleagues in Parliament	63	15	11
Ability to handle foreign affairs	62	8	6
Respect of leaders of other countries	49	10	6
Determination to pursue policies, even when they are unpopular	49	11	6
Skill developed from long experience in politics	45	10	5
Sincerely held principles and views which he will not compromise	42	12	6
Ability as speaker on TV	36	29	12
Background of a happy family life	26	24	6

Thus two of Mr Kinnock's top three scoring qualities were at the bottom of the public's list of priorities, though the item thought to apply most to Mr Kinnock is third in the table, and in fact he did better than the other three party leaders on this dimension. As far as the third column in the table is concerned, the 35 per cent thinking 'understanding of ordinary people' was very important and that it applied to Mr Kinnock was the highest such score for any of the qualities for any of the leaders. Among Labour supporters, the items on which Mr Kinnock scored lowest tended to be on those on which he also obtained low scores among the general public.

In December, yet another series of image dimensions were measured:

Table 2.37: Mr Kinnock's Qualities

Q. Which of the qualities on this card would you say
  Mr Kinnock has:

	General public	Con	Lab	Alliance
Likeable as a person	49	40	67	45
Listens to reason	46	35	65	43
Caring	42	34	62	36
Determined	35	24	56	28
Sticks to principles	25	14	45	19
Shrewd	25	23	26	24
Decisive	19	10	34	17
Tough	17	11	27	15
None of these; don't know	19	31	4	22

Mr Kinnock, therefore, scored highly as a caring, likeable person who would listen to reason. However, in sharp contrast to Mrs Thatcher he was not thought to be tough or decisive — even among Labour supporters.

The Left–Right Scale

Although some members of the general public are not entirely at home with the political concept of left and right, a significant number are conversant enough with the concept to enable us to look meaningfully at their perception of the Labour Party on such a scale, particularly as an extension of the idea of extremism (in both parties). Table 2.38 shows the public's perceptions of Labour on an eight-point verbal scale, ranging from 'far left' to 'far right', with 'middle-of-the-road' as a volunteered reply.

It is obvious from the table, that Labour is seen — as it should be — as a party on the left of politics. In the last three years, the figure never dropped below two in three of the public, with around one in five not being able to place Labour on the scale. The main interest lies in whereabouts Labour was thought to be in the 'left' segment. At the time of the 1983 election, one in two of the public saw Labour as either being on the far left or substantially left: half as many again as had held the same view at the beginning of 1983. By October, with the new leader, the proportion fell back to one in three but since then has crept up to around 40 per cent.

One in two (52 per cent) of Labour supporters in September said

Table 2.38: Left–Right Scale — the Labour Party

Q. Whereabouts on this scale would you place the Labour Party?

| | 1983 | | | | | 1984 | | | 1985 | |
	Jan	**June**	**Sept**	**Sept/ Oct**	**Oct**	**May**	**Sept**	**Sept**	**Sept**	**Sept**
Far left	11	24	20	18	13	14	15	17	18	19
Substantially left	23	26	26	26	21	28	24	22	24	24
Moderately left	26	16	14	18	23	20	21	20	18	18
Slightly left	8	8	6	6	9	8	9	7	8	8
All left	68	74	66	68	66	70	69	66	68	69
Middle-of-the-road	1	1	1	1	3	2	2	2	2	1
Slightly right	2	2	2	3	3	3	3	3	3	3
Moderately right	4	3	4	4	3	4	4	3	3	3
Substantially right	1	1	2	2	2	1	2	2	2	1
Far right	1	1	2	1	2	2	3	2	2	1
All right	8	7	10	10	10	10	11	10	10	8
Don't know	21	18	24	22	22	19	19	23	19	18

that they were voting Labour mainly for negative reasons: that is out of dislike of the Conservatives. Just over one in four (29 per cent) said it was mainly for positive reasons: because of what they liked about Labour. In June 1983, the replies had been very similar: 51 per cent and 31 per cent respectively.

The Consequences of a Labour Victory

In the run-up to the 1983 general election, Gallup asked electors what they thought the consequences would be of a victory for each of the three main party groups. Majorities expected a Labour victory to bring more power for the unions, more help for the nationalised industries and higher inflation. The question was repeated in May 1985, with similar results on these three dimensions while other dimensions showed some favourable shifts in opinion.

Table 2.39: Consequences of a Labour Victory

Q. If the Labour Party won the next general election, do you think there would be more or less ..., or wouldn't things change?

	May 1983 More	Less	No change	Don't know	May 1985 More	Less	No change	Don't know
Union power	77	4	13	5	71	7	13	9
Government help for the nationalised industries	76	6	7	11	73	9	7	11
Inflation	64	11	16	9	52	18	18	12
Direct taxation for example, income tax	50	21	17	11	42	26	19	14
Control of incomes	42	17	25	16	37	22	24	17
Government control over people's lives	38	16	33	13	29	25	32	15
Industrial disputes	38	30	23	9	30	34	23	12
Immigrants	33	11	41	15	30	19	36	14
Encouragement for small businesses	30	38	20	12	32	31	23	14
Unemployment	24	38	29	9	21	47	21	11
Law and order	20	19	48	12	20	21	44	15
Personal freedom	18	25	45	12	24	21	42	13

Majorities of the public, therefore, still expected more government help for the nationalised industries, more union power and more inflation, though the proportions taking that view had fallen over the two years. This favourable shift of opinion was evident on all the other dimensions, with the sole exception of law and order. The biggest favourable shifts were on the question of inflation and on government control over people's lives.

A Concerned, Responsible Party?

Between the early part of the year and mid-year the public increasingly saw Labour as a more concerned, more responsible party, but then reversed the trend in Gallup's pre-conference study so that Labour was worse off than it had been seven months earlier.

Table 2.40: Labour as a Concerned Party

Q. Do you think the Labour Party is becoming more
   concerned for the interests of people like yourself, less
   concerned, or is there no change?

	Feb/Mar	June	Sept
More concerned	30	40	23
Less concerned	25	18	22
No change	39	34	49
Don't know	6	8	6

The mid-year improvement and subsequent decline was spread almost evenly across all groups of the public, but was slightly more marked among those aged under 35. Among this group the proportion saying that Labour was becoming more concerned for the interests of people like themselves rose from 31 per cent to 45 per cent in June, and then fell to a low of 22 per cent. Even among Labour supporters, morale fell 14 points between June and September.

Labour's image as a responsible party also rose and fell in parallel with the results from the 'concerned party' question.

The decline in Labour's image on this dimension was less marked among Labour supporters than among the public as a whole, but more marked among the under-45s.

Table 2.41: Labour as a Responsible Party

Q. Do you think the Labour Party is becoming more
   responsible in its approach to the important issues facing
   the country, less responsible, or is there no change?

	Feb/Mar	June	Sept
More responsible	26	35	25
Less responsible	28	19	25
No change	39	37	43
Don't know	7	8	7

Labour's Future

As part of its pre-conference study, Gallup also asked a number of questions dealing with aspects of the future for Labour. The malaise that was apparently affecting the party in the summer can be seen in the replies to a question on where Labour will be in the mid-1990s.

Table 2.42: Labour's Future

Q. Looking ahead to, say, ten years from now, what is your best guess for the future of the Labour Party?

	Sept 1983	Sept 1984	Sept 1985
The Labour Party is a spent force whose future can only be downhill	23	13	17
Labour will continue to be the main opposition party but it won't hold power again	24	22	19
Labour will form some sort of coalition with the SDP/Liberal Alliance in order to form a government	17	19	27
Labour will form a government on its own in the next ten years	28	37	27
Don't know	9	9	10

The proportion, therefore, who thought that Labour would form a government on its own had fallen ten points in a year, mainly shifting into the 'coalition' category. Even among Labour supporters, 12 per cent saw Labour's days in power as being over and 24 per cent thought it would form a government only in coalition with the Alliance parties.

A majority (57 per cent) of the general public thought that the trade unions would dominate a future Labour government under Neil Kinnock, though 30 per cent thought otherwise. Among Labour supporters, a majority (61 per cent) said the party would not be dominated by the unions, but 22 per cent said they would. This impression was no doubt engendered by the miners' dispute and Labour's support for it. This can be seen in the replies to a final question on some of the proposals being discussed which concerned what would happen if a Labour government were returned at the next election. Two in three (68 per cent) of the public —

including 41 per cent of Labour supporters — said that they disapproved of the idea of a future Labour government reinstating all miners sacked for activities arising from the miners' strike. Similarly, 67 per cent of the public and 37 per cent of Labour supporters disapproved of paying to the National Union of Mineworkers and other unions any money confiscated as a result of fines, etc. or legal costs. On the other hand, the public was evenly divided on the issue of conducting a complete review of all cases of miners jailed as a result of the dispute, with 45 per cent each approving or disapproving. Among Labour supporters, the figures were 66 per cent and 23 per cent respectively.

Labour's Defence Policy

It is generally accepted that one of the reasons Labour lost the 1983 election was partly a credibility problem on defence and partly an actual dislike of their policies, particularly of unilateral disarmament. In the week leading up to Labour's annual conference, therefore, Gallup asked a number of questions about Labour's defence policy, and at the same time asked similar questions of a separate sample but without any mention of the policies as being proposed by Labour.

The first question was designed simply to measure approval of the various policies, and Table 2.43 shows the proportions approving. Thus only on two items, Britain's membership of NATO and the 'first use' question, did Labour have majority approval among the general public. On the third item, cruise missiles, a plurality of the public were in approval of the policy. Among Labour supporters, majorities approved of all policies with the exception of reducing Britain's forces for non-European purposes. Only on the first two in the table did majorities of Conservatives approve, and among Alliance supporters the first three policies obtained majority support.

When the questions were asked 'blind', that is without mention of the policies as belonging to the Labour Party, approval was slightly higher for seven of the policies, but the differences were not statistically significant. Similarly, seven of the policies were more popular among Conservatives in the 'blind' study, but again the differences tended to be small. There was also a tendency for both Labour and Alliance supporters to give slightly higher approval scores.

Part of the argument about cruise missiles being sited in Britain

Table 2.43: Approval of Labour's Defence Policies

Q. Here are some of the ideas from the Labour Party's defence policy. Could you tell me whether you approve or disapprove of them?

	General public	Con	Lab	Lib/ SDP
Britain to continue as a member of NATO	77	86	69	81
Obtain an agreement from NATO not to be first to use nuclear weapons in the event of a war breaking out	67	53	75	74
Send cruise missiles back to the United States	50	28	67	54
Remove all US nuclear bases from Britain	40	16	60	42
Cancel the Trident submarine missiles programme	40	17	59	42
Press NATO to withdraw all short-range nuclear weapons from Europe	36	17	58	33
Britain's defence to be based on not having nuclear weapons	34	15	54	32
Get rid of the Polaris nuclear submarines in Britain	33	13	53	31
Reduce Britain's defence forces for operation outside Europe	32	15	44	34

revolves around the question of 'Whose finger on the trigger?' In fact, it has been a question whenever foreign missiles have been brought to this country. The people who approved of returning cruise missiles to the United States — 50 per cent of the general public — were then asked whether they would accept the missiles if the British government had more control over their use. This group was evenly divided on the idea of a 'dual-key' arrangement: 23 per cent accepting the missiles in Britain, 23 per cent still opposing them and 4 per cent undecided.

A third question was then asked of everybody which dealt with the likelihood of a future government following a non-nuclear defence policy. Again the question was asked in two forms, but the results were significantly different:

Table 2.44: Non-Nuclear Defence

Q. *Do you think a future (Labour) government would or*
would not follow a defence policy based on not having
nuclear weapons?

	'Blind'	Labour
Would	30	42
Would not	44	35
Don't know	26	23

More people, therefore, could see a future Labour government adopting a non-nuclear defence strategy than saw this happening through a future anonymous government. This was also true of supporters of the three main parties. A non-nuclear policy would obviously not be popular with Britain's NATO partners, particularly America. Yet despite the potential damage to the 'special relationship', a significant minority of the public, especially Labour supporters, felt that a non-nuclear defence policy should be introduced.

Table 2.45: British/United States Relations

Q. *Do you think a future (Labour) government should or*
should not introduce a non-nuclear defence policy, if it
might lead to harming our relationship with the United
States?

	'Blind'	Labour
Should	37	29
Should not	47	50
Don't know	16	21

The difference between the proportions replying 'should' to the two questions was statistically significant, and came about from a decline among both Conservatives and Alliance supporters when it came to a Labour government action. The figures for Labour supporters were very similar across the two questions.

On the other hand, a majority to the public felt that Britain should stay in NATO if it were unable to persuade its allies to adopt a non-nuclear defence policy, be it Labour's policy or that of an unnamed government. Just over one in two opted for continued

NATO membership, while one in four said Britain should not stay in NATO. In contrast to their replies to other questions on defence spending — when they tended to take a negative attitude — the public were divided on the issue of expenditure on conventional forces being the price of adopting a non-nuclear defence policy. Again, the two forms of question were asked and similar findings emerged. Around one in four thought more should be spent on conventional forces, one in four said spend less, and just over one in three thought the same amount should be spent on defence.

Finally, people were asked, 'Would you support or oppose the introduction of National Service as the price for putting less emphasis on nuclear weapons in Britain's defence policy?' Three in five (59-60 per cent) supported the idea, while just under one in three (29-30 per cent) were opposed. Analysis by party showed Labour voters as less likely to support the introduction of National Service.

The Alliance

Since the heady days of winter 1981, when the two Alliance parties combined attracted more than half the public's support in terms of voting intentions, their success at by-elections has fallen far short of these expectations. By the summer of 1982, support for the Alliance had fallen to 23 per cent; it then dropped slightly lower when 1983 arrived, eventually picking up in time to take around one-quarter of the votes at the general election. Their apparent success in gaining votes (though this was not translated into seats) plus Labour's leadership problems temporarily put them ahead of Labour but still behind the Conservatives. In 1984 they fell back, achieving a best score of 27½ per cent, still in third place in December. The Alliance's victory in the Brecon and Radnor by-election in early July, in particular, boosted support for the two parties in 1985; enough to push the Conservatives into third place four times and to put the Alliance in first place in the September study (with interviewing conducted midway between the two parties' conferences). The relatively poor showing of the Liberals and the SDP in the winter of 1984/5 and the effect of Brecon and Radnor are reflected in the replies given to specific questions about voting for the Alliance in three quite different electoral scenarios.

Table 2.46: Support for the Liberal/SDP Alliance

Q. Would you be likely to vote for the Alliance between the Liberals and the Social Democrats if you thought they ...? (Proportion answering 'yes'.)

	Sept 1984	Jan 1985	July 1985	Aug/Sept 1985
Would get a majority	47	42	53	54
Were likely to hold the balance	44	39	50	50
Would win only a few seats	23	20	28	31

Whom were the Alliance more likely to attract in these situations? Of the other two main parties, Labour supporters were slightly more likely than Conservatives to say that they would consider voting for the Alliance, and they were also numerically larger. Those who toyed with the idea also tended to be loosely attached to a political party; and again there were large numbers of such people. In September, when Alliance voters were asked what was stronger, 35 per cent said it was what they liked about the Alliance, and 45 per cent what they disliked about Labour or the Conservatives. Within the Alliance group of voters, Liberals tended to be voting more for positive reasons, while SDP supporters tended to be voting more for negative reasons. Despite their quite different histories and backgrounds, the two halves of the Alliance were seen as very similar on the left–right scale.

Table 2.47: Left–Right Scale: Liberal Party and Social Democratic Party

Q. Whereabouts on this scale would you place the Liberal Party?
Q. And the Social Democratic Party?

	Liberal	SDP
Far left	1	1
Substantially left	1	1
Moderately left	6	6
Slightly left	15	15
All left	23	23
Middle-of-the-road	14	11

Slightly right	20	19
Moderately right	10	10
Substantially right	1	2
Far right	1	1
All right	32	32
Don't know	31	33

Thus one in three was unable to place the two parties on the scale, a higher proportion than those unable to place either the Conservative or Labour parties on the scale. Though among those who could, both parties were seen as more of a party of the right than of the left, with just over one in ten seeing them as middle-of-the-road parties. Gallup also asked people whether they would vote for the Alliance if it merged into one party and had one leader, both ideas attracting a significant degree of popularity among non-Alliance supporters.

Among those who were currently Alliance supporters, the idea of a merged party and a single leader was slightly more popular among Liberals; and among non-Alliance people it was Conservatives who appeared most interested in the two ideas.

Table 2.48: A Merged Alliance Under One Leader

Q. *Would you be more likely or less likely to vote for the Alliance:*

	General public	Lib/SDP	Rest
a) if the Liberal Party and the Social Democratic Party merged to form one party?			
More likely	41	59	32
Less likely	8	7	9
No difference	45	30	52
Don't know	7	4	8
b) if the partners in the Alliance had one leader rather than two, as at present?			
More likely	45	59	38
Less likely	5	3	5
No difference	45	33	51
Don't know	6	5	6

One in two of the public in September saw the Alliance as two parties, while 39 per cent saw it as one party. On the other hand, one in two Alliance supporters considered the Alliance as one party, and 43 per cent as two parties. Liberals, in the Alliance group, were slightly more likely to see the Alliance as two parties. David Steel was the public's definite choice as the best leader for the Alliance, and was also chosen by a narrow margin by Alliance supporters. Among the public as a whole, 50 per cent said Mr David Steel would be the best leader, while 34 per cent picked Dr Owen. Among Alliance supporters, the figures were 49 per cent and 43 per cent respectively. Dr Owen's defection from the Labour Party still appears to rankle where some Labour supporters are concerned. Whereas Conservatives were almost evenly divided on the subject of the two Alliance leaders, with Mr Steel narrowly ahead, Labour supporters chose Mr Steel by a margin of more than two to one over Dr Owen. Similarly, when questioned on who would be the best Alliance prime minister if they won the next general election, 48 per cent of the general public opted for Mr Steel and 34 per cent for Dr Owen. Again, on the subject of which of the two best understood the economy and how it worked, Mr Steel, with 35 per cent, was narrowly ahead of Dr Owen, with 33 per cent. Finally, 61 per cent of the public thought that Mr Steel would prove a good prime minister and 50 per cent thought Dr Owen would. Among Alliance supporters, the figures were 74 per cent and 73 per cent respectively.

In December, three questions showed both the strengths and the weakness of the Alliance. Two in three (69 per cent) of the public saw the Alliance as a moderate party, while 4 per cent thought it was extreme. Similarly, 66 per cent thought the Alliance was good for all classes, while 7 per cent thought it was good for one class only. Yet a significant minority — 42 per cent — of the public thought the Alliance had vague policies, as did 26 per cent of Alliance supporters. Slightly fewer of the general public — 32 per cent — thought it had clear policies, though naturally more (61 per cent) Alliance supporters shared this view.

The Next Election

An idea that had been in circulation for some time now — though not taken particularly seriously by the Labour Party — was the making of an anti-Tory electoral pact between the Alliance and Labour. Majorities of the public and of the two 'parties' concerned thought the idea to be a good one.

Table 2.49: An Anti-Tory Pact

Q. *Do you think it would be a good idea or a bad idea if Labour and the Liberal/SDP Alliance came to an agreement not to fight each other in certain seats at a general election?*

	General public	Con	Lab	Lib/SDP
A good idea	54	40	68	55
A bad idea	34	47	24	38
Don't know	11	13	8	7

Compared with 1984, the public's view on the chances of the Alliance had improved significantly. In September 1984, 41 per cent thought the Alliance might have a chance of taking over from the Labour Party as the main challenge to the Conservatives, and the proportion thinking the number of votes for the Alliance would go up at the next election rose from 50 per cent in September 1984 to 70 per cent a year later. Over the same period, the proportion thinking the number of Alliance MPs would go up rose from 40 per cent to 59 per cent. This shift of opinion is reflected in the replies to another question asking people whether they agreed or disagreed with the idea that the Liberal/SDP Alliance will probably hold the balance of power after the next general election. In June 1984, 34 per cent of the public agreed and 52 per cent disagreed. By the following March the gap had narrowed to 38 per cent and 45 per cent respectively; and in June the figures reversed, so that 48 per cent agreed while 36 per cent disagreed. The Brecon and Radnor result probably accentuated the trend, and in July an actual majority (53 per cent) agreed, with 29 per cent disagreeing. By November the Alliance was in decline in terms of public support, and the figures on this statement moved to 45 per cent and 38 per cent respectively. In the November study, agreement with the statement was naturally highest among Alliance supporters (72 per cent) with only one in three of both Labour supporters and Conservatives sharing the same view.

In May, Gallup asked the public's views on the effect of an Alliance victory. Around one in three of the public were undecided on the impact of such an event, but on balance it was thought that it would mean more government help for the nationalised industries, more inflation, more personal freedom, more encouragement for small businesses, and more law and order, as well as less unemployment and less government control over people's lives. Thus, two years after the 1983 general election, the public were less pessimistic about the effects of an Alliance victory on inflation and industrial disputes.

Table 2.50: Consequences of an Alliance Victory

*Q. If the Alliance between the Liberals and the Social
Democrats won the next general election, do you think
there would be more or less ..., or wouldn't things
change?*

	May 1983				May 1985			
	More	Less	No change	Don't know	More	Less	No change	Don't know
Encouragement for small businesses	43	8	17	32	48	6	18	28
Government help for the nationalised industries	30	12	22	37	34	11	24	31
Inflation	40	7	20	33	28	16	25	31
Law and order	20	8	41	31	22	7	43	28
Personal freedom	13	7	47	32	21	5	44	29
Control of income	21	11	30	37	19	15	33	33
Direct taxation, e.g. income tax	19	11	28	42	17	18	31	34
Industrial disputes	25	12	28	35	17	23	31	29
Unemployment	18	24	27	31	15	32	26	27
Union power	13	20	35	33	13	22	36	29
Immigrants	11	9	42	38	10	16	42	32
Government control over people's lives	10	15	42	33	8	23	38	31

The public, however, saw the Alliance as doing better in the next election than it had prior to the 1983 general election. More saw the Alliance either winning or coming second in their area. One in two of the public — and 61 per cent of Alliance supporters — thought it would be an easy victory, virtually the same pattern of replies as in April 1983.

Table 2.51: The Election Placings

Q. Leaving aside your own hopes, which party do you think will in fact win in your area in the general election?

Q. And which party do you think will come second in your area?

Q. And which party do you think will come in third place?

	Winners		Second		Third	
	April 1983	Sept 1985	April 1983	Sept 1985	April 1983	Sept 1985
Conservative	46	42	23	22	12	23
Labour	37	40	25	19	21	30
Alliance	5	11	30	45	41	30
Other	0	1	3	2	3	2
Don't know	12	7	20	12	24	14

With the polls showing a three-horse race for large periods of the year, the idea resurfaced of a coalition following the next election, particularly an anti-Tory coalition, though without any real impetus behind it. Seven in ten Conservatives or Labour supporters approved of a coalition with the Alliance to form a joint government on its own, or if the Alliance won the most seats but not enough to form a government on its own. Alliance supporters were less enthusiastic about a coalition with either the Conservative Party or the Labour Party — in the two scenarios described above. A little under two in three approved of a coalition with the Conservatives, while fewer (56 per cent) approved of a coalition with Labour.

The Two Davids

Mr Steel and Dr Owen have tended to be ahead of Mrs Thatcher and Mr Kinnock in the popularity stakes since the 1983 general election, with a few exceptions. Mr Kinnock's initial measurement in October 1983 was only two points below that of Mr Steel but 10 points better than Dr Owen's. The beginning of 1984 saw Dr Owen slightly down on Mrs Thatcher's ratings, though doing slightly better than Mr Kinnock. Through most of 1983 and 1984 Mr Steel enjoyed a higher personal rating than Dr Owen, with one exception in October 1984 when the media publicity surrounding the party conferences pushed Dr Owen into a two-point advantage.

Both Alliance leaders started 1985 as significantly more popular than either Mrs Thatcher or Mr Kinnock, improved on their positions during the summer yet had exceptionally poor ratings in the October post-conferences study. Mr Steel's — at 53 per cent — was his lowest since the election in 1983 and ten points down on his score in August, just two months earlier. Dr Owen, too, after equalling his best rating in September, fell twelve points in a month to register one of his poorest ratings since being elected party leader. Undoubtedly, the timing of the party conferences — with the two Alliance parties having theirs first, followed by Labour and then the Conservatives — focused the media limelight more on Mr Kinnock and Mrs Thatcher in October.

Comparisons of image dimensions in September 1984 and July 1985 mirrored the improvement in popularity of the two Alliance leaders in the summer. The statements included in the question, as seen below, were all negative, and the proportions applying them to Messrs Steel and Owen went down or remain unchanged. Dr Owen's poor rating overall, especially compared to David Steel's, was reflected in the replies to another question asked in late October.

In early November, as part of a larger study of the qualities looked for in a prime minister (as mentioned elsewhere), people were asked which of 14 qualities could be said to apply individually to

Table 2.52: Image of Mr Steel and Dr Owen

Q. Which of these statements would you say are true of Mr Steel/Dr Owen?

	Steel		Owen	
	Sept 1984	July 1985	Sept 1984	July 1985
I don't find him interesting on TV	19	14	19	14
Newspaper stories about him are dull	17	16	15	14
He never does anything of importance	17	11	13	11
He never says anythng of importance	16	11	12	11
He doesn't give a clear lead to his party	15	12	14	11
He doesn't seem a big enough man for the job	14	13	8	9
You can't trust what he says	13	10	15	13
I wouldn't want to have him as a friend	13	10	15	13
He doesn't stand for the party's traditional policies	6	6	7	6
He doesn't seem to be particularly clever	6	5	5	6
He shows no sympathy for ordinary people	4	4	7	6
He doesn't seem to have any real friends	4	3	5	5
None of these; don't know	49	53	52	55

Table 2.53: The Two Davids, Their Personalities and Policies

Q. Which of these statements comes closest to your view of Mr Steel/Dr Owen?

	General public Steel	Owen	Lib Steel	SDP Owen
I like ... and I like his policies	34	28	83	73
I like ... but I dislike his policies	27	19	8	7
I dislike ... but I like his policies	6	9	1	11
I dislike ... and I dislike his policies	18	23	4	2
None of these	15	21	3	7
Summary				
Like personality	61	47	91	80
Dislike personality	24	32	5	13
Like policies	40	37	84	84
Dislike policies	45	42	12	9

Mr Steel and Dr Owen. As expected, both politicians obtained a fairly low-profile image, with 29 per cent being the highest figure achieved by Dr Owen and 28 per cent being the highest for Mr Steel — both for the same dimension. In fact, 33 per cent either thought Mr Steel had none of the qualities or were still undecided, while 34 per cent similarly mentioned no qualities for Dr Owen. The following table shows the public's image of Mr Steel on the prime ministerial qualities:

Table 2.54: Mr Steel's Qualities

Q. Which, if any, of these do you think applies to Mr Steel?

	'Very important' quality	Mr Steel has:	'Very important' and Mr Steel has:
The country's interests above party advantages	79	18	15
A clear view and purpose for the future of this country	78	17	14
Understanding of ordinary people	74	26	19

Table 2.54 continued

Ability to handle economic and financial affairs	72	10	7
A team of first-rate men and women as ministers or potential ministers behind him	72	8	7
Ability to handle problems at home	67	11	8
The respect and loyalty of his colleagues in Parliament	63	20	14
Ability to handle foreign affairs	62	8	5
Respect of leaders of other countries	49	10	6
Determination to pursue policies, even when they are unpopular	49	8	5
Skill developed from long experience in politics	45	17	7
Sincerely held principles and views which he will not compromise	42	10	5
Ability as speaker on TV	36	28	11
Background of a happy family life	26	18	4

Among Liberals, Mr Steel's top quality was a clear view and purpose (mentioned by 43 per cent) followed by the country's interests above party advantage (38 per cent) and ability as a speaker on television (36 per cent). Their hope must be that this latter ability will help to improve the public's attitude towards Mr Steel on some of the other qualities.

The public had an image of Dr Owen similar to the one it had of Mr Steel, with a few exceptions. Dr Owen, for example, scored slightly lower on his understanding of ordinary people but higher on his ability to handle foreign affairs: an obvious memory of his Labour days.

Table 2.55: Dr Owen's Qualities

Q. Which, if any, of these do you think applies to Dr Owen?

	'Very important' quality	Dr Owen has:	'Very important' and Dr Owen has:
The country's interests above party advantages	79	16	13
A clear view and purpose for the future of this country	78	19	16

Understanding of ordinary people	74	19	14
Ability to handle economic and financial affairs	72	11	8
A team of first-rate men and women as ministers or potential ministers behind him	72	6	5
Ability to handle problems at home	67	12	9
The respect and loyalty of his colleagues in Parliament	63	17	10
Ability to handle foreign affairs	62	19	12
Respect of leaders of other countries	49	12	7
Determination to pursue policies, even when they are unpopular	49	10	6
Skill developed from long experience in politics	45	21	8
Sincerely held principles and views which he will not compromise	42	11	5
Ability as speaker on TV	36	29	10
Background of a happy family life	26	16	4

Among SDP or Alliance supporters, the item on which they rated Dr Owen best was his ability as a speaker on TV (mentioned by 41 per cent) followed by 'a clear view' (36 per cent) and an understanding of ordinary people (34 per cent) — an altogether different image from that held by Liberals of Mr Steel.

As part of the normal monthly political study in December, yet another set of image dimensions were tested, showing similar yet different patterns of replies concerning Mr Steel and Dr Owen:

Table 2.56: Mr Steel/Dr Owen's Qualities

Q. Which of the qualities on this card would you say Mr Steel/Dr Owen has?

	General public	Con	Lab	Lib/SDP
Mr Steel:				
Likeable as a person	53	45	45	74
Listens to reason	43	35	32	62
Caring	42	37	32	61
Determined	27	19	25	39
Shrewd	22	23	15	30
Sticks to principles	22	17	17	33
Decisive	16	12	12	28
Tough	9	7	6	14
None of these; don't know	27	31	37	11

Table 2.56 continued

Dr Owen:

Determined	35	28	25	51
Likeable as a person	35	29	22	52
Listens to reason	32	28	22	48
Caring	31	29	20	48
Shrewd	29	29	20	39
Decisive	23	18	15	38
Sticks to principles	22	18	13	35
Tough	18	13	13	31
None of these; don't know	34	37	46	15

The similarities between the two Alliance leaders are the 'caring, likeable' dimensions, though Mr Steel scores higher than Dr Owen on both. Alternatively, Dr Owen has a slightly tougher image, suggesting a possible lack of the human touch.

Brecon and Radnor

Every now and then — thankfully rarely — one or more of the polls comes unstuck in a by-election or general election, and we at Gallup still have memories of 1970 and of the later Glasgow Hillhead by-election. In 1985 it was the turn of MORI, who had otherwise had a good record in election studies of all sorts. Both they and NOP suggested a comfortable majority for Labour in Brecon and Radnor, basing their predictions on interviewing conducted close to polling day. Beaufort Research, in a slightly earlier study for HTV, saw Labour neck and neck with the Alliance, with only one point separating them. On the actual day, the Alliance captured the seat with a 2-per-cent lead over Labour, with the Conservatives in third place.

Gallup were asked by the *Daily Telegraph* to conduct a postmortem poll in the constituency to see what shifts of opinion had taken place during the campaign period. During the weekend following the by-election, a representative sample of 796 electors were interviewed. As is usual in such studies, a slightly greater proportion said they had voted than had actually done so on the the previous Thursday. In the shares of votes among those who claimed to have voted, there was a slight shortfall of Conservatives, with a slight exaggeration in the numbers of Labour and Alliance supporters. In the subsequent analyses, the sample was adjusted to be representative of the voting patterns in the by-election. Of those who voted, three in four said they had finally made up their minds which way to vote a long time beforehand, while 13 per cent said they had made up their minds during the early part of the campaign and a further 12 per cent said they had done so in the final few days. Among both Labour supporters and Conservatives, more than 80 per cent had made up their mind some time before the election. In the case of Alliance supporters, however, the proportion was a little under 60 per cent, with almost one in five saying they had made up their minds in the last few days of the campaign.

One in four of all voters said that during the campaign they had considered voting for one of the other parties, one half of them mentioning the Alliance. This latter group accounted for one in five of those who had actually voted for either the Conservative or Labour candidate. Amongst Alliance voters, 14 per cent said they had considered voting Conservative but had not done so and 12 per cent had considered voting Labour. Because the 'floaters' were relatively few in number, we cannot go into too much detail as to why they considered a party and then rejected it; but there are some indications. Among those who considered voting for the Conservative candidate, one in three said their reason for not voting that way was because of dissatisfaction with the Government and one in four said they did not like the candidate in question. The two main reasons given for considering but later rejecting the Labour candidate were Labour extremism and dislike of Labour's policies, each mentioned by one in five of this group. One in four of those who considered voting Alliance eventually decided to stick with their first choice.

Gallup also asked people about they voting intentions four weeks before the by-election and how they generally thought of themselves politically. The following table shows the replies given to the three questions:

Table 2.57: Party Support Trends in Brecon and Radnor

Q. Were you able to go and vote in last Thursday's by-election, or were you prevented from doing so? If you did vote, for which party did you vote?

Q. Casting your mind back to, say, four weeks ago, had you decided then to vote or not to vote? Which party were you intending to vote for at that time?

Q. Leaving aside this particular election, would you say you generally think of yourself as Conservative, Labour, Alliance, Nationalist, or what?

	Consider self	4 weeks before	Polling day
Conservative	38	30	27
Labour	36	34	34
Alliance	22	33	36
Other	3	2	2

The table seems to suggest that not much happened over the campaign period, with a drop of just three points in the Conservatives support and an increase of three points for the Alliance. Yet this simple approach disguises substantial shifts within the electorate which counterbalance one another to a very large degree. For example, one in ten of the people who had decided at the beginning of the campaign to vote Conservative voted for some other candidate. Four per cent of Labour supporters similarly changed their minds, as did 9 per cent of Alliance supporters. Overall, one in five electors did something other than what they had decided to do four weeks earlier. In the longer term, of course, the shifts were even more extreme. The following table shows the internal shifts between what people considered themselves to be politically and how they actually voted in the by-election. The question wordings are as shown in the previous table.

Table 2.58: Electoral Shifts in Brecon and Radnor

	Considered self to be:				
	Con	Lab	Alliance	Other	No party
Did not vote	16	17	18	16	58
Voted:					
Conservative	59	1	1	6	8
Labour	2	73	6	4	11
Alliance	22	8	75	39	21
Other	1	0	1	36	3

Thus it can be seen that it was among the Conservatives that the biggest defection occurred in the constituency, with one in five of them voting for the Alliance. This can be explained partly by the relatively loose attachment this Conservative group had to the party. Among this self-labelled Conservative group, 25 per cent said that their attachment to the party was very strong, 48 per cent fairly strong, and 26 per cent not very strong. The 25 per cent 'very strong' group compares with 42 per cent among Labour supporters and 19 per cent for the Alliance, a party barely four years old.

The Ideal Prime Minister

In October, Gallup returned to a topic studied 17 years earlier: what qualities were looked for in a prime minister? The techniques used then — the Stapel Scale — produced very sensitive results but meant asking the equivalent of more than 40 questions to cover just two party leaders. Given four leaders now, it was decided to simplify the method while still adhering to the spirit of the original. The 1985 results were as follows:

Table 2.59: Qualities in a Prime Minister

Q. *How important do you yourself think it is that a prime minister should have each of these: very important, quite important, not very important, or not at all important?*

	Very	Quite	Not very	Not at all	Don't know
The country's interests above party advantage	79	16	1	0	4
A clear view and purpose for the future of this country	78	17	1	0	4
Understanding of ordinary people	74	21	2	0	3
Ability to handle economic and financial affairs	72	23	2	1	4
A team of first-rate men and women as ministers or potential ministers behind him/her	72	22	2	0	4
Ability to handle problems at home	67	25	4	1	4
The respect and loyalty of his/her colleagues in Parliament	63	29	4	1	3
Ability to handle foreign affairs	62	29	4	1	4
Respect of leaders of other countries	49	37	9	1	4
Determination to pursue policies, even when they are unpopular	49	31	10	3	6
Skill developed from long experience in politics	45	35	12	3	4
Sincerely held principles and views which he/she will not compromise	42	33	14	6	5
Ability as speaker on television	36	39	19	4	3
Background of a happy family life	26	35	26	9	4

In 1968, using a slightly different methodology, the rank orders were very similar, with a few exceptions. 'Ability for handling problems at home', for example, was rated slightly more highly, as was 'sincerely held principles'. Analysis of the 1985 data showed, as expected, some significant differences in the level of importance given to each of the attributes by supporters of the various parties: for example, Conservatives attached less importance to the third quality in the list, 'understanding of ordinary people'. Naturally, given the personality of Mrs Thatcher, Conservatives were inclined to see 'determination to pursue policies even when they are unpopular' and 'sincerely held principles and views which she will not compromise' as being more important than the general public did.

When asked which of the 14 qualities was the most important for a prime minister to possess, 'the country's interests' (mentioned by 30 per cent) dominated the public's choice. This was followed by 'a clear view' (17 per cent) and 'understanding of ordinary people' (13 per cent). No other quality was mentioned by more than one in twelve of the public. All four (or three) parties' supporters agreed with the public on what was the most important quality, and then the answers diverged. The second and third qualities selected were:

Conservatives : A clear view and purpose (16 per cent)
: Sincerely held principles (11 per cent)

Labour : A clear view and purpose (17 per cent)
: An understanding of ordinary people (17 per cent)

Liberal : A clear view and purpose (20 per cent)
: A first-rate team (13 per cent)

SDP/Alliance: An understanding of ordinary people (18 per cent)
: A clear view and purpose (17 per cent)

Televising the House of Commons

At the end of November, the House of Commons voted yet again on the issue of admitting television cameras for a trial period; and yet again it voted to keep them out, despite earlier indications that the Commons might follow the lead of the upper chamber. The vote against the proposal, however, was in contrast to the views of the general public, of whom a majority thought it would be a good idea.

Table 2.60: Televising the House of Commons — A Good Idea?

Q. Do you think it would be a good idea or a bad idea to televise the proceedings of the House of Commons?

	General public	Con	Lab	Lib/SDP
Good idea	58	55	68	54
Bad idea	27	35	17	31
Don't know	15	10	15	15

Men were slightly more inclined to see it as a good idea (63 per cent) than women were (53 per cent), and there tended to be a generation gap. People aged between 35 and 44 were most in favour, with 67 per cent of them saying it was a good idea; while those aged 65 or over were most against, 35 per cent saying it was a bad idea.

When asked why they held that particular view, those thinking it was a good idea were almost single-minded in saying that it would enable the public to see their representatives at work (87 per cent). Another 14 per cent thought it might help to improve the image of MPs by making them behave properly. Those thinking televising the House would be a bad thing were less decisive. One in three (32 per cent) said that too much arguing took place in the Commons for this to be shown on television, while 21 per cent said either that it was boring or would not interest the public, and a further 20 per cent thought it might mean some MPs playing to the camera or trying to hog it. Just under one in ten (9 per cent) thought there was enough coverage already, on the radio or in newspaper reports, and slightly fewer (6 per cent) thought it might inhibit some MPs from speaking their minds.

Members of Parliament

A number of studies carried out throughout 1985 showed the public's low regard for its elected representatives. Out of 14 professions, Members of Parliament came tenth for honesty and ethical standards as far as the public was concerned.

Table 2.61: Honesty of Groups

Q. How would you rate the honesty and ethical standards of the people in these different fields — very high, high, average, low or very low? (The figures have been compressed.)

	High	Average	Low	Don't know
Doctors	75	20	4	2
Police officers	55	31	11	3
Lawyers	46	30	11	13
University teachers	38	28	7	27
Psychiatrists	37	19	8	36
Engineers	34	44	2	20
Government ministers	22	38	30	9
Civil servants	20	51	20	9
Business executives	20	41	19	20
Members of Parliament	17	40	35	7
Building contractors	12	43	32	12
Advertising executives	10	37	32	21
Journalists	10	31	47	13
Trade union leaders	9	33	50	8

These figures in March reflected to some degree a study conducted in February on the subject of the public's confidence in various institutions, where the police were at the top of the list and trade unions at the bottom.

Table 2.62: Confidence in Institutions

Q. Please look at this card and tell me for each item listed how much confidence you have in them: is it a great deal, quite a lot, not very much, or none at all?

	A great deal	Quite a lot	Not very much	None at all
The police	40	43	12	5
The armed forces	39	47	8	6

The Church	20	36	29	15
The legal system	13	46	30	12
Major companies	10	43	32	15
Parliament	10	38	39	13
The Civil Service	8	36	41	14
The education system	8	35	46	11
Trade unions	7	18	45	31
The press	5	23	52	20

Comparisons are also available for April 1983, a year after the Falklands War. The proportion having a great deal of confidence in the armed forces had dropped from 52 per cent to 39 per cent. A similar fall had occurred, on the same dimension, for Parliament: from 17 per cent to 10 per cent.

In August. even more hostile attitudes towards Members of Parliament emerged, with around three in four of the public thinking most parliamentary candidates made promises they did not intend to keep, told lies and were more concerned with power than they were about the nation.

Table 2.63: Members of Parliament

Q. I am going to read a few statements. For each, can you please tell me if you tend to agree or disagree with it or if, perhaps, you have no opinion about the statement.

	Agree	Disagree	No opinion
Most Members of Parliament will tell lies if they feel the truth will hurt them politically	79	12	8
Most Members of Parliament care more about keeping power than they do about the best interests of the nation	75	16	9
To win elections, most candidates for Parliament make promises they have no intention of fulfilling	72	23	5
Most Members of Parliament care more about special interests than they care about people like you	67	19	14
Most Members of Parliament make a lot of money by using public office improperly	46	31	23
Most Members of Parliament have a high personal moral code	42	35	23
Most Members of Parliament care deeply about the problems of ordinary citizens	32	57	11

Analysis by party affiliation suggests that some people, particularly non-Conservatives, were answering more in terms of members of the government than Members of Parliament in general. For example, on the question of MPs caring more about special interests, Conservatives were 16 points below the general public in agreeing and 12 points below on the question of MPs being more concerned about power. Labour supporters, on the other hand, took a much more cynical view of Members of Parliament. A month later, Gallup asked people how much confidence they had in the politicians from each of the four parties. Comparisons with May 1983, when the questions had last been asked, showed a significant drop in confidence in Conservative politicians and an increased confidence in Alliance politicians.

Table 2.64: Confidence in Politicians

Q. On the whole, how much confidence do you have in Conservative/Labour/Liberal/Social Democratic politicians to deal wisely with Britain's problems — very great, considerable, little or very little?

	Conservative		Labour		Liberal		SDP	
	1983	1985	1983	1985	1983	1985	1983	1985
Very great	11	5	5	5	4	3	2	5
Considerable	34	25	20	20	21	30	12	31
Little	20	20	21	24	27	27	23	23
Very little	19	24	23	22	20	16	20	14
None at all (vol.)	14	24	27	25	17	13	28	15
Don't know	2	3	3	4	11	11	15	11

At the time, the Liberal/SDP Alliance was riding high in the polls due to the immediacy of their party conferences and the attendant media publicity. Labour and the Conservatives were ten points behind, vying with each other for second place, but analysis of the confidence question suggests that Labour's position was not so good as it appeared. Among each party's own supporters, the proportion saying they had at least considerable confidence in their party's politicians were:

Conservative: 81 per cent
SDP: 78 per cent
Liberal: 76 per cent
Labour: 67 per cent

Over one in four (29 per cent) of Labour supporters said they had little — or worse — confidence in their party's politicians. When the questions were repeated in late October, with the party conferences over, the main differences were a slight increase in confidence in Labour's politicians and a slight loss of confidence in politicians of both parties making up the Alliance.

Attitudes towards Conservative politicians showed no significant changes compared with the pre-conference study. The public's relative lack of confidence in politicians from the various parties was matched by a lack of interest in January in how the parties chose their parliamentary candidates. Thus, 59 per cent were not very interested or not interested at all. Three in four of the public, however, did think that the way candidates were chosen was important, and the same proportion thought that a sitting Member of Parliament should have to go before the local party for approval. Only one in ten thought the incumbent should be automatically readopted. Similarly, three in four of those saying the sitting MP should seek reapproval thought there should be several other people on the short list in competition with the MP, though one in five thought the party should simply be asked to decide whether or not it want to renominate the MP, without considering others. As previous studies had shown, the public wanted the widest possible group of people to be involved in the choosing of new parliamentary candidates: 37 per cent thought all supporters who normally voted for the party should be involved and 41 per cent wanted all members of the constituency party to have a vote. Just over one in ten (11 per cent) wanted this confined to a committee of constituency party leaders, and even fewer — 4 per cent — to the national party headquarters.

Experience, effectiveness, local knowledge and political views were the characteristics thought to be most important when it came to choosing a parliamentary candidate. One in two (51 per cent) of the public thought it was more important for an MP to devote himself to looking after constituency concerns than it was for him to make a real contribution nationally in Parliament (35 per cent). Labour supporters tended to see the latter as slightly more important than the public overall. Then, in order to measure the 'presidential' aspects of a general election, the public was asked which was more important: the policies and character of party leaders nationally or the policies and character of the candidates in the constituency. One in two (52 per cent) said the party leaders were more important, while

Table 2.65: Parliamentary Candidates' Characteristics

Q. Which of these do you think important in choosing a
parliamentary candidate?

Q. Which two of these characteristics is most important?

	Important	Most important
Experience of local council problems	63	46
Ability to have an impact in Westminster	58	43
Views on major political issues	56	44
Knowing and being known in the constituency	56	35
Pleasing personality and manners	24	5
Attitudes towards the party leader	19	7
Personality of wife/husband	7	1
None of these; don't know	4	5

41 per cent opted for the candidates. Conservatives, Labour supporters and Alliance supporters tended to mirror the pattern of replies
for the public as a whole, while one in two Liberals put more emphasis
on the candidates in the constituency.

One in two (49 per cent) of the public claimed to know the
name of the MP for their constituency, ranging from 45 per cent
among Labour supporters to 57 per cent among Alliance supporters. Three in four of the public, however, knew their MP's
party: 44 per cent Conservative, 29 per cent Labour and 2 per cent
Alliance. Just over one in two (53 per cent) of the public thought
that they lived in a safe seat, 32 per cent thought they lived in a
marginal constituency, and 14 per cent were undecided. One in ten
also said that they were a dues-paying member of a political party:
5 per cent Labour, 4 per cent Conservatives and 1 per cent Liberal
or SDP.

The Views of Members of Parliament

In December, Gallup interviewed 329 Members of Parliament —
200 Conservatives, 107 Labour and 22 from other parties — and
asked their views on a number of issues. A majority (55 per cent)
of all the MPs polled, for instance, agreed with the government's
decision to withdraw from Unesco, though the parties were poles
apart on this question: whereas 85 per cent of Conservative MPs
thought the decision was the correct one, 87 per cent of Labour

MPs took the opposite view. On a question about the Anglo-Irish agreement, however, MPs from the two main parties held similar views. Overall, one in two (53 per cent) thought that the government would be able to implement the agreement, 17 per cent thought that it would be implemented but only after major modifications had been made, and 24 per cent thought it unlikely that it would ever be implemented. Three in five (62 per cent) Conservatives and 41 per cent of Labour MPs saw the agreement being implemented, though 31 per cent of the latter group thought it never would be.

The Geneva summit meeting was rated a success overall by nine in ten Conservative MPs but only by one in two Labour Members. On specific issues, however, with two exceptions, MPs felt that little had been accomplished either in the way of reducing East-West tension or for future co-operation. On the other hand, majorities among all MPs felt that at best 'not very much' had been accomplished on the questions of human rights issues (90 per cent), 'Star Wars' (85 per cent), regional conflicts (76 per cent) or nuclear arms control (71 per cent).

It came as no surprise that in their answers to two questions on defence — unilaterialism and cruise missiles — the MPs begged to differ. The vast majority (94 per cent) of Conservatives thought that unilaterialism was a bad idea, while 81 per cent of Labour MPs thought it was a good idea. Similarly, while 99 per cent of Conservatives thought cruise missiles should continue to be stationed in Britain, 90 per cent of Labour MPs thought they should not. There were also major differences between the MPs on the Strategic Defence Initiative or 'Star Wars': nine in ten (93 per cent) of Conservatives thought the British Government should co-operate with the United States in SDI research, while 84 per cent of Labour MPs took the opposite view.

Similarly, 84 per cent of Conservative MPs thought British Companies should co-operate in the research regardless of whether or not any formal agreement existed between the governments of the two countries, while 57 per cent of Labour MPs thought they should not. Naturally, 60 per cent of Labour MPs saw it as making war more certain.

The MPs were also unable to agree on questions closer to home. Eight in ten (81 per cent) Conservatives, for example, felt that the benefits of Britain's membership of the Common Market outweighed the disadvantages, but 70 per cent of Labour MPs saw the disadvantages outweighing the benefits. On a question concerning a possible Channel link, 80 per cent of Conservatives were in favour, compared with only 31 per cent of Labour MPs, 57 per cent of whom were opposed. Neither could they agree on what form such a link should take. The most popular was a twin-bored tunnel for both road and rail services, preferred by 52 per cent of Conservatives and by 32 per cent of Labour MPs. This was followed by a twin-bored tunnel for a rail shuttle and a passenger service, 21 per cent and 38 per cent respectively.

There was a degree of agreement on one aspect of the government's taxation policy, but not on another. Nine in ten Conservatives and 71 per cent of Labour MPs felt that it was important to alter the tax thresholds; but while 59 per cent of Conservatives attached some importance to reducing the standard rate of tax, only 10 per cent of Labour MPs did so. In fact, 80 per cent thought that it was either not very important or not at all important. Both groups of MPs, however, emerged with the same proportion — 81 per cent each — opposed to the idea of proportional representation. Only 13 per cent of Conservatives and 15 per cent of Labour MPs were in favour of changing the voting system. This compared with two in three MPs from the 'minor' parties.

Party Differences

Around one in three of the general public thought there was a great deal of difference between the two main established parties and the two partners in the Alliance, while one in two thought there was a great deal of difference between the four parties.

The cynics, those who thought there was not much difference between the parties, amounted to 15 per cent in June. The public were first asked about differences between the Liberal Party and the Conservatives and Labour separately.

Table 2.66: Differences Between the Liberal Party and the Conservative/Labour Parties

Q. Considering everything the Conservative and Liberal parties stand for, would you say that there is a great deal of difference between them, some difference, or not much difference?

Q. *And considering everything the Labour and Liberal parties stand for, would you say there is a great deal of difference between them, some difference, or not much difference?*

| | Conservative/Liberal | | | Labour/Liberal | | |
	Public	Con	Lib	Public	Lab	Lib
A great deal	31	32	33	38	35	34
Some	36	34	39	32	34	31
Not much	28	28	24	24	27	31
Don't know	5	7	5	5	5	4

The public overall were more likely to see a greater difference between the Liberals and Labour than between the Liberals and the Conservatives. Liberal supporters, on the other hand, saw their own party as being more like the Labour Party than the Conservative Party. The public saw even less of a difference when comparing the Social Democratic Party with both the Conservative and Labour parties:

Table 2.67: Differences between the SDP and the Conservative/Labour Parties

Q. *Thinking about the Conservative and Social Democratic parties would you say there is a great deal of difference between them, some difference, or not much difference?*

Q. *And thinking about the Labour and Social Democratic parties would you say there is a great deal of difference between them, some difference, or not much difference?*

| | Conservative/SDP | | | Labour/SDP | | |
	Public	Con	SDP	Public	Lab	SDP
A great deal	32	34	35	32	34	40
Some	31	31	42	31	30	40
Not much	25	22	18	24	25	16
Don't know	12	13	5	13	11	4

Therefore, when comparing the Social Democratic Party with the two main established parties, the public saw the two pairs of parties as having the same degree of difference. The Conservatives and Labour supporters also saw the Social Democratic Party in a similar light when making the comparison. In contrast, SDP supporters tended to see a slightly larger difference between their party and Labour than between it and the Conservative Party.

Finally, people were asked what differences there were between the four parties. Not surprisingly, they saw greater differences between the four parties than they had in the earlier questions.

Table 2.68: Differences Between the Four Parties

Q. *And considering the Conservatives, Labour, Liberal and Social Democratic parties as a whole, would you say there is a great deal of difference between them, some difference, or not much difference?*

	General public	Con	Lab	Lib	SDP
A great deal	51	54	50	49	61
Some	27	29	25	34	28
Not much	15	12	18	13	7
Don't know	6	5	7	4	3

It would appear that Social Democrats, having decided to support the most recently formed party, claimed to be able to detect more differences between the four parties — possibly in order to rationalise their choice.

Tactical Voting

The volatility in the public's support for the three main parties mentioned earlier in this chapter can also be seen in the replies to a question spanning more than 35 years. In December 1949, Gallup asked: 'In politics, which do you think is the best thing to do — to choose a party and stick to it, or to make up your mind at each election according to the way things are going?', and repeated the question in January 1985. In the run-up to the 1950 general election, the public were almost evenly divided in their replies to the question, with 45 per cent saying it was better to choose a party and stick to it and 46 per cent saying it was better to take events into account. At the beginning of 1985, the proportion of 'loyalists' among the public had fallen to 34 per cent while that of 'opportunists' had risen to 61 per cent. Labour voters in January — like the general public in 1949 — were evenly divided on the question. 'Loyalists' amounted to 39 per cent of Conservatives, 23 per cent of Liberals and 12 per cent of SDP supporters.

In an election situation, however, the public claimed to be less fickle in their voting behaviour. Three in four said in June that they would stick to their party even if they thought the party they most disliked was likely to win in their constituency and the party they favoured most had no chance of winning. Yet one in five said they would seriously consider voting for the party in second place. Which were the disliked parties? In September, 39 per cent said the Conservatives were the party they would very much not want to win, 34 per cent said Labour and 4 per cent the Alliance. Two-and-a-half years earlier, Labour had been slightly in the lead as the party people did not want to win.

1985 saw yet another attempt to muzzle the opinion polls following the Brecon and Radnor by-election and the failure of some of the normally more reliable polls. Compared with 1983, before the election, the public in 1985 saw opinion polls as slightly less influential in both general elections and in by-elections.

Table 2.69: The Influence of Opinion Polls

Q. How much influence do you think opinion polls have on people in general elections: a lot, a fair amount, a little, or none at all?

Q. And what about in by-elections: a lot, a fair amount, a little, or none at all?

| | General elections | | By-elections | |
	April 1983	Sept 1985	April 1983	Sept 1985
A lot	14	12	15	11
A fair amount	28	25	22	22
A little	34	34	32	32
None at all	17	22	23	27
Don't know	6	7	8	8

Possibly with Brecon and Radnor in mind, and their loss in the by-election, Labour supporters tended to see the polls as slightly more influential than did either Conservatives or Alliance supporters. Three months earlier, the public were asked how they would react to a change in the voting method to a transferable vote system.

Table 2.70: Transferable Voting

Q. Let us suppose that our method of voting were changed so that you were asked to place two parties in order of preference, that is to put a '1' for the party you normally vote for and a '2' for your second choice. If this were the case, which party would be your second choice?

	First choice:			
Second choice:	Conservative	Labour	Alliance	Other
Conservative	0	8	37	9
Labour	9	0	40	36
Alliance	75	71	0	37
Other	2	7	2	3
Don't know	4	4	5	7
No second choice	10	11	15	7

Thus, around three in four Conservatives and Labour supporters would choose the Alliance as their second vote, with a potentially significant impact on the many constituencies where no party achieved a majority of the votes and the Alliance came in first or second.

Electoral Reform

In one of their party political broadcasts in early December, 'starring' John Cleese, the Social Democrats concentrated on the concept of proportional representation and the unfairness, as they saw it, of the electoral system. In May, questions had been asked on the topic, repeated from June 1983, and these were subsequently repeated in November 1985. On balance, the public were satisfied with the present way of choosing MPs, though there had been a slight decline in the degree of satisfaction and an increase in the number of undecideds.

Conservatives expressed most satisfaction with the present system, 71 per cent saying they were either 'very satisfied' or 'quite satisfied'. The proportion so satisfied dropped to 60 per cent among Labour supporters and, further still, to 47 per cent among Alliance supporters. The public also attached less importance to changing

Table 2.71: Satisfaction with the Electoral System

Q. At present the candidate who wins the most votes in an election becomes the MP. How satisfied are you with this system of choosing MPs? Are you:

	June 1983	May 1985	Nov 1985
Very satisfied	24	19	17
Quite satisfied	35	42	41
Not very satisfied	25	21	19
Not at all satisfied	14	12	12
Don't know	2	6	10

Table 2.72: Importance of Changing System of Choosing MP

Q. How important do you think it is for us to change the system of choosing MPs?

	June 1983	May 1985	Nov 1985
Very important	29	23	22
Quite important	19	24	21
Not very important	16	22	25
Not at all important	26	21	21
Don't know	9	10	12

the system, despite the decline in satisfaction with the system.

As might be expected, Conservatives attached the least importance to the making of any changes in the electoral system. One in three (31 per cent) thought that it was at least quite important, compared with 39 per cent of Labour supporters and 56 per cent of Alliance supporters. However, a majority of the general public (59 per cent) and of all three parties said that they would be in favour of a system whereby the number of seats won in the House of Commons was proportional to the number of votes it won nationally. Seven in ten (71 per cent) of Alliance supporters favoured the idea. The public was, on balance, favourable to the idea of coalition government being a by-product of a change in the electoral system. Just under one in two (43 per cent) said the idea of a government being made up of more than one political party made them more favourable to a change in the present system, while 32 per cent said that it made them less favourable. A majority of Alliance supporters said it made them feel more favourable; Labour supporters were almost evenly divided on the question; and Conservatives tended to be less favourable to the idea.

On the other hand, the public in May was less favourable to a change if it meant that there would be larger constituencies with more than one MP. While one in three (31 per cent) said that such a consequence would make them feel more favourable to the change, 43 per cent said it would make them feel less favourable. A similar pattern of replies emerged in the June 1983 study, when the figures were 34 per cent and 52 per cent respectively. The idea of keeping the present constituencies but having voters list candidates in their order of preference was favourably received by 61 per cent of the general public, two points up on the proportion doing so in June 1983.

Two further questions asked in November, but not earlier, dealt with the idea of having a referendum on the question of proportional representation. One in two (49 per cent) of the public thought the Alliance would be entitled to demand a referendum on the issue if they campaigned on the basis of a reform of the electoral system but won only enough seats to be part of a joint government, and 23 per cent said they would not be entitled to do so. Naturally, two in three Alliance supporters thought the Alliance would be entitled to call for a referendum, a view accepted by slightly more than two in five Conservatives and Labour supporters. When asked what should happen if the Alliance won enough seats to form a government on its own, 52 per cent said that a referendum should still be held, though 20 per cent said it should not. The analyses by party affiliation would go some way to gladden the hearts of political cynics: more Conservatives and Labour supporters thought that a referendum should still be held in answer to the second question than thought that the Alliance would be entitled to demand a referendum in answer to the first question — an increase among both parties of around ten points. Yet fewer Alliance supporters (the number was down by eleven points) thought that a referendum would still be necessary after gaining power.

The final question on the topic was asked in mid-December and showed a much more evenly divided public on the question of proportional representation than in the earlier surveys. Analysis by age showed one in two of the under-45s wanting a change in the voting

Table 2.73: A Change to Proportional Representation

Q. *Some people say that we should change the voting system to allow smaller political parties to get a fairer share of MPs. Others say that we should keep the voting system as it is to produce effective government. Which view comes closer to your own?*

	General public	Con	Lab	Alliance
Change voting system	45	31	42	64
Keep current system	47	64	50	30
Don't know	8	5	8	6

system, while a majority of those aged 45 and over opted for the status quo.

Local Elections

On 2 May, in the county council elections, the Alliance made substantial gains at the expense of both the Conservative and Labour parties, winning the balance of power in 20 out of 26 counties. A week earlier, Gallup put a number of questions to the public about their local councils. A majority (58 per cent), for example, were 'very satisfied' or 'fairly satisfied' with the way their local council was running the area, but 21 per cent were not very satisfied and another 14 per cent were not satisfied at all. Dissatisfaction with local councils increased with age, with 27 per cent of 18- to 34-year olds not very satisfied or not at all satisfied, the proportion rising to 42 per cent among senior citizens. Whether a sign of cynicism or frustration, the public were fairly evenly divided on the issue of whether it mattered which party won the local elections. Just under one in two (47 per cent) said it mattered a lot, 17 per cent that it mattered a little, and 34 per cent said it didn't matter. At a time when the GLC and the government were involved in a propaganda battle on the question of the Council's abolition in 1986, the public — in particular, Labour supporters — thought that the government had too much control over local councils.

Despite the (then unknown) success of the Alliance in the county council elections, the public overall saw them doing neither better

Table 2.74: Independence of Local Councils

Q. Do you think that, in general, the local councils have too much independence from national government, not enough independence — or are things about right?

	Public	Con	Lab	Lib	SDP
Too much	12	18	7	15	13
Not enough	45	32	57	55	40
About right	31	39	28	20	33
Don't know	12	11	9	10	14

nor worse than the Conservative or Labour councils. Forty-four per cent thought they would do much the same as the other parties, 24 per cent thought they would do better, and 19 per cent thought they would do worse. Even one in three Alliance supporters thought their parties would do no better than the Conservatives or Labour councils.

The replies to two other questions brought good news for the Alliance, though the concept behind the questions is unlikely to come to fruition in the near future. People were asked what should happen if no party obtained a majority in the local elections, and one in four said the party with the most seats should take responsibility for running the council. Almost two in three, however, thought two of the parties should get together to share responsibility for running the council as a coalition. When a similar question was asked about general elections, slightly more people (32 per cent) opted for the status quo but 58 per cent still wanted a coalition goverment. In both these questions, Conservatives were more likely than average to support the idea of the party with the most seats taking over.

The vast majority (72 per cent) of the public thought that the cost of housing was going up. Almost two in three (63 per cent) of those saying housing costs had risen blamed it on the general rise in the cost of living. One in five said it was due to the rise in local rates, and 15 per cent said the chief reason was the increasing cost of mortgages. The general public was similarly concerned about the level of rates in their area. Two in three (68 per cent) were either 'somewhat concerned' or 'very concerned', 20 per cent were 'not very concerned', and 8 per cent 'not at all concerned'. Alliance supporters tended to be the most concerned about the level of rates in their area. Majorities of the general public, and of Alliance supporters and Labour supporters, lay the blame for rate increases on the government rather than their local council.

Table 2.75: Government to Blame for Rate Increases

Q. Whom do you think is more responsible for recent increases in rates: your local authorities or the government at Westminster?

	General public	Con	Lab	Lib	SDP
Local authorities	30	53	15	21	32
Government	55	29	74	68	56
Don't know	14	18	10	11	12

One in two home-owners also blamed the government, while one in three blamed the local authorities. Among council tenants, blame for the government went up to a ratio of three to one.

Yet despite the concern about rising rates, the public preferred to pay possibly more in rates than have a cut in services. This applied to people of all political persuasions.

Table 2.76: Extension of Local Services

Q. People have different views about whether it is more important to reduce rates or keep up local government spending. How about you? Which of these statements comes closest to your own view?

	General public	Con	Lab	Lib	SDP
Rates being cut even if it means some reduction in local services such as schools, housing and welfare services	15	19	13	17	12
Things should be left as they are	29	30	28	23	35
Local services such as schools, housing and welfare services, should be expanded even if it means some increases in rates	50	42	55	51	47
Don't know	6	9	4	9	6

There was a slight generation gap in the replies to this question, with a majority of the under-45s wanting extended local services and the proportion dropping to just over one in three among senior citizens.

On the other hand, the public, on balance, approved of governments limiting the amount of rate increase that a local council can levy: two in five (43 per cent) approved of such limits, and slightly fewer (39 per cent) disapproved. As expected, a majority of Conservatives approved of the idea and a majority of Labour supporters disapproved. Alliance supporters shared the more balanced view of the general public. The public was also almost evenly divided on questions of a local income tax and a poll tax. Just over one in three (35 per cent) approved of having a local income tax to replace rates, against 37 per cent disapproving. Not surprisingly, Conservatives were more inclined to approve of the idea, but not by a majority as were Alliance supporters.

Labour supporters, on balance, disapproved of the idea of a local income tax. The general public were more favourable to the idea of a poll tax — 'a charge of so much per person in each household' — to replace the rates; but again it did not receive majority approval. Just over two in five (44 per cent) approved of the idea — including majorities of Conservatives and Alliance supporters — and 39 per cent disapproved. Among Labour supporters, more disapproved (46 per cent) than approved (33 per cent). The idea of the poll tax was particularly attractive to people aged 45 and over.

As always, there was majority support for the idea of a local council being required to have a referendum, seeking approval from its electors if it wanted to pass a major rate increase. Seven in ten approved of a referendum, with only 17 per cent disapproving. Whether 70 per cent would actually bother to go and vote is doubtful and was not questioned, but the idea of increased involvement was obviously attractive to electors. Finally, Gallup asked people their views on the privatisation of local services, and on balance they were against the idea. A little under one in two (48 per cent) disapproved of the practice of services being carried out by private contractors, while slightly fewer (43 per cent) approved. Around two in three Conservatives agreed with the privatisation of local services, two in three Labour supporters disagreed, and Alliance supporters, on balance, were marginally in favour. Among those people agreeing with privatisation, refuse collection — mentioned by 56 per cent of the group — topped the list of services to be privatised. This was followed by street cleaning (34 per cent), road repairs and housing repairs (each mentioned by 33 per cent) and public transport (29 per cent).

'Traditional Values'

One of the catch phrases that came into prominence in 1985 was 'traditional values', used particularly by Mrs Thatcher, and Mr Tebbit made allusion to such values in his Disraeli Lecture towards the end of the year. But what did such a term mean to the general public? To a significant minority — as shown below — it meant absolutely nothing, particularly when used by a politician.

Table 2.77: The Meaning of 'Traditional Values'

Q. *When you hear people talking about 'a return to traditional values', what does it mean to you'? Anything else?*

Q. *When you hear politicians talking about 'a return to traditional values', what does it mean to you? Anything else?*

	People	Politicians
Morals	14	8
Law and order	14	8
Good old days, the past	13	9
Cheaper prices, money with value	10	5
Discipline	6	2
More employment	6	6
Consideration/concern for others	6	3
Fair pay for fair day's work	5	2
Importance of family	4	2
'Victorian' values	3	2
Poverty, low wages	3	3
Hard work	2	1
Less emphasis on welfare state	2	2
Other	13	12
Nothing; don't know	36	53

A solicitor interviewed in the survey where the 'politicians' question was asked, neatly summed up the cynical view many of the general public had: 'Means whatever they intend it to mean'. It is noticeable that the proportion answering 'nothing' or ' don't know' was significantly higher when asked about 'politicians' than when the questions related to 'people'.

This was true for all groups of people, but the difference was greatest among women and older people. The idea of 'traditional values' also meant different things to different people. Almost no Conservatives, for example, took it to mean 'Victorian' values, though Labour and Alliance supporters tended to do so, usually seeing it as a return to the Poor Law and squalor for the working classes. Also, over twice as many Conservatives and Alliance supporters saw it as meaning law and order, morals or discipline than did Labour supporters.

British Gas

In contrast to 30 years ago, when a number of important industries were nationalised, the mid-1980s have seen the policy reversed, with the privatisation of profitable nationalised industries. After British Telecom came British Gas, to be followed by other such institutions. On balance, the public in May were against the proposed sell-off of British Gas. Just over one in three (35 per cent) thought it was a good idea, but 45 per cent said it was a bad idea. Those in favour of the idea said that they were so through a belief in private enterprise (46 per cent), that people should have the chance to buy shares (25 per cent), that it would help to reduce or stabilise prices (16 per cent), or that it would make the industry more efficient (11 per cent).

The top four reasons given by those opposed were that private enterprise was bad (50 per cent), that privatisation would bring about increases in prices (17 per cent), that British Gas was a paying concern already (15 per cent), and that people would make money on the shares (13 per cent).

When asked what should be done with the money from the sale, only 24 per cent wanted to use it to cut taxes. Almost three times as many (67 per cent) felt it should be invested in the National Health Service and used for the building of new hospitals or the modernisation of existing ones. Two in five (38 per cent) wanted more investments in public works such as sewage, roads or housing, and the same proportion wanted the money to be spent on school building, improvements or additional educational facilities.

Around one in five (22 per cent) felt that it should be used to improve social security benefits. On balance, the public felt that the new privately owned gas body would give a better service, though prices would rise faster than under British Gas. One in three (31 per cent) thought a better service would be given, 21 per cent saw no change, and 24 per cent felt the service would be worse under the new gas body. On the other hand, 35 per cent thought gas prices would rise faster under the privately owned gas body than they did under British Gas, 33 per cent felt they would rise at the same rate, and 16 per cent thought they would rise more slowly.

A repetition of the questions later in the year, in mid-November, found little in the way of significant shifts of opinion. Among the group of people who thought the privatisation of British Gas was a bad idea (47 per cent of the public), there were fewer mentions of private enterprise being a bad thing and more mentions of an increase in prices. This was echoed by the replies to the only other question showing any differences. In the final question on prices, the proportion thinking they would rise at a faster rate than they did under British Gas had increased from 35 per cent in May to 42 per cent in mid-November.

3   The Economy

The Most Urgent Problem of All

Since July 1981, the question of unemployment has dominated the replies to questions about the most urgent problems facing the country. Only twice during the Falklands crisis in 1982 did the proportion mentioning unemployment drop below 50 per cent, and even then it still topped the list of the public's concerns. Throughout 1985, as can be seen in the table opposite, no other problem came remotely near the figures for unemployment. The government has consistently held the view that the taking of extraordinary measures to create employment would be artificial and counter-productive in the long run, as well as endangering their counter-inflationary policy. The aim was a healthy economy within which a true demand for more jobs would appear, substantially reducing the dole queues. But as the dole queues lengthened, their successful 1979 poster campaign of Britain 'not working' under Labour came back to haunt them.

The public also had different priorities to the government. When asked in August which should be given greater attention, trying to curb inflation or trying to reduce unemployment, almost five times as many said reducing unemployment (77 per cent) as said curbing inflation (16 per cent). Even a majority of Conservatives put unemployment before inflation. However, on the more personal level of what was of most concern to members of the public themselves and their families, inflation (54 per cent) emerged above unemployment (43 per cent).

In June, August and again in November, around eight in ten of the public thought that it was very important that unemployment was drastically reduced, though this was slightly down on the 85 per cent who had held the same view in February 1983. However, the public had no illusions about the problem being solved in the near future, if at all.

Table 3.1: Most Urgent Problems

Q. What would you say is the most urgent problem facing the country at the present time? What is the next most urgent?

	Jan	Feb	Mar	Apr	May	June	July	Aug	Sept	Oct	Nov	Dec
Top problem												
Unemployment	75	70	83	80	80	77	79	81	78	76	77	77
Strikes	10	13	1	1	0	1	0	1	1	0	0	1
Cost of living	2	5	3	2	4	5	4	2	2	2	2	2
Other economic	2	3	2	1	2	1	1	1	1	1	1	2
Defence	3	1	1	2	2	2	2	1	1	1	1	1
Law and order	1	1	2	3	2	5	2	2	5	9	9	8
Health	0	1	1	2	2	2	2	1	1	1	1	1
Immigrants	0	0	0	0	0	1	1	1	3	3	2	1
Top two problems:												
Unemployment	85	82	91	89	88	87	87	89	89	87	88	88
Strikes	25	23	4	4	2	2	2	2	2	3	1	2
Cost of living	14	19	17	15	14	16	15	14	11	9	10	9
Other economic	10	13	10	7	8	7	8	6	6	6	6	6
Defence	15	9	7	9	12	9	8	10	8	6	8	7
Health	7	7	12	14	12	10	13	12	7	11	7	11
Pensions	5	5	1	5	6	7	5	4	5	4	7	6
Law and order	4	3	9	10	9	18	9	9	18	27	28	19
Education	4	5	7	7	6	5	5	5	6	6	5	6
Housing	3	6	7	8	10	7	10	12	8	7	8	12
Immigrants	1	1	2	2	1	3	3	2	8	9	5	4

Table 3.2: Unemployment for Another Five Years?

Q. How long do you think it will be before unemployment is
   drastically reduced?

	Nov 1984	Feb 1985	Aug 1985	Nov 1985
In the next 6 months	0	0	1	1
Over 6 months–1 year	0	1	0	0
Over 1 year–1½ years	1	1	0	1
Over 1½ years–2 years	2	1	2	2
Over 2 years–2½ years	2	2	3	4
Over 2½ years–3 years	3	4	2	3
Over 3 years–4 years	5	5	3	7
Over 4 years–5 years	7	11	7	10
Over 5 years–10 years	16	18	16	16
Over 10 years	20	19	17	14
Never	22	20	25	16
Don't know	22	18	23	25

As can be seen from the above table, up to six in ten of the general
public saw the problem as being around for at least five years, with
one in four seeing it as insoluble. It could be that the public was, to
some degree, beginning to take a fatalistic attitude towards unemployment, with a significant minority adopting the view that high
unemployment is unavoidable.

Table 3.3: The Inevitability of Unemployment

Q. Do you generally agree, generally disagree, or neither
   agree nor disagree that high unemployment is something
   we'll just have to learn to live with as best we can?

	Agree	Disagree
June 1984	55	38
March 1985	48	36
June 1985	39	56
July 1985	42	53
November 1985	46	49

A majority (58 per cent) of Conservatives in November agreed with
the statement, while majorities both of Labour supporters (56 per

cent) and Alliance supporters (55 per cent) disagreed. There was also a generation gap: around one in two (52 per cent) young adults disagreed with the idea of the inevitability of unemployment while 54 per cent of senior citizens agreed.

In mid-December, the vast majority of the general public expressed criticism of the way the government had handled the unemployment problem but a majority felt that they had handled the problem of inflation well.

Table 3.4: Government's Handling of Inflation and Unemployment

Q. On the whole, do you think the Conservative government since 1983 has handled the problem of inflation ...?

Q. And as for unemployment: on the whole, do you think the Conservative government since 1983 has handled the problem of unemployment ...?

	Inflation	Unemployment
Very well	15	1
Fairly well	42	12
Not very well	24	32
Not at all well	14	52
Don't know	5	3

Of some concern for the government should be the result that a majority (58 per cent) of Conservatives thought that at best the government had handled the problem of unemployment not very well. At the same time, the general public were asked which of the two problems — the threat of rising prices or the threat of unemployment — represented the greatest threat to themselves and their families. The figures were very similar to those found earlier in the year: 49 per cent saw rising prices as the greatest threat and 44 per cent unemployment. Conservatives and senior citizens were inclined to cite inflation as the greater personal problem, while unemployment came top among both Labour and Alliance supporters and among people aged under 45.

Other questions in June on unemployment reinforced the concern it engendered among the general public. The vast majority (82 per cent) felt that the government was not doing enough to stop unemployment from rising, and 75 per cent thought that the government should always aim at keeping unemployment as low as possible, even if this meant some inflation with rising prices. Just over one in two (57 per cent) thought that unemployment was always a bad thing, though 37 per cent felt that it could be justified as necessary during a period of adjustment. Altogether, 28 per cent of the public said that either they or someone in their family were directly affected by unemployment, and 38 per cent felt that they or their family would be affected by the rising unemployment. In September, Gallup asked people whether they or anyone in their immediate family had either been unemployed or had had great difficulty in getting a job in the last three to four years. Just under one in two (44 per cent) answered positively to this question, compared to 38 per cent in June 1983.

In December, people were asked to agree or disagree with a number of statements, some of which dealt with unemployment. Three in four of the general public thought that the government should spend more money on creating jobs and that as a rule a person was not at fault when he or she became unemployed.

Table 3.5: Agreement with Unemployment Statements

Q. *Please say whether you agree or disagree with each of these statements, or say if you are not sure either way. (Figures show 'agree' or 'disagree' results only.)*

The government should spend more money to create jobs	Public	Con	Lab	Lib/SDP
Agree	79	56	96	88
Disagree	12	32	1	6
The government should set firm guidelines for wages and salaries				
Agree	59	57	62	61
Disagree	28	31	24	26
The high level of unemployment in Britain is mainly the British Government's fault				
Agree	49	10	77	50
Disagree	42	84	14	40

Much of our unemployment has
been caused by trade union
leaders

Agree	47	68	29	47
Disagree	35	18	50	35

The rise in unemployment has
helped Britain's products to be
more competitive

Agree	22	34	16	19
Disagree	48	37	53	54

When someone is unemployed
it's usually his/her own fault

Agree	9	18	6	7
Disagree	81	68	88	86

In addition to the obvious party differences in the above table, there were generation differences. On the question of guidelines for wages and salaries, for example, 55 per cent of the under-35s agreed with the idea, but agreement rose to 65 per cent among senior citizens. There was also a tendency with increasing age to attach more blame to trade union leaders as a cause for unemployment. One in three (39 per cent) of young adults did so, compared with 61 per cent of people aged 65 and over.

But what of the views of those with a job on the spectre of unemployment? For a decade Gallup has asked them two questions about job security and their chances of re-employment if they were to lose their current job.

Table 3.6: Views of Those in Employment about Unemployment

Q. *Do you think that your present job is safe, or do you think that there is any chance you may become unemployed?*

Q. *In the case of your becoming unemployed, do you think you would be able to find a new job fairly quickly or do you think it might take longer?*

	Present job safe	Chance of unemployment	New job quickly	May take longer
June 1985	61	33	45	48
January 1982	66	29	31	61

Table 3.6 continued

November 1980	66	27	32	56
September 1980	58	38	38	54
July 1980	64	30	45	47
May/June 1980	68	27	48	44
September 1977	71	20	40	41
Sept/Oct 1976	70	24	42	45
September 1976	67	25	45	41
August 1976	71	24	42	44
March 1976	68	25	42	43
February 1976	64	26	42	43
October 1975	62	29	38	44

The table shows that the proportion thinking that their present job was secure peaked in 1976/77 but has since fallen, so that the June 1985 study represents the low point, with the exception of September 1980. On the other hand, despite the relatively high proportion thinking there was a chance they might become unemployed, they felt reasonably happy about getting a new job quickly.

One proposed way of reducing the level of unemployment was that the unemployed should be made to take a new job, even if this meant less money or lower status. One in two (51 per cent) agreed with the idea, though 43 per cent disagreed. Among those in a job, 62 per cent said they would be prepared to accept less money or lower status to get a job. Two in three (65 per cent) of the general public also thought that those in work should be prepared to accept changes in order to share work. On a question on increased taxation to help with the problem of unemployment, 32 per cent said they would be prepared to pay more in tax while 55 per cent said not. This may have been because 13 per cent felt that the unemployment benefit was too high and 32 per cent about right, though 38 per cent thought it was too low.

A further question in May threw more light on the public's attitude towards unemployment benefit, showing their division of opinion:

Table 3.7: Unemployment Benefits

Q. Opinions differ about the level of benefit for the unemployed. Which of these two statements comes closest to your own opinion:

	Total	Con	Lab	Lib	SDP
Benefit for the unemployed is too low and this causes hardship	41	22	65	38	33
Benefit for the unemployed is too high and this discourages people from finding jobs	32	53	17	26	32
Neither	19	19	13	26	24
Don't know	8	5	6	10	11

In addition to the political differences in the replies to these questions, with Conservatives and Labour supporters poles apart, there was a generation effect. While a majority (52 per cent) of young adults thought the benefits were too low, and 25 per cent thought they were too high, senior citizens were divided on this question (28 per cent and 41 per cent respectively).

Of particular significance is the impact of unemployment on young people, whose lives it could blight for ever. That unemployment had become a youth problem is highlighted by the replies given to a question asked not in 1985 but a year earlier, with a comparison of twenty years ago:

Table 3.8: The Young and Unemployment

Q. Do you think that nowadays the children of people like yourself starting work for the first time, will find a job without any trouble, will have some difficulty but will find one in the end, or will they find it almost impossible to get one?

	July 1965	July 1984
Without any trouble	46	4
With some difficulty	42	54
Almost impossible	4	39
Don't know	8	3

It is almost as if the replies have been turned on their heads in the 1984 study. The number of those who felt that their children starting out on their first job would find one without any trouble had fallen from 46 per cent to a mere 4 per cent. At the same time, the number of those thinking it would be almost impossible had increased tenfold: from 4 per cent to 39 per cent.

Youth Survey

With this in mind, and given the increasing number of young unemployed, Gallup conducted a study in July among youngsters aged 15 to 16 who were still at school. The survey showed a mixture of despair, disillusionment and self-help, and the answers to this wide-ranging questionnaire focusing mainly on unemployment suggested a potential powder-keg for the future. The popular image of shiftless youngsters hanging around on street corners was not confirmed by the attitudes of this sample to finding work. The vast majority (82 per cent) felt it was better to take a low-paid job than stay unemployed, though 13 per cent thought it was better to stay on the dole. There also tended to be majority support for the idea of training courses. Gallup asked its sample how far they agreed with three statements about unemployed people.

Table 3.9: Training Courses

Q. Here are some statements about young people under 18 who have left school and cannot find jobs. Please tell me for each statement how strongly you agree or disagree.

	Agree	Disagree	Neither; don't know
It would be better for young people under 18 who cannot get jobs to go on a good training course with a training allowance, or to carry on with suitable further education rather than be unemployed, receiving benefit and doing nothing	83	8	9
It would be better if the government spent money on providing more opportunities for further education or good training courses with a training allowance rather than spending it on paying out on unemployment or supplementary benefit	74	13	13
If there were suitable places available on good training courses, young people up to the age of 18 who are unemployed should be expected to take them up and not be paid unemployment or supplementary benefit	46	36	18

Two in three (68 per cent) of the youngsters were willing to move away from their home town if that was the only way they could get a job, while 30 per cent were not very willing. This mobility idea was less popular in the North and in Scotland.

The young persons, like the general public, were split when it came to discussing the level of unemployment benefits. While 45 per cent thought the benefits for the unemployed were too low and caused hardship, 30 per cent felt the benefits were too high and discouraged people from working. The same question put to the public at large revealed a similar pattern. The youngsters were also critical of the government's policy on unemployment, sometimes more critical than their elders: for instance, slightly more youngsters (87 per cent) thought reducing unemployment should be the government's priority, compared with 78 per cent among the public as a whole.

One in four (23 per cent) of the youngsters thought it would be easy to find their first job, while 71 per cent expected some difficulty. This latter proportion rose to 76 per cent among girls, and among the young in the North and in Scotland. When asked how long it would be before they got a job after leaving school, 17 per cent said up to a month, 21 per cent up to three months, 15 per cent up to six months, and 20 per cent longer than six months. Finally, the 15- and 16-year-olds were asked whether they agreed or disagreed with seven statements:

Table 3.10: Attitudes of the Young

Q. How far do you agree or disagree with each of these statements?

	Agree	Disagree	Neither; don't know
Everybody should have the right to a job	93	3	4
The pressures of life on young people are much greater today than they were for their parents	73	14	14
People will have to get used to living without working a full week	50	30	19
Taxes should be raised to provide the money to help the jobless	42	36	22

Table 3.10 continued

The use of violence is sometimes justified in order to bring about political change	32	47	20
The young are too pampered and have things too easy these days	30	58	11
It will be easier for me to have a successful career than it was for my father	23	63	14

Given the replies to the questions on their employment prospects, it should come as no surprise to learn that nine in ten of the youngsters held the view of the right to a job, and this is also reflected in the perceived difficulty of making a successful career for themselves compared with their father. Of perhaps greater concern are the one in three who advocated violence for the sake of achieving political change. Where this view was least popular, among young Alliance supporters, the proportion was 21 per cent rising to 39 per cent among young Labour supporters.

A number of the questions dealing with unemployment and future prospects can be divided up according to whether the replies given to them are optimistic or pessimistic. Two in particular were analysed in this way: firstly, the one relating to the ease or otherwise with which the youngsters would find their first job, and secondly that concerning the future impact of rising unemployment on themselves or their families. One in three (34 per cent) gave a pessimistic response to both these questions, 21 per cent gave optimistic replies to both, and 46 per cent gave answers that were a mixture of the two. Pessimists were more likely to be girls, 15-year-olds, Labour-inclined and living in the northern part of the country.

What possible media influences were there on these youngsters? Two in three of them read a daily paper every day, while the same proportion claimed to read a Sunday paper every week. Around one in seven (15 per cent) either read a daily paper less often than once a week or never read one, and for Sunday newspapers the proportion rose to 26 per cent. The *Sun*, at 31 per cent, topped the list of national dailies, followed by the *Daily Mirror* (22 per cent), the *Daily Mail* (13 per cent) and the *Daily Express* (10 per cent).

One in four read a local newspaper. A similar pattern emerged on the Sundays, with the *News of the World* (31 per cent) being the most popular, followed by the *Sunday Mirror* (24 per cent), the *Sunday People* (15 per cent), the *Sunday Express* (14 per cent) and the *Mail on Sunday* (13 per cent). As far as television was concerned, 60 per cent said they watched a news broadcast every day, though 15 per cent either saw one less than once a week or never watched. On average, news broadcasts on television were watched on about four-and-a-half days a week. The level of listening to news broadcasts on radio was distinctly lower, with only 36 per cent listening to one every day and on fewer than three days in an average week.

'*A Job for the Boys*'

The disillusionment evinced in the youth survey can be partly explained by the view, widely held among the general public, that it is not what you know but who you know. Three in four (74 per cent) of the public in March thought that it was true to say that many people got jobs because of who they knew not what they knew. This 'truism' was accepted by all sectors of the public; and among this group, 35 per cent felt that it happened very often, 45 per cent often, and 17 per cent thought it did not happen very often.

'A job for the boys' was also seen as a phenomenon that was an ever-increasing part of the British way of life, though views on this question varied according to the political party supported. Among the public at large, the proportion saying the process was happening more often than it did 20 years ago (42 per cent) outnumbered those who thought it was happening less often (26 per cent) with 23 per cent seeing no change over the period concerned. Conservatives were evenly divided on whether it was happening with any greater or lesser frequency, and a majority (54 per cent) of Labour supporters thought it was happening more often than it did 20 years ago. Alliance supporters, on balance, tended to agree with their Labour counterparts.

Despite this perceived increase since the mid-1960s, the public saw it as a worldwide problem rather than as yet another symptom of the 'British disease'. Just over two in five (44 per cent) thought Britain was no different from the rest of the world in this respect, 13 per cent thought it happened more in Britain, and 9 per cent more in the other countries. Finally, Gallup asked people whether either they or a member of their family had ever got a job because of somebody they had known at the job. Just over one in three (37 per cent) and 54 per cent of young adults (18–34) said they had.

The Economic Situation

One of the perplexing problems for the government in 1985 must have been the stubborn reluctance on the part of the general public to accept two economic facts: that inflation had fallen to a relatively low point and that the level of pay increases was running ahead of inflation. The year began, for example, with 59 per cent of the public saying that the government was not doing enough to control the rise in prices, 66 per cent thinking that the rise in prices was bound to continue, and 63 per cent feeling that the government was not handling the economic situation properly. At the same time, 49 per cent felt that wages had gone up less than food prices, despite government pronouncements to the contrary.

Since the beginning of 1979, Gallup has been asking a series of questions on the public's attitudes towards the economy, particularly with regard to prices and wages. The questions were asked three times in the first half of 1979 and monthly from then on. The figures in the following tables have been simplified in the form of quarterly averages.

As can be seen, Mrs Thatcher began her first term in office with only 17 per cent thinking her government was doing enough to

Table 3.11: Government Control of Rising Prices

Q. Do you think the government is or is not doing enough to control the rise in prices? (Figures are quarterly averages for percentage saying 'Is')

	Quarter:			
	1	2	3	4
1979	21	—	17	21
1980	18	21	21	24
1981	25	22	22	20
1982	23	32	34	39
1983	43	47	40	37
1984	38	37	33	35
1985	31	29	32	32

control rising prices, and for the following two years the figures were only marginally better. Then, as they say, the Argentinians invaded the Falklands — and the whole political world was turned on its head. The proportion of people approving of the government's policy on prices rose by nine points between the first and second quarters of 1982: the biggest shift in either direction in a single quarter over the whole period. Inspection of the individual months' figures show that as early as March — before the invasion — there were the beginnings of an increase in optimism about price rises. The Falklands crisis, coming when it did, probably accelerated the movement. The figures continued to improve in the government's favour, peaking in the second quarter of 1983. In June of that year, an actual majority (51 per cent) felt that the government was doing enough to control the rise in prices — the only time in the seven-year period. From then on, almost the only way to go was down, so that in the second quarter of 1985 the proportion had fallen to 29 per cent.

The last seven years has seen the public in an almost fatalistic mood about prices, probably reflecting a reaction to the substantial increases in oil and petrol prices and their subsequent effect on inflation. Only once in the period — in November 1982 — did less than one in two of the public think that the rise in prices was bound to continue. Otherwise, the proportion has tended to fluctuate between 51 per cent and 73 per cent on a monthly basis. This period has also been one of quite significant shifts in the perceived rises and falls in wages and food prices.

The replies to the two questions below can be seen to follow very similar patterns: peaking around the end of 1979 and the beginning of 1980, and bottoming out in 1983 and 1984.

Table 3.12: Increasing Wages and Food Prices

Q. *Thinking about wages, compared with a year ago, would you say they had risen a great deal, quite a lot, moderately, very little, or not at all?*

Q. *Now what about food prices generally? Compared with a year ago, would you say they had risen a great deal, quite a lot, moderately, very little, or not at all?*

(Figures are quarterly averages for percentages saying 'A great deal' or 'Quite a lot'.)

Table 3.12 continued

	Wages				Food prices			
	Q1	Q2	Q3	Q4	Q1	Q2	Q3	Q4
1979	21	25	29	34	73	77	85	86
1980	33	36	34	25	89	86	84	73
1981	20	16	16	12	63	69	69	70
1982	10	8	7	7	63	62	56	53
1983	10	8	7	6	44	44	42	46
1984	6	7	6	10	49	50	53	52
1985	8	8	9	9	53	57	52	50

However, the food price figures show a relatively sharp increase from the third quarter of 1983 continuing through 1984, but no matching increase in the perceived rate of wage rises.

The replies to a third question shows a similar disparity in the perception of wage rises and food price rises:

Table 3.13: The Public's Perception of the Wages and Food Prices Relationship

Q. Generally speaking, would you say that over the last year wages have gone up less than food prices, wages have gone up more than food prices, or wages and food prices have just about kept pace with each other? (Figures are quarterly averages.)

		Wages have gone up less than food prices	Wages have gone up more than food prices	Both the same
1979:	Q1	52	12	30
	Q2	51	17	25
	Q3	55	12	24
	Q4	52	14	25
1980:	Q1	54	11	25
	Q2	50	15	26
	Q3	53	12	27
	Q4	49	15	29
1981:	Q1	49	14	28
	Q2	54	11	25
	Q3	59	9	25
	Q4	60	7	25
1982:	Q1	62	8	23
	Q2	60	5	25

	Q3	57	7	27
	Q4	52	8	33
1983:	Q1	47	11	33
	Q2	42	12	36
	Q3	43	12	34
	Q4	47	12	31
1984:	Q1	49	10	31
	Q2	50	9	31
	Q3	52	8	28
	Q4	46	12	31
1985:	Q1	51	11	30
	Q2	53	8	27
	Q3	49	9	31
	Q4	44	12	32

Throughout the seven years, therefore, the proportion thinking that
wages had gone up less than food prices was always the largest of the
three positive replies, and it was only in the middle two quarters of
1983 that the proportion saying wages and food prices had kept pace
with each other closed on the former. It is hardly surprising, given this
earlier result, that a majority of the public over the period thought
that they had less disposable income in their pockets than a year
before. Gallup asked: 'When you've paid all the things you can't get
out of paying, for example, rent, rates, fares etc., would you say the
amount left in your pocket is more than a year ago, the same as, or
less?' At no time did the proportion saying they had more in their
pocket rise above 16 per cent, while the proportion saying they were
worse off was never less than 52 per cent and reached 74 per cent
more than once. Against this background, it was almost inevitable
that the public would be critical of the government's performance as
far as the economy was concerned, though criticism was somewhat
muted in the spring of 1983 in the run-up to the general election.

Table 3.14: Government's Handling of the Economy

*Q. Do the government's policies for tackling the economic
situation give you a feeling that they are or are not
handling the situation properly? (Figures are quarterly
averages for percentage saying 'Are'.)*

	Q1	Q2	Q3	Q4
1979	27	—	32	34
1980	27	32	29	26

Table 3.14 continued

1981	24	23	21	20
1982	25	34	33	38
1983	36	44	39	34
1984	31	33	29	31
1985	26	23	23	25

Again, one can see the improvement in the figures in the spring of 1982 — though actually preceding the Falklands crisis — followed by a peaking a year later and a subsequent decline to the levels of 1981. The political importance of the replies to this question is the closeness of the fit with support for the government, though they do not appear to be having any predictive capabilities. A charting of the above figures, along with that of the quarterly figures for support for the Conservatives, follows a similar pattern, with the 'economy' line always on a lower level than the 'political' line by around five points. Finally, this suite of questions contains one about the perceived fairness of the government's economic policies. The overwhelming majority of the public from the end of 1979 onwards took the view that the government's economic policies were not fair to all concerned. During the fourth quarter of 1979 and again in the second quarter of 1983 the proportion thinking the policies were fair peaked at 27 per cent, significantly higher than the 15 per cent average found in 1985.

Table 3.15: Importance of Inflation and Economic Situation

Q. How important is it to you that:
inflation is cut to below 5 per cent?
the economic situation substantially improves?

	Inflation			Economy		
	June	Aug	Nov	June	Aug	Nov
Very important	52	47	44	71	70	64
Quite important	29	35	33	22	22	27
Not very important	11	10	11	3	3	3
Not at all important	4	4	6	1	1	2
Don't know	4	4	6	3	3	5

The public was significantly more concerned about an improvement in the general economic situation than it was about controlling inflation in 1985, though the latter was thought to be a more achievable objective.

As can be seen, the proportion saying that these two economic aims were very important was falling throughout 1985, though improving the general economic situation was consistently seen as being more important than reducing inflation to below 5 per cent. Most of the time, however, inflation was either down to this level anyway or very close to it, so it is not surprising that less importance was being attached to it. The public were also more optimistic about achieving the aim of reducing inflation, though significantly less so about the economic situation as a whole.

Table 3.16: The Economic Future

Q. How long do you think it will be before:
   inflation is cut to below 5 per cent?
   the economic situation substantially improves?

	Inflation			Economy		
	Feb	Aug	Nov	Feb	Aug	Nov
In the next 6 months		3	7	1	1	2
Over 6 months–1 year		9	17	2	2	4
Over 1 year–1½ years		7	8	2	2	3
Over 1½ years–2 years		9	9	4	4	5
Over 2 years–2½ years		9	5	5	5	6
Over 2½ years–3 years	NA	4	3	6	4	5
Over 3 years–4 years		3	3	7	5	6
Over 4 years–5 years		6	3	13	9	12
Over 5 years–10 years		6	4	19	17	12
Over 10 years		7	4	12	13	9
Never		11	8	6	9	6
Don't know		26	28	23	30	29

Thus, after Mr Lawson's autumn Budget announcement the proportion thinking inflation would be reduced to below 5 per cent within a year doubled from 12 per cent to almost one in four. At the same time, the proportion thinking the economic situation would substantially improve within a year rose from 3 per cent to 6 per cent. One in four, however, still thought it would take at least five years or perhaps would never be achieved.

Despite Mrs Thatcher's claims that she knew best, that there was light at the end of the tunnel or that we were in our sixth year of economic recovery, three in four of the general public felt that the government should change its economic policies in some way. Only 20 per cent thought the present policies should be continued with. At the same time, two in three (68 per cent) of the public felt that the current economic situation could be solved if a government really tried to apply the right measures. A year earlier, 59 per cent had held the same view. On the other hand, just under one in four (23 per cent) in September 1985 thought the economy was a problem that no government could really solve, compared with 31 per cent a year earlier.

There was therefore an increase in the proportion thinking the economic situation would get worse under the Conservatives.

Table 3.17: A Worsening Economy

Q. *In the long term, do you think that the Conservative government's policies will mean that the economic situation will get better, will get worse, or will remain the same?*

	Sept 1984	Sept 1985
Get better	29	23
Get worse	38	42
Same	27	30
Don't know	6	5

Not surprisingly, three in five (62 per cent) Conservatives thought the economic situation would get better, but two in three (69 per cent) Labour supporters and one in two (49 per cent) Alliance supporters said that things would get worse.

This finding is echoed in the replies to another question, on whether or not 'the country's economy is worse off now than it was five (or six) years ago when the Conservatives came into goverment.' In June 1984, 48 per cent agreed with this statement, with the figure rising to 54 per cent in March 1985, to 57 per cent in June, to 56 per cent in July, before finally declining slightly to 49 per cent in November. In the last-mentioned study, 73 per cent of Conservatives disagreed with the statement, but majorities of both Labour supporters (79 per cent) and Alliance supporters (53 per cent) agreed. One message the government was slowly getting over was that 'with inflation under control, the economy will pick up smartly now'. In June 1984, a minority (23 per cent) agreed with the statement, rising to 26 per cent in March 1985, 28 per cent in both June and July, to 32 per cent in November. Over the same period, disagreement fell from 55 per cent to 46 per cent. On the other hand, majorities of the public rejected the idea that more jobs *and* low inflation is not possible.

Table 3.18: More Jobs *and* Low Inflation

Q. *Do you generally agree, generally disagree, or neither agree nor disagree that it is possible to have more people in jobs and low inflation at the same time?*

	Agree	Disagree
June 1984	50	26
March 1985	57	20
June 1985	55	23
July 1985	54	23
November 1985	61	18

Perhaps surprisingly, around three in five supporters of all parties including Conservatives, agreed with this statement.

Wages and Prices

Gallup has also been asking monthly for the last three years and during the first half of 1982 three questions on the public's perception of wage increases and inflation. The following table shows the quarterly averages among the employed population for the three questions and for two derived statistics:

Table 3.19: Perception of Wage and Price Rises

Q. *Over the next twelve months, what percentage increase, if any, do you expect to get in your wages or salary?*

Q. *Bearing in mind the present economic situation, inflation and unemployment, what level of wage or salary increase do you think workers should aim for?*

Q. *Over the next twelve months, what percentage increase in prices do you expect?*

		(i)	(ii)	(iii)	(iii-i)	(iii-ii)
					Own	Overall
		Increase	Increase		standard	standard
		for self	for workers	Inflation	of living	of living
1982						
	Q1	6.7	9.9	10.0	−3.3	−0.1
	Q2	5.9	9.5	9.2	−3.3	+0.3
	Q3	−	−	−	−	−
	Q4	−	−	−	−	−
1983						
	Q1	4.8	7.2	6.1	−1.3	+1.1
	Q2	4.3	7.0	6.3	−2.0	+0.7
	Q3	4.4	7.0	6.2	−1.8	+0.8
	Q4	4.4	7.2	6.4	−2.0	+0.8
1984						
	Q1	4.5	7.0	6.2	−1.7	+0.8
	Q2	4.6	7.3	6.3	−1.7	+1.0
	Q3	4.6	7.3	6.3	−1.7	+1.0
	Q4	5.2	7.7	6.6	−1.4	+1.1
1985						
	Q1	4.8	8.0	6.6	−1.8	+1.4
	Q2	4.7	8.0	6.8	−2.1	+1.2
	Q3	5.1	8.0	6.7	−1.6	+1.3
	Q4	4.9	7.8	5.9	−1.0	+1.9

The first three columns show the answers to the questions themselves; the fourth column is the difference between the third and the first columns, that is the difference between how much increase in pay they expect to get compared with the increase in prices; and the final column is the difference between the third and the second columns, that is the difference between how much workers in general should aim for and inflation. One can be said to be a measure of the individual's standard of living, while the other reflects the shift in the standard of living of all workers.

A number of trends are apparent in the figures: one being that the perceived increases for self are always less than the overall increase for workers, which in turn has tended to be above the perceived future increase in prices. This has produced a situation in which workers have come to expect any pay increase they may get to be at a rate lower than that of inflation, while workers in general were thought, on average, to be doing better than inflation. The differences therefore suggest that despite the perception of a declining standard of living at the personal level workers as a whole are doing slightly better than inflation. Of concern to the government must be the third column in the table, particularly the 1985 results showing an expectation of inflation above the 1984 level and at a level higher than the contemporary rise in prices. Such a view does little to damp down the demand for wage increases. On the other hand, the figures for the final quarter of 1985 are the best in the four-year period for the perceived inflation rate and the two 'standard of living' indices. It remains to be seen how these will be reflected politically in 1986.

Consumer Confidence

For over 25 years Gallup have been measuring consumer confidence, and in fact now have three separate monthly series. The first of these dates back to 1960 and is a relatively simple tool for measuring the public's attitude towards the economy: prices, business activity, unemployment, wages and consumer spending. In 1974 a more sophisticated series was begun which has run parallel to the earlier set of questions. In more recent years, Gallup in Britain have been the supplier of a third series for the EEC as part of a European-wide consumer economic climate study. The series are important not only in terms of trying to understand peaks and troughs in consumer spending but also in terms of seeing to what degree confidence in the economy generally is correlated with support for the government. The upturn, for example, in the electoral fortunes is paralleled to some degree by the first question in the series on perception of how the economy has behaved in the past twelve months.

Table 3.20: Perception of the Economy over the Last Twelve Months

Q. *How do you think the general economic situation in this country has changed over the last twelve months? (Quarterly averages.)*

		Got a lot better	Got a little better	Stayed the same	Got a little worse	Got a lot worse
1983:	Q1	2	21	17	26	32
	Q2	3	31	19	21	23

Table 3.20 continued

	Q3	2	28	26	22	20
	Q4	1	26	27	23	19
1984:	Q1	1	26	25	24	21
	Q2	2	26	22	25	21
	Q3	2	17	22	28	29
	Q4	1	16	22	30	28
1985:	Q1	1	11	19	30	36
	Q2	1	17	20	28	31
	Q3	1	15	22	29	30
	Q4	2	19	23	26	27

The significant improvement in the spring of 1983 can be seen in the table above, when the proportion saying the economic situation had got better increased from 23 per cent in the first quarter to 34 per cent in the second quarter. The figures then remained static for almost a year, until the fall in the third quarter of 1984 and the low at the beginning of 1985, with only 12 per cent thinking things had got better. By the end of the year, however, this latter figure had risen to 21 per cent. A similar pattern can be seen in the replies to a second question about future economic prospect, but this does not show the improvement in mid-1985 found in the earlier figures.

Table 3.21: Perception of the Economy over the Next Twelve Months

Q. *How do you think the general economic situation in this country will develop over the next twelve months? (Quarterly averages.)*

		Get a lot better	Get a little better	Stay the same	Get a little worse	Get a lot worse
1983:	Q1	2	27	26	21	15
	Q2	4	36	24	14	10
	Q3	2	32	26	21	13
	Q4	2	29	30	22	12
1984:	Q1	2	30	29	20	12
	Q2	2	29	28	20	13
	Q3	2	21	28	25	17
	Q4	2	23	28	24	15

1985:	Q1	2	23	27	23	19
	Q2	2	23	28	23	18
	Q3	2	20	30	24	17
	Q4	2	24	30	21	15

Thus, there was an improvement in the second quarter of 1983 when more people thought that things would improve over the next 12 months than thought they would get worse. Again, there was a slight decline in the third quarter and the figures then remained fairly static until a more substantial fall in the third quarter of 1984. In contrast to the earlier question, there does not appear to have been any significant improvement in 1985 on the public's view of the future. This is surprising in one sense, in that the proportion of people expecting a more rapid increase in future prices declines from a peak in the first quarter of 1985. Given that prices are a powerful determinant in economic attitudes, one would have expected this improvement to have been reflected in the other questions on the economy.

Table 3.22: Perception of Future Price Rises

Q. By comparison with what is happening now, do you think that in the next twelve months (quarterly averages):
  a) there will be a more rapid increase in prices?
  b) prices will increase at the same rate?
  c) prices will increase at a slower rate?
  d) prices will be stable?
  e) prices will fall slightly?

		(a)	(b)	(c)	(d)	(e)
1983:	Q1	16	34	29	14	2
	Q2	15	33	27	17	2
	Q3	22	36	25	12	2
	Q4	21	39	24	11	1
1984:	Q1	21	42	22	10	1
	Q2	21	42	21	11	1
	Q3	26	42	19	9	1
	Q4	25	44	19	8	1
1985:	Q1	29	44	17	7	0
	Q2	27	44	17	8	0
	Q3	21	46	18	10	1
	Q4	21	44	20	12	1

At its most optimistic over the last three years, 19 per cent of the public in the second quarter of 1983 thought that prices would remain stable or actually fall; while at the other extreme, 15 per cent thought there would be a more rapid increase in prices. This latter proportion rose to 29 per cent at the beginning of 1985, but then slowly declined to the levels of 18 months to two years before. Two other questions, similar to the first two, were also asked, dealing with the financial situation of the person's household, both over the last twelve months and in the next twelve months. These showed a much flatter picture over the last three years. For example the proportion thinking the financial situation of their household had got better was 17 per cent at its lowest in the second quarter of 1985 and never higher than 21 per cent. Similarly, the proportion thinking there would be an improvement in their household's financial position ranged between 21 per cent and 25 per cent.

One consequence of the public's pessimism about the economy was a decline in the proportion of the public thinking it was a good time to buy major consumer durables. Translated into behaviour, rather than an attitude, the omens would be bad for the manufacturers of such products.

Table 3.23: The Climate for Buying Major Consumer Durables

Q. *Do you think that there is an advantage for people to make major purchases (furniture, washing machine, TV set, etc.) at the present time? (Quarterly averages.)*
   a) *Yes, now is the right time*
   b) *It is neither the right time nor the wrong time*
   c) *No, it is the wrong time — the purchase should be postponed*

		Right time	Neither	Wrong time
1983:	Q1	53	13	23
	Q2	46	16	23
	Q3	51	16	19
	Q4	53	15	20
1984:	Q1	51	16	20
	Q2	47	19	20
	Q3	45	19	24
	Q4	46	18	23

1985:	Q1	47	18	24
	Q2	44	20	24
	Q3	45	20	23
	Q4	42	22	23

The 1983 general election appears to have made people think it would be better to wait, in anticipation of Conservative policies favourable to the consumer to be transformed later in the year into a 'buyers' market'. Then the proportion declined again, with a contemporaneous increase in the proportions saying it was the wrong time or that it ws neither the right time nor the wrong time. For most of the period, around one in two of the public said that they were just managing to make ends meet on their income, while around one in three said that they were able to save. But a minority — increasing slowly, though not at a statistically significant rate — said that they were either having to draw on their savings or were running into debt.

At the same time, majorities of the public thought that the level of unemployment would increase, and never more than one in five saw the level declining.

Table 3.24: Unemployment on the Increase

Q. *How do you think the level of unemployment (I mean the number of people out of work) in the country as a whole, will change over the next twelve months? Will it: (Quarterly averages.)*

		Increase sharply	Increase slightly	Remain the same	Fall slightly	Fall sharply
1983:	Q1	26	47	14	9	1
	Q2	17	40	20	16	1
	Q3	23	45	17	12	1
	Q4	15	41	23	17	1
1984:	Q1	17	39	24	15	1
	Q2	17	41	24	15	1
	Q3	19	45	22	10	1
	Q4	18	46	20	11	1
1985:	Q1	20	46	21	10	1
	Q2	19	44	23	11	1
	Q3	19	43	23	12	1
	Q4	16	41	25	14	1

Thus, in the second and fourth quarters of 1983 the public thought
the level of unemployment would diminish somewhat, yet it gradu-
ally increased through 1984 and 1985. Not only was the government failing to calm public concern about unemployment; the
public was also failing to see the cost of living getting any easier. In
fact, the very opposite trend took place once the 1983 general
election was out of the way: the public's perception was one of a
significant increase in the cost of living.

Table 3.25: The Rising Cost of Living

Q. *Compared to what it was twelve months ago, do you think
the cost of living is now: (Quarterly averages.)*

		Very much higher	Quite a bit higher	A little higher	About the same	Lower
1983:	Q1	14	26	40	16	2
	Q2	12	24	40	19	3
	Q3	12	24	41	20	2
	Q4	11	25	45	17	1
1984:	Q1	11	26	44	15	1
	Q2	13	27	44	13	1
	Q3	14	28	44	13	1
	Q4	14	28	43	13	1
1985:	Q1	16	29	41	12	1
	Q2	18	32	39	10	1
	Q3	16	31	39	12	1
	Q4	14	28	41	14	1

By the second quarter of 1985, one-half of the public thought that
the cost of living, compared with twelve months earlier, was at best
'quite a bit higher', with around one in six people seeing it as 'very
much higher'. It was not surprising, therefore, that on balance the
public thought that they would be spending less on major purchases in the near future. A consistent one in five thought they
would be spending more on such things as furniture, washing
machines, televisions, etc. in the next twelve months, while one in
three thought they would be spending less.

Despite the feeling that it was a relatively good time to save, the
public tended to think it unlikely that they would be able to save
any money in the next twelve months. Around 45 per cent of the

Table 3.26: The Climate for Savings

Q. In view of the general economic situation, do you think this is: (quarterly averages.)
a very good time to save?
quite a good time to save?
rather an unfavourable time to save?
a very unfavourable time to save?

		Very good	Quite good	Rather unfavourable	Very unfavourable
1983:	Q1	17	34	26	14
	Q2	16	37	23	13
	Q3	18	38	21	12
	Q4	19	37	23	11
1984:	Q1	20	34	23	12
	Q2	21	33	23	12
	Q3	22	32	22	13
	Q4	22	32	23	12
1985:	Q1	28	25	23	13
	Q2	24	31	22	12
	Q3	26	31	20	12
	Q4	23	34	20	12

public over the three years thought it was likely that they or another member of their household would be able to save some money, while a little over one in two thought it unlikely. This is in contrast to the increasing proportion thinking it was a good time to save.

The Budget

Mr Nigel Lawson's second Budget, in marked contrast to his first, was one of the most unpopular to have taken place since the late 1940s, when Gallup began to measure the public's rating of the chancellor's policies. Only three Budgets had been less well received than that of 1985, with 41 per cent thinking that it was fair. The 'popularity' of the Chancellor of the Exchequer, too, went from majority approval in 1984 to majority disapproval in 1985. Only Sir Geoffrey Howe in 1981 scored lower, personally, than Mr Lawson.

Table 3.27: Rating of the Chancellor of the Exchequer and the Budget 1949-1985

Q. Do you think that ... is doing a good job or a bad job as Chancellor of the Exchequer?
Q. Do you think the Budget is a fair one or not?

| | | Chancellor of the Exchequer | | | | Budget | |
		Good job	Bad job	Don't know	Fair	Not fair	Don't know
Lawson	Mar 1985	33	51	16	41	51	8
	Mar 1984	57	26	17	60	36	4
Howe	Mar 1983	51	36	13	53	39	8
	Mar 1982	49	39	13	56	38	6
	Mar 1981	24	61	15	22	73	5
	Mar 1980	51	29	19	57	36	7
	June 1979	38	30	32	44	49	7
Healey	April 1978	57	27	16	68	24	8
	Nov 1977	58	23	19		NA	
	April 1977	38	46	16	36	54	10
	April 1976	60	23	17	63	23	14
	April 1975	44	36	20	51	37	12
	Nov 1974	53	23	24	59	27	14
	Mar 1974	43	22	35	56	32	12
Barber	Mar 1973	57	23	20	55	34	11
	April 1972	57	17	26	64	27	9
	Mar 1971	56	18	26	61	29	10
Jenkins	April 1970	61	19	20	66	24	10
	April 1969	49	32	19	59	32	9
	Mar 1968	41	28	31	43	47	10
Callaghan	April 1967	51	26	23	56	23	21
	May 1966	61	18	21	60	24	16
	April 1965	48	24	28	51	34	15
	Nov 1964	48	24	28	56	33	11
Maudling	April 1964	47	33	20	41	48	11
	April 1963	59	19	22	59	24	17
Selwyn Lloyd	April 1962	42	30	28	48	34	18
	April 1961	36	31	33	33	51	16
Heathcoat	April 1960	43	28	29	41	47	12
Amery	April 1959	58	18	24	56	34	10
	April 1958		NA		62	23	15
Thorneycroft	April 1957	50	23	27	42	40	18
Macmillan	April 1956	42	33	25	43	43	14

Butler	April 1955	57	18	25	50	32	18
	April 1954	53	31	16		NA	
	April 1953	63	31	6	50	37	13
	April 1952	49	25	25		NA	
Cripps	April 1949	57	24	19		NA	

Gallup also asked people whether they approved or disapproved of five of the main Budget proposals. Majorities approved of the increase in the price of cigarettes and the raising of the tax thresholds (59 per cent approving of each and 33 per cent disapproving). Fewer (49 per cent) approved of the increases in wine, beer and spirits, though 40 per cent disapproved, in line with the public's view of a similar measure in 1984. Substantial majorities disapproved of the increase in the price of petrol (79 per cent) and in the road tax (76 per cent).

The Budget was put forward as one for jobs, but the public believed that it would fail in that respect and that it would fail to achieve five other possible objectives. Three in four (76 per cent) thought it would not reduce unemployment, and even 56 per cent of Conservatives held this view. Similarly, 74 per cent of the general public thought it would not encourage people to work harder; neither would it make it easier for people like themselves to manage (73 per cent). Three in five (62 per cent) said it would not help the economy to expand, and almost as many (56 per cent) felt that it would not reduce inflation.

Given this initial reaction to the Budget, it came as no surprise that 39 per cent of the public said it had made them less favourably inclined towards the government and only 7 per cent more favourably inclined. One in two said that it had made no difference to them. When asked whether the financial and economic situation would be better or worse if we had a Labour government, and the same question was asked separately for an Alliance government, the public was evenly divided on the former and lukewarm on the latter. One in three (30 per cent) thought the situation would be better under Labour, matched by the 32 per cent thinking it would be worse. As far as the future under the Alliance was concerned, 27 per cent thought things would improve and 15 per cent thought they would deteriorate.

Taxation

Gallup also attempted to make an assessment of the public's view of the Government's taxation policy by putting the question in the table below. The card mentioned in the question actually consists of a five-point 'agree-disagree' scale with a central 'neither agree nor disagree' answer, but for the sake of space the replies have been collapsed and the 'neithers' ignored.

Table 3.28: Government Taxation Policy

Q. I am going to read out some things people have said about the government's taxation policy. Using this card, would you tell me whether you agree or disagree with them?

	Nov 1979	Mar 1980	Mar 1981	Mar 1982	Mar 1983	Mar 1985
They've given a bit to everyone						
Agree	41	51	26	49	51	39
Disagree	47	38	62	42	39	47
They try to give you the money you have earned						
Agree	35	40	23	29	33	27
Disagree	50	45	62	57	54	59
People who want to work will gain						
Agree	50	54	37	44	49	42
Disagree	36	34	47	43	36	42
They look after the middle classes						
Agree	53	58	47	59	60	59
Disagree	31	28	37	28	27	31
They are giving people the incentive to work harder						
Agree	34	38	18	23	31	21
Disagree	53	50	72	64	56	68
Not fair to the lower-paid						
Agree	59	56	66	60	60	67
Disagree	27	33	24	29	25	26
The rich get richer, the poor get poorer						
Agree	71	66	70	75	74	79
Disagree	18	23	20	17	17	13

The deterioration in attitudes between 1983 and 1985 reflects the adverse shift between 1979 and 1981, then two years into the previous government's term of office. Between 1979 and 1981, five of the statements moved in a negative direction, while one on 'the rich' remained static and the one on 'the middle classes' improved — if a decrease in the number of those agreeing can be said to be an improvement. Similarly, between 1983 and 1985 six of the statements showed negative shifts, while the one on the middle classes remained static.

In the longer term, three attitudes have persisted so far through Mrs Thatcher's two terms. The first of these, never dropping below two in three of the public, was the feeling that 'the rich get richer, the poor get poorer'. The second, allied, statement receiving majority agreement was that the government was 'not fair to the lower paid'. Finally, in 1985 two in three disagreed with the idea that the government was 'giving people the incentive to work harder'. Back in 1980, only one in two disagreed.

In December, the public were almost evenly divided on the government's success in keeping taxes down but were more critical of their success in improving people's living standards.

Table 3.29: Government's Success on Taxes and Living Standards

Q. On the whole, do you think the Conservative government since 1983 has been successful or unsuccessful at keeping taxes down generally?

Q. And has it been successful or unsuccessful at improving your standard of living?

	Taxes	Living standards
Very successful	5	5
Fairly successful	41	27
Fairly unsuccessful	23	29
Very unsuccessful	21	29
Don't know	10	10

Conservatives, naturally, tended to think the government had been fairly successful in its handling of these two issues, but around one in five expressed criticism of the Government on both of them. In answer to three statements about taxation, around two in three of the general public thought that high tax levels act as a disincentive, that there sould be a redistribution of wealth, and that too many people rely on the Welfare State.

Table 3.30: Agreement with Taxation Statements

Q. *Please say whether you agree or disagree with each of these statements. Or say if you are not sure either way. (Figures show 'agree' or 'disagree' results only.)*

	Public	Con	Lab	Alliance
High income tax makes people less willing to work hard				
Agree	66	70	62	69
Disagree	26	25	27	25
Too many people these days like to rely on government handouts				
Agree	61	86	46	58
Disagree	29	10	44	30
Income and wealth should be redistributed towards ordinary working people				
Agree	60	34	81	60
Disagree	24	48	5	24

There were also generational differences in the replies to these statements, particularly on the 'handouts' statement. While 49 per cent of young adults aged under 35 agreed with the statement, almost twice as many (79 per cent) senior citizens did so. Similarly, a greater than average proportion of people aged 65 and over agreed with the 'lack of incentives' statement. On the other hand, agreement with the statement on the redistribution of wealth tended to decline with increasing age.

Gallup repeated in 1985 a trade-off question dating back to the 1979 general election, where people were asked to choose between three options on the level of taxes and government expenditure. The replies to this question show a dramatic shift in opinion over the period.

Table 3.31: Taxes and Expenditure on Services

Q. *People have different views about whether it is more important to reduce taxes or keep up government spending. How about you? Which of these statements comes closest to your own view?*

	March 1979	Feb 1983	Feb 1985
Taxes being cut, even if it means some reduction in government services, such as health, education and welfare	34	23	16
Things should be left as they are	25	22	18
Government services such as health, education and welfare should be extended, even if it means some increases in taxes	34	49	59
Don't know	7	6	6

It can be seen, therefore, that the public has gone from being evenly divided on the question in 1979 to a situation in which there is a clear majority in 1985 wanting more government spending on services, even if it meant more taxation. Even among Conservatives, almost twice as many opted for more services (46 per cent) as wanted tax cuts (25 per cent). Roughly two in three Labour and Alliance supporters wanted an extension of government services.

Despite government protestations that expenditure on such things as hospitals and education had gone up during their period in office, the public stubbornly stuck to the view that the government was still not spending enough on the services. Only on armaments and defence was it felt that the government was spending too much.

Table 3.32: Government Spending

Q. *Do you think the government is spending too much, too little or about the right amount on:*

	Too much	Too little	About right	Don't know
Armaments and defence	53	9	27	11
Roads	5	63	24	9
Education and schools	4	74	15	7
National Health Service	2	77	17	5
Old-age pensions	1	70	24	5

That the government had failed in its efforts to get its message across
is confirmed by the replies to this question among Conservatives.
Majorities felt that too little was being spent on old-age pensions,
roads, education and schools, and on the National Health Service,
nor did the public as a whole attach great importance to reducing
taxes.

Table 3.33: Importance of Taxation Aims

Q. *How important is it to you that:*
   there are tax cuts right across the board?
   the standard rate of income tax drops to 25p?

| | Tax cuts | | | | Standard rate | | | |
	Feb 1983	June 1985	Aug 1985	Nov 1985	Feb 1983	June 1985	Aug 1985	Nov 1985
Very important	37	33	34	29	38	39	37	30
Quite important	30	29	32	29	31	26	29	31
Not very important	22	19	20	22	18	18	17	20
Not at all important	8	14	10	14	7	11	9	12
Don't know	4	5	5	6	5	6	7	7

The proportion answering 'very important' to either of these questions was significantly less than the same degree of importance
attached to drastically reducing unemployment (78 per cent), substantially improving the economic situation (70 per cent), and reducing inflation to below five per cent (47 per cent).

Looking into the future, only one in ten up to August saw general
tax cuts within the next twelve months, and even fewer saw the standard rate dropping over the same period. But after Mr Lawson's
autumn Budget statement, one in four expected tax cuts in 1986 and
one in eight thought there could be a drop in the standard rate of
income tax.

Table 3.34: A Bleak Future for Taxes

Q. *How long do you think it will be before:*
   there are tax cuts right across the board?
   the standard rate of income tax drops to 25p?

	Tax cuts				Standard rate			
	Nov 1984	Feb 1985	Aug 1985	Nov 1985	Nov 1984	Feb 1985	Aug 1985	Nov 1985
In the next 6 months	6	6	1	11	0	1	1	4
Over 6 months–1 year	9	6	10	15	1	1	3	9
Over 1 year–1½ years	4	7	7	7	2	2	4	6
Over 1½ years–2 years	4	5	8	7	1	2	5	7
Over 2 years–2½ years	4	5	9	6	3	2	6	5
Over 2½ years–3 years	2	5	3	3	2	3	3	3
Over 3 years–4 years	3	4	3	3	3	2	3	3
Over 4 years–5 years	4	6	6	4	3	4	5	6
Over 5 years–10 years	6	5	7	4	6	6	7	6
Over 10 years	6	6	4	3	12	10	8	6
Never	18	19	12	7	30	40	22	13
Don't know	35	27	30	28	38	27	33	32

The public's expectations about the future for taxes were in sharp contrast to their perception of one of Mrs Thatcher's main themes in 1979 and to what had happened to taxes in the meantime. Two in three (68 per cent) remembered that the Conservatives were aiming to cut taxes; yet almost as many (59 per cent) said that taxes and National Insurance contributions had gone up over the past six years. Two in five (41 per cent) also thought that the taxes they paid were not fair, while 15 per cent thought they were and 22 per cent thought they were about right.

Government Spending Priorities

In May, a number of other questions were asked about government spending which confirmed the public's concern about the National Health Service, educational facilities and old age pensions.

Table 3.35: Goverment Spending Priorities

Q. Here are some items of government spending. Which of them, if any, would be your highest priority for extra spending, and which next?

	Top	Top two
Health	38	62
Education	18	43
Help for industry	17	28

Table 3.35 continued

Housing	9	25
Social security benefits	7	16
Police and prisons	3	7
Roads	3	6
Defence	2	6
Public transport	1	3
Overseas aid	1	2
None of these	1	1
Don't know	0	0

There was a generation gap on this question as far as spending on education was concerned, with only 9 per cent of people aged 65 or over saying it should be given the highest priority; this group also thought that higher priority should be given to help for industry. When it came to the social benefits this elderly group was very much in people's minds, and retirement pensions topped the list of priorities for extra spending.

Table 3.36: Government's Social Benefits Priorities

Q. Thinking now only of the government's spending on social benefits like those on the card, which, if any, of these would be your highest priority for extra spending, and which next?

	Top	Top two
Retirement pensions	40	64
Benefits for the disabled	24	54
Benefits for the unemployed	16	33
Child benefits	10	23
Benefits for single parents	8	20
None of these	1	1
Don't know	1	1

Again there was a generation gap in the replies to this question, as well as political differences. Among young adults aged under 35, the unemployed, pensioners and the disabled were given almost equal priority being chosen by a little under one in four. On the other hand, 61 per cent of senior citizens thought retirement pensions should be given the highest priority, followed by benefits for the disabled (25 per cent). A slightly greater than average proportion of Conservatives gave priority to benefits for the disabled (31 per cent), and slightly fewer than average (11 per cent) gave priority to benefits for the unemployed. Labour supporters, on the other hand, were more concerned about the unemployed (23 per cent) than were the general public as a whole.

Finally, in mid-December, people were asked their attitudes to five possible government policies, ranging across private education and private medicine, poverty, and funding of the National Health Service. Around nine in ten of the public felt that the government should do more for pensioners, do more for the National Health Service, and do more to reduce poverty. On the other hand, the public did not, on balance, want to see an end to private education; neither did they want a growth in private medicine in Britain.

Table 3.37: Political Attitudes

Q. Do you think the government should or should not do each of the following things, or doesn't it matter either way?

	Should	Should not	Doesn't matter	Don't know
Put more money into the National Health Service	89	7	1	3
Increase the standard of living of pensioners	87	7	3	3
Spend more money to get rid of poverty	86	8	2	5
Encourage the growth of private medicine	25	56	8	11
Get rid of private education in Britain	20	59	16	6

It is probably not necessary to comment on the political analyses of the first three items, given the overwhelming public support for each of them. However, almost one in five Conservatives (16 per cent) were opposed to more money being spent on the National Health Service. There was also a generation gap on the 'poverty' statement. Whereas 89 per cent of the under-35s thought more money shold be spent to get rid of poverty, the proportion fell to 78 per cent among those aged 65 or over, with 13 per cent opposed to the idea. The other two statements, on private medicine and private education, revealed, as was expected, distinct differences between supporters of the main parties. For example, on the question of getting rid of private education in Britain, four in five Conservatives (82 per cent) were opposed and only 6 per cent were for the proposal. Among Labour supporters, however, 37 per cent were for the idea and 36 per cent were opposed. Alliance supporters were similar in their views to Conservatives: 64 per cent against the idea and 15 per cent for. When it came to encouraging the growth of private medicine, Conservatives were almost evenly divided, with 41 per cent in favour and 40 per cent opposed. On the other hand, majorities of Labour and Alliance supporters were opposed to a growth in private medicine. Among Labour supporters, 15 per cent were in favour and 66 per cent opposed, with 25 per cent and 59 per cent respectively for Alliance supporters.

The Welfare State

Other findings have shown majorities of the public feeling that not enough was being spent on the National Health Service, education, and pensions in particular, and that unemployment benefits were probably on the low side. On the wider question of benefits over-all, the public held what otherwise might appear to be conflicting views, as the table below shows:

Table 3.38: False Benefits Claims and Failures to Claim

Q. I will read two statements. For each one, please say whether you agree or disagree, strongly or slightly.
  a) Large numbers of people these days falsely claim benefits
  b) Large numbers of people who are eligible for benefits these days fail to claim them

	False claims	Failure to claim
Agree strongly	45	51
Agree slightly	23	34
Disagree slightly	12	5
Disagree strongly	11	3
Don't know	9	7

Obviously a large number of people were in agreement with both of the statements, but there were some internal differences. Slightly more Conservatives agreed strongly with the first statement (53 per cent) than agreed strongly with the second (46 per cent). The reverse was true for Labour supporters: 37 per cent and 54 per cent respectively. There was also a generation gap, with more young adults holding the second statement to be true than thought the first was. Among senior citizens, slightly more agreed strongly with the first statement than agreed with the second.

The public was less decisive on a question in May on who benefited most from the National Health Service in terms of value for money:

Table 3.39: Value for Money in the NHS

Q. Turning now to the National Health Service: on the whole, which of these three types of family would you say gets best value from their taxes out of the National Health Service?

	Total	Con	Lab	Lib	SDP
Those with high incomes	36	23	47	44	32
Those with middle incomes	16	18	16	13	20
Those with low incomes	28	36	20	30	29
Don't know	19	23	16	14	20

Given the political analysis above, it is not surprising that the social classes also took different views on who gets the most from the National Health Service. Dividing the public into three almost equal groups, the top third thought that people with low incomes (35 per cent) did better than those with high incomes. The bottom third, however, held the opposite view: 44 per cent thought those with high incomes did better and 24 per cent thought those with low incomes did better.

The public rejected — by a margin of nearly two to one — the idea that the National Health Service should not be universally available to all sectors of the population, though Conservatives were almost evenly divided on this question.

Table 3.40: A Segregated National Health Service

Q. It has been suggested that the National Health Service
should be available only to those with lower incomes. This
would mean that contributions and taxes could be lower,
and most people would then take out medical insurance or
pay for health care. Do you support or oppose this idea?

	Total	Con	Lab	Lib	SDP
Support	34	41	29	32	26
Oppose	60	51	67	62	69
Don't know	6	7	5	6	4

In contrast to the replies to the earlier question, there were no
significant differences between the social classes, and opposition
was actually slightly above average among people in the top group.

In early June, the Secretary of State for the Social Services,
Norman Fowler, announced an overhaul of the Welfare State,
including the controversial proposal to phase out earnings-related
pension schemes. A fortnight later, 62 per cent of the public said
that they had read or heard something about the proposals, and a
majority of this aware group were less than impressed with them.
While 27 per cent thought the government's plans were a good
thing, more than twice as many (59 per cent) thought they were a
bad thing. Not surprisingly, a majority (58 per cent) of aware
Conservatives thought the plans were a good idea, though 24 per
cent thought otherwise. Nine in ten Labour supporters knowing
something of the plans thought they were a bad thing, as did six in
ten Alliance supporters.

While 5 per cent aware of the plans thought that they would be
better off from the proposed changes, 45 per cent said that they
would be worse off, and 43 per cent thought that they would not
be affected. People at the bottom of the social scale, in particular,
thought that they would be worse off.

Table 3.41: Effect of the Government's Plans

Q. Do you think that in the long run you will be better off
through the proposed changes, worse off, or will it have
little effect on you?

	(ABC1) top third	(C2) middle third	(DE) bottom third
Better off	5	4	6
Worse off	34	47	64
Not affected	53	44	22
Don't know	8	5	8

Three in five Conservatives thought that they would not be affected by the plans, though slightly more felt that they would be worse off (17 per cent) than thought they would be better off (12 per cent). Two in three Labour supporters and almost one in two Alliance supporters thought that they would be worse off. Despite public attitudes about feather-bedding civil servants, the public was almost evenly divided on the question of the index-linking of their pensions. Forty-two per cent thought that index-linking for public servants should be stopped after the state earnings-related pension scheme was ended, but 47 per cent thought that it should not. Even among Labour supporters, 40 per cent were in support of the continuation of index-linking for civil servants.

In line with their basically negative overall view of the government's plans, the public also held a number of specific negative views as well as some positive ones:

Table 3.42: Attitudes Towards the Proposals

Q. *I am going to read some of the things that have been said about the proposals. Do you tend to agree or tend to disagree that:*

	Agree	Disagree	Don't know
The proposals will lead to more means tests	74	16	10
The proposals will mean less money available for social security benefits	65	18	18
The system of social security benefits will be simplified	56	32	12
People will no longer be worse off taking a job than if they lived on security benefits	56	28	17

Table 3.42 continued

The proposals will lead to more people living in poverty	54	33	13
The government has proposed the changes mainly to provide the money to cut taxes at the next election	50	31	20
Benefits will be aimed to give extra aid for those in greatest need	47	42	11

Among Conservatives, the statements achieving the highest agreement scores were:

a simplified system (77 per cent)
people no longer worse off taking a job (74 per cent)
benefits aimed at those in greatest need (74 per cent)

On the other hand, Labour supporters scored highest in agreement on:

less money available (86 per cent)
more means tests (85 per cent)
more people living in poverty (82 per cent)

Three weeks after the proposals, Gallup repeated some questions first asked for the Department of Health and Social Security at the turn of the year. The first of these asked employed people about the fairness of the amount they paid in respect of social security pensions and benefits they were entitled to receive. One in two (49 per cent) felt the amount they paid was either 'very fair' or 'quite fair', but almost as many (41 per cent) felt that it was 'not very fair' or 'not at all fair'. Six months earlier, the figures had been 59 per cent and 27 per cent respectively. The government's plans therefore appear to have soured the public's 'value for money' attitude towards what they paid and what they received in return. The proposals did, however, increase public awareness of the state earnings-related pension scheme (SERPS for short). Whereas at the beginning of the year 45 per cent were aware, the proportion had risen to 62 per cent by late June.

Overall, 51 per cent of the public in both studies said that they or their spouse belonged to a pensions scheme by an existing employer or by a former employer. Among these people, three in four (73 per cent) said that it was very important to them to belong to an employer's pension scheme so that they could have a pension in addition to the state pension. Hardly suprisingly, people who were not part of an employer's pension scheme attached less importance to having an additional pension, 47 per cent thinking it very important to have one. A majority (58 per cent) of the public thought that 'National Insurance contributions/stamps are different from income tax because they pay for benefits like pensions and unemployment, when a person needs them', though 28 per cent took a less charitable view, feeling that 'National Insurance contributions/stamps are a deduction from a person's pay just like income tax.'

Another effect of Norman Fowler's review in early June was to change to some degree the public's view of the social security system as compared to the early part of the year.

Table 3.43: Perception of the Social Security System

Q. Here are two statements which describe the social security system. Please read them both and tell me which statement you feel best describes the future social security system after the government's recent proposals. *

	Dec 1984/Jan 1985	June 1985
Is simple to understand and administer. Deals promptly with claims and is likely to make fewer mistakes. Is more likely to reach all the people it is intended to help but does not try to deal with the special needs that individuals may have	32	43
Tries to deal with the special needs individuals may have but is more complicated to understand and administer. Deals less promptly with claims and is likely to make more mistakes. Is less likely to reach all the people it is intended to help	52	32
Neither	3	6
Don't know	12	19

*The earlier question related to the 'present social security system'

A majority (53 per cent) of Conservatives thought the first description best suited the future social security system, while 26 per cent opted for the second. Labour and Alliance supporters tended to be more evenly divided between the two descriptions. When asked which of the two descriptions they thought was the better system, the first was the overwhelming favourite on both occasions — 69 per cent in the earlier study and 59 per cent in June. Only 13 per cent and 17 per cent respectively opted for the second of the two descriptions.

Another of the proposals outlined by Norman Fowler was family credits in the pay packets of low-income working families, though the public tended to favour financial help for all families with children. There were differences, however, between the party supporters and between the generations.

Table 3.44: Importance of Helping All Families with Children

Q. *How important do you think it is for the state to give financial help to all families with children, whatever their level of income?*

	Very	**Fairly**	**Not very**	**Not at all**
General public	30	24	21	19
Conservative	19	26	26	26
Labour	43	22	16	12
Liberal/SDP	27	25	24	20
18–34	39	29	18	9
35–44	35	25	26	11
45–64	26	25	21	24
65+	18	16	23	35

On the other hand, if the system were to be changed, one in two (49 per cent) of the public felt that more should be given to lower-income families, and 27 per cent thought less should be given to well-off families. A small minority (6 per cent) wanted more to be given to larger families, while 13 per cent thought that the present system should not be changed. Again there were differences of opinion between supporters of the three main parties, but these were less significant than those across the age groups. A majority (59 per cent) of young adults, for example, opted for giving more to lower-income families. Senior citizens, however, were almost evenly split between giving more to lower-income families (37 per cent) and giving less to well-off families (35 per cent).

The public was also concerned about giving people on low incomes more help with their housing costs and towards the cost of bringing up their children. Sixty-two per cent felt that the system should do more to help low-paid working families, 28 per cent felt that they should be helped as at present, 2 per cent thought that less should be done to help them, and 3 per cent thought that they should not be helped in this way. Again, there were differences by political affiliation and a generation gap. The proportion thinking more should be done to help low-paid working families was 49 per cent among Conservatives, 61 per cent among Alliance supporters and 72 per cent among Labour supporters. A slightly wider range was found across the ages: 73 per cent of the 18–34 year olds said do more for the low-paid, dropping to 61 per cent of the 35–44s, 60 per cent of the 45–64s, and to 47 per cent of those aged 65 or over.

Alienation

Pessimism about the economy was mirrored in the replies to a question in June on how various groups had prospered, or otherwise, under the present Conservative government. The well-to-do and the middle classes were thought to be better off, as were those investing on the stock market; but the rest of the population were thought to be worse off.

Table 3.45: Six Years of Conservatism

Q. In general terms, would you say ... were better off or worse off than they were six years ago when the Conservatives took over as government?

	Better off	Worse off	No difference	Don't know
The well-to-do	72	9	12	7
Middle-class people in managerial and executive jobs	52	16	24	8
People investing on the stock market	49	6	9	36

Table 3.45 continued

Skilled manual workers	26	40	23	11
People like yourself	22	50	26	1
Pensioners	20	52	23	5
Unskilled manual workers	13	66	14	7

Overall, these figures can be summarised along the lines to be found elsewhere in this book: the rich get richer while the poor get poorer. Analysis by party supported showed Conservatives, to a high degree backing their party, though not wholeheartedly: just under one in two (44 per cent) felt that they were better off, 32 per cent saw no change, and 22 per cent thought that they were worse off. The vast majority (72 per cent) of Labour supporters and 54 per cent of Alliance supporters thought that things had got worse for them. Even among the middle classes — the ABC1s of the market research industry — normally the solid base for the Conservative Party, more (43 per cent) said they were worse off than said things had improved for them (27 per cent). It is hardly surprising, given these findings, that an earlier survey conducted in February found a substantial degree of alienation, with three in four feeling that 'the rich get richer and the poor get poorer'.

Table 3.46: Alienation

Q. I want to read you some things some people have told us they felt from time to time. Do you tend to feel or not to feel:

	Total	Con	Lab	Lib/SDP
a) Most people with power try to take advantage of people like yourself				
Feel	63	46	83	66
Not feel	31	49	12	29
b) The people running the country don't really care what happens to you				
Feel	56	28	80	68
Not feel	38	67	17	25
c) You are left out of things going on around you				
Feel	40	21	60	39

Not feel	52	71	34	51
d) The rich get richer and the poor get poorer				
Feel	77	49	97	90
Not feel	19	42	2	7
e) What you think doesn't count very much any more				
Feel	60	43	74	63
Not feel	29	44	18	25

Overall, the average member of the general public felt that three of the five statements were true: slightly up on a year ago. Among Conservatives the average dropped to two in five, was just over three among Alliance supporters, and almost four for Labour supporters.

Poverty

In recent years, Gallup has been looking in more detail at the concept of 'Two Nations' from a number of aspects, and one of these in 1985 dealt with poverty in Britain. Perhaps because of the prevailing economic climate, the public took a far more liberal view towards the poor in 1985 than they had eight years earlier.

Table 3.47: Poverty: Beyond One's Control

Q. In your opinion, which is more often to blame if a person is poor — a lack of effort on his/her own part or circumstances beyond his/her control?

	1977	1985
Lack of effort	33	21
Circumstances	30	49
Both	31	28
Don't know	6	3

As one might expect, replies to this question tended to follow party lines. The pattern of replies for Conservatives, for example, followed the pattern for the general public in 1977. On the other hand, majorities of each of the other major parties thought that poverty was

beyond one's control. Three in four (73 per cent) of the public —
including more than 80 per cent of Labour and Alliance supporters —
felt that the money and wealth in this country should be more evenly
distributed among a larger percentage of the people, while one in five
of the public thought the distribution was fair now. Conservatives
were more evenly divided on this question, 39 per cent seeing the distribution of wealth as fair and 51 per cent thinking it should be more
evenly distributed. Similar divisions of opinion occurred on the
extent of poverty in Britain.

Table 3.48: The Poverty Line

Q. *What percentage of British people would you say are
living below the poverty line today? Your best guess will
do.*

	General public	Con	Lab	Lib/SDP
Under 15	18	29	9	17
15–20	18	19	15	21
21–30	18	19	19	20
31–49	12	8	13	17
50 or more	17	9	29	12
Don't know	17	17	16	13

Three in four (73 per cent) of the public thought that the proportion of the British public living below the poverty line* was
increasing from year to year, though 9 per cent felt it was decreasing
and 11 per cent said it was staying the same. Among Conservatives,
58 per cent thought the proportion was increasing, compared with 85
per cent of Labour supporters and 81 per cent of Alliance supporters.

It is fairly obvious that the government was to a very large degree
blamed for the perceived poverty in Britain. Since June 1984, people
have been asked whether they agreed or disagreed with the statement: 'The rich are getting richer and the poor are getting poorer
under this government.' Between June 1984 and November 1985,
the proportion agreeing with the statement never fell below 69 per

---

*Views on this vary, but it has been estimated that around eight million of the
population (15 per cent) come into this category. For further information on the
subject, see *A New Deal for Britain's Poor* (Child Poverty Action Group, 1985)
and *Poor Britain* by Joanna Mack and Stewart Lanley (Allen & Unwin, 1985).

cent, and rose to 77 per cent at its highest. The overwhelming majority of Labour supporters (94 per cent) and Alliance supporters (83 per cent) agreed with this statement, and even 34 per cent of Conservatives did so, though 53 per cent disagreed.

Trade Unions

1985 saw the end of one of the longest-running miners' strikes and the start of one of the longest-running teachers' disputes. Yet despite this high-profile muscle-flexing of two unions at the extremes of the movement, there is little doubt that the unions no longer had the public's 'respect' from days past. Gone was the time when the General Secretary of the TUC was said to wield the most power in the country. In June 1984, for example, only 14 per cent of the public agreed with the statement 'The government now has the unions firmly under control', but as the miners' dispute dragged on the proportion agreeing trebled to 42 per cent in March 1985. Yet still the public saw the unions as too powerful in Gallup's annual study prior to their summer conference.

Just over one in two (53 per cent) — including 44 per cent of union members — thought the unions were too powerful, against only 12 per cent for both the public and members saying they were not powerful enough. In the future, however, it was thought that the unions would be less powerful: while 22 per cent felt the unions would be more powerful, 33 per cent saw them as being less powerful. The figures for union members were 13 per cent and 39 per cent respectively: a pessimistic though perhaps realistic view, given the failure of the miners' strike and the then lack of success of the teachers.

That the government was hostile to trade unions — fond of 'union-bashing', as the movement would put it — was apparent to the public in the replies to one of Gallup's questions. Seven out of ten members of the public and eight in ten trade unionists took this view. Even among Conservatives, slightly more saw the government as being hostile to the unions (47 per cent) than took the opposite view (42 per cent). It was hardly surprising, therefore, that 47 per cent of the general public thought that relations between the government and the unions would worsen, and that only 14 per cent felt they would improve. The figures were even more depressing among trade unionists: 58 per cent and 9 per cent respectively. On balance, though, the public saw trade unions as a good thing, with their 1985

Table 3.49: Standing of the Trade Unions

Q. *Generally speaking, and thinking of Britain as a whole, do you think that trade unions are a good thing or a bad thing?*

		A good thing	A bad thing	Don't know
August	1985	65	24	10
	1984	61	30	10
	1983	63	25	12
	1982	59	30	11
	1981	56	28	16
	1980	60	29	11
July	1979	51	36	13
August	1978	57	31	12
	1977	53	33	14
	1976	60	25	14
	1975	51	34	16
	1974	54	27	19
	1973	61	25	14
	1972	55	30	16
	1971	62	21	17
	1970	60	24	17
	1969	57	26	17
	1968	66	18	16
	1967	60	23	17
	1966	63	20	17
	1965	57	25	18
	1964	70	12	18
	1963	62	21	17
September	1961	57	27	16
	1960	59	16	25
August	1959	60	23	17
	1958	61	15	24
	1957	53	21	26
	1956	61	20	19
	1955	67	18	15
	1954	71	12	17

rating the highest for almost twenty years. The average rating for the 1980s so far was five points above the average for the 1970s and equal to that of the 1960s.

In no group analysed — even among Conservatives — did less than one in two think the unions were a good thing. As usual, however, this endorsement did not extend to the trade union leadership. More than one in two (56 per cent) of the general public and 53 per cent of union members saw the leadership as being unrepresentative of the views of the ordinary trade union member. Minorities of the public (29 per cent) and of the membership (38 per cent) felt that they were representative. This negative attitude towards trade union leaders can also be seen in the replies to a battery of statements about unions.

Table 3.50: Attitudes Towards Trade Unions

Q. I'm going to read you a few statements. For each, please tell me if you tend to agree or disagree with it.

	Agree	Disagree	Don't know
Trade unions improve wages, working conditions and job security for workers	76	16	8
Trade unions get power or money for union leaders	69	14	17
Trade unions ensure fair treatment for workers	68	22	10
Most workers who are not in management jobs would be better off belonging to a union than not belonging to one	62	23	15
Trade union leaders are out of touch with the workers they represent	62	28	10
It is true in this country that if you work hard, eventually you will get ahead	47	47	6
Trade unions control, dominate or run business	42	41	17
Trade unions may have been needed at one time in Britain, but not any longer	23	68	8
Wages and working conditions would have reached today's level even without the efforts of trade unions	22	68	10

Thus the two most widely accepted criticisms of unions concern their leaders: that they are getting power or money from their position, and that they are out of touch with the members. Majorities of the public accept that the unions are fulfilling their traditional role of looking after the workers, and that there is still a place for them in the Britain of the 1980s. Among trade union members, 58 per cent agreed that the leaders were out of touch and even more — 69 per cent — felt that trade unions got power or money for union leaders. Mention has already been made elsewhere about the feeling of alienation and cynicism pervading the views of the British public. It is also worth noting that they were evenly divided on the statement: 'It is true in this country that if you work hard, eventually you will get ahead.' A majority of Conservatives, senior citizens and home-owners agreed with this sentiment. On the other hand, majorities among Labour and Alliance supporters, young adults and the 45–64 age group and union members disagreed.

As a measure of the regard — if not the respect — which the public holds the unions, 81 per cent agreed that 'Because of a few rotten apples among them, trade unions have tended to get a bad reputation', though 11 per cent thought that 'Most trade unions deserve to have a bad reputation.' Perhaps this was because the most urgent problem facing the country was also seen to be the most urgent problem facing the unions when they met at their annual conference. Two in five said it was unemployment: twice as many as a year earlier, when strikes had dominated the public's view of the unions' problems. The public was almost evenly divided on the question of a law banning strikes in the key public service industries such as gas, electricity and water: one in two (51 per cent) approved, against 43 per cent disapproving. Majorities of both Conservatives and Alliance supporters approved of the idea, while Labour supporters and — not unnaturally — union members disapproved.

The unions and Labour got together to discuss and publish new plans for co-operation in the event of Labour winning the next general election. To begin with, the public's awareness of the plans was on the disappointingly low side, at 40 per cent, and it was hardly encouraging that awareness among union members and Labour supporters was barely above average. Secondly, among those aware of the plans, majorities felt that they would not be a practical help in solving the country's problems, and that the unions would dominate a future Labour government under Neil Kinnock. Labour supporters tended to disagree with both these views, but more than two in five union members agreed with the probable lack of success and the domination of Labour.

The Sterling Crisis

As the pound dropped against the dollar through the winter of 1984/5, the financial pundits vied with one another at trying to forecast the date when parity — or something worse still — would be reached. At the beginning of the year it was already down to $1.1185, and in the slightly longer term had added £1,400 billion to the cost of the Trident nuclear system since June 1984. By the end of February the pound had fallen even further, to a new low of $1.0575; and then it dropped to below $1.05. Within a month the worst was over and the pound was up to $1.23, eventually reaching $1.45. In early March, therefore, Gallup asked a number of questions on the public's perception of the problem, the first of which dealt with the British economy.

Table 3.51: The Economy in Poor Health

Q. How would you describe Britain's economic health at the present time? Would you say that it is very good, fairly good, fairly poor or very poor?

	Total	Con	Lab	Lib/SDP
Very good	3	5	1	1
Fairly good	35	56	23	28
Fairly poor	39	32	40	49
Very poor	19	6	33	18
Don't know	3	2	3	3

The public were almost evenly divided on the subject of Britain's economic future: 24 per cent thought the economy would improve over the next few years, 32 per cent that it would get worse and 40 per cent that things would not change. Not surprisingly, 50 per cent of the Conservatives were optimistic about the future of the economy and 8 per cent were pessimistic. Labour supporters, on the other hand, held the opposite view, with 6 per cent optimists and 54 per cent pessimists. Among Alliance supporters, just under one in five were optimistic against one in three pessimists.

The vast majority (86 per cent) of the public saw the dollar as being a strong currency, while 8 per cent thought it was weak. This was hardly surprising, given the media coverage of the pound's decline. The public were equally single-minded on the effect on Britain of a strong dollar. Almost three in four (73 per cent) of those who thought the dollar was strong felt that it would be a bad thing for Britain, while 10 per cent thought it would be a good thing and 7 per cent thought it would have no effect one way or the other. Slightly more than two in five (44 per cent) saw the strength of the American dollar relative to the pound as mainly the result of deliberate US policy, 6 per cent saw it as mainly the result of deliberate British policy, and 35 per cent thought that it was mainly due to market conditions beyond the control of either government.

4   The Environment

In October 1982, as part of a Europe-wide study, Gallup asked a number of questions about the environment. These were subsequently repeated in May 1985, and the answers to them revealed an increasing level of concern about the way human beings were harming the ⟨ planet. People were first asked whether they had any reason to complain about their immediate surroundings in terms of such things as drinking water, noise, air pollution, open spaces, lost farmland or damage to the landscape. On all these items, majorities of the public said that they had no reason to complain, as in 1982. The areas of greatest complaint were the loss of good farmland (23 per cent saying they had at least a fair amount to complain about); and damage done to landscape (31 per cent complaining); in 1982 the figures had been 17 per cent and 21 per cent respectively. Analysis by party supported showed that, on balance, Conservatives were less concerned about their environment than were the public as a whole.

The scope of the questions was then widened to cover not only damage done to Britain's environment but that done to the earth as a whole. The following table shows the degree of public concern on nine environmental issues:

Table 4.1: Concern about Environmental Damage

Q. Now, about the country as a whole. I would like to find out how worried or concerned you are about a number of problems I am going to mention: a great deal, a fair amount, not very much, or not at all?

	A great deal	A fair amount	Not very much	Not at all	Don't know
Disposal of nuclear waste	66	20	4	6	4
Disposal of industrial chemical waste	57	28	7	5	3
Damage caused to sea life and beaches by spillage or discharge by oil tankers	55	31	8	4	2

Table 4.1 continued

Pollution coming from outside this country, such as acid rain from another country's polluted air; damage to beaches and fisheries due to foreign oil tankers wrecked offshore or discharging oil; water polluted by individual waste brought in by rivers from other countries	46	29	11	9	4
Pollution of water of rivers and lakes	39	37	12	9	4
Air pollution	29	36	16	16	3

Q. Finally, more generally, how concerned or worried are you about the following: a great deal, a fair amount, not very much, or not at all?

	A great deal	A fair amount	Not very much	Not at all	Don't know
The depletion of world forest resources	49	30	10	8	2
The extinction in the world of some plants and animal species	45	33	13	8	1
The possible atmospheric damages affecting the world's weather brought about by gas (carbon dioxide) emitted from burning coal and oil products)	34	32	17	12	4

As before, Conservatives tended to express less concern about these issues. Yet among the public at large, a number of significant increases in concern had taken place in the brief period that had elapsed since the 1982 study. The largest of these was the 14-point increase in the proportion saying that the disposal of nuclear waste caused them a great deal of concern: up from 52 per cent in 1982 to 66 per cent in 1985. This was followed by twelve-point increases in concern about the disposal of industrial chemical waste and — perhaps a related problem — pollution of rivers and lakes. Concern about damage to sea life and beaches had risen by 10 per cent, about the depletion of world forest resources by 9 per cent and about pollution — acid rain, for example — by 8 per cent.

Finally, two trade-off questions were asked on the subject of what people would be prepared to pay in order to protect the environment. The first of these dealt with the cost to industry of measures designed to protect the environment: whether it was more important to protect the environment or to keep prices down. Three in five (60 per cent) felt that the environment was more important, while 23 per cent put prices first; in 1982, the figures had been 50 per cent and 40 per cent respectively. Analysis of the 1985 study by party supported reverses the image of the unconcerned Conservatives: two in three (68 per cent) of them gave the environment first priority compared to 54 per cent of Labour supporters.

The second question asked people to decide between the environment and economic growth. Again, a majority (57 per cent) felt that protection of the environment should be given priority, even at the risk of holding back economic growth; in 1982, the figure had been 49 per cent. On the other hand, 32 per cent felt that economic growth should be given priority even if the environment suffered to some extent (compared with 41 per cent in 1982). In contrast to the earlier question on prices, there were no significant differences between the replies of Conservatives or Labour supporters. There was, however, a generation gap: while young adults, aged from 18 to 34, opted for the environment as opposed to prices by a margin of 63 per cent to 28 per cent, senior citizens were almost evenly divided (44 per cent to 41 per cent respectively).

Science

What do people think of science? In December 1984 and January 1985, Gallup investigated the topic on behalf of the magazine *New Scientist*. People were asked, for example, to name three famous scientists, living or dead. Albert Einstein topped the list (with mentions from 28 per cent), followed by Sir Isaaac Newton (13 per cent), Sir Alexander Fleming (11 per cent) and Marie Curie (9 per cent). Budding scientists may find it a sobering thought to learn that only one living scientist — Sir Clive Sinclair — gained enough votes to put him in the top eighteen as far as public awareness was concerned. Space exploration, mentioned by just 17 per cent of the public, was thought to be the most important scientific achievement since the war. No other achievement was mentioned by 10 per cent or more of the sample.

On the whole, respondents felt that science was a good thing. Just under one in two (45 per cent) thought that science and technology did more good than harm, 38 per cent said that the good and harm balanced each other out, and 11 per cent said that it did more harm than good. The overwhelming majority (83 per cent) agreed that scientific knowledge was good in itself and that it was the way in which it was applied that created problems. On the other hand, 73 per cent felt that scientific discoveries could have very dangerous effects. Nuclear energy topped the list of the potentially dangerous scientific discoveries, mentioned by two in three (66 per cent) of those who believed in the potentially dangerous effects of science. Second on the list were biotechnology and genetic engineering (38 per cent), national defence and armaments (25 per cent), and pharmaceutical research and the development of new drugs (also 25 per cent).

Given the place of nuclear energy on the 'danger list', it came as no surprise to see that it figured low on the public's list of priorities for research spending.

Table 4.2: Expenditure on Scientific Research

Q. Let us suppose that it was you who had to decide how much of the available money for research should go to tackling the following problems. When deciding how the money should be spent, which do you think should be given priority? And which do you think should have the money limited or even reduced?

	Given priority	Limited/reduced
Medical research	72	2
New forms of energy	41	6
Pharmaceutical research and the development of new drugs	39	9
Control and reduction of pollution	37	5
Agriculture and plant science	27	13
Information technology and computers	19	14
Biotechnology and genetic engineering	12	23
Nuclear energy	11	36

National defence and armaments	11	35
Space exploration	5	42
Robotics	4	31
Astrology	1	42

Despite the great interest shown in the stars and the pronouncements of clairvoyants, the public did not rate the 'science' as being worthy of additional funds. However, as far as the wider field of scientific research was concerned, the public was responsive to a need to allocate more money. Just under one in two (44 per cent) thought the government should spend more money on scientific research, while 34 per cent said the amount already spent was about right and 12 per cent said less should be spent. When the question was repeated, but in terms of British companies spending money, very similar figures emerged. Perhaps because of the high cost of scientific research — or, maybe, because some saw Britain as already well ahead in this field — only 59 per cent of the public wanted Britain to seek to be a world leader in science.

On balance, Britain's institutions — the scientific community included — were not particularly highly rated. For instance, three in five (60 per cent) of the public said that they had hardly any confidence in the way trade unions were run.

Table 4.3: Confidence in Institutions

Q. I am going to name some institutions in this country. As far as the people running these institutions are concerned, would you say you have a great deal of confidence, only some confidence, or hardly any confidence at all in them?

	A great deal	Some	Hardly any	Don't know
Medicine	57	35	4	4
Military	29	45	18	8
Legal system	25	48	20	7
Scientific community	19	50	12	18
Television	16	57	24	4
Major companies	16	56	19	9
Parliament	13	44	38	5
Organised religion	12	38	41	9
Civil service	9	50	33	7
Trade unions	7	27	60	7
Press	6	44	45	5

Major companies were slightly more highly regarded by men than by women, while the reverse was true for organised religion.

Finally, Gallup asked a couple of questions on the place of science in Britain's schools. Around one in two (48 per cent) of the general public — and 72 per cent of young adults aged between 16 and 24 — felt that enough science was taught at school, while 36 per cent of the public said this was not the case. The vast majority of people (89 per cent) did think that everyone should study at least some science up to the age of 16.

Nuclear Energy

Both the studies discussed so far — on the environment and on science — contained indications of public disquiet about nuclear energy. Two in three expressed a great deal of concern about the disposal of nuclear waste, and nuclear energy headed the 'danger list'. As part of its normal, ongoing public opinion research, Gallup has collected other data over a number of years on the public's attitude towards nuclear power. This shows increasing anxiety about nuclear energy — anxiety which as yet is not being dispelled by the nuclear industry.

Two of the questions in the repertoire of trend questions, both dating back almost a decade, deal with the growth of nuclear energy and the anxiety it arouses:

Table 4.4: The Growth of Nuclear Energy

Q. *At present, about 10 per cent of the total electricity in Great Britain comes from nuclear power. What do you think should be the development of nuclear power generation in this country?*

	May 1976	Sept 1979	Jan 1980	May 1983	Oct 1984	Mar 1985
They should increase nuclear power generation	39	45	41	30	35	34
They should not develop any more at present	21	21	28	36	33	33

They should stop generating nuclear power	15	17	18	19	21	20
Don't know	25	17	14	15	11	12

A number of significant shifts in the replies to this question can be seen in the table above. The first of these was the gradual decline in the number of 'don't knows' from May 1976 to the March 1985 study. The second was the increase between 1979 and 1980 in the proportion not wanting any further expansion of nuclear energy, followed by a decline in the number of those actually supporting an increase in the generation of nuclear power. Overall, the proportion wanting a halt, at least temporarily, rose from 36 per cent in 1976 to 53 per cent in March 1985.

A second question attempted to measure the public's reaction to a nuclear power station being sited in their locality. Again, replies to this question showed a negative shift in opinion over the nine-year period.

Table 4.5: Local Nuclear Power Stations

Q. *What would you do if a nuclear power station were to be built in your area?*

	May 1976	Sept 1979	Jan 1980	May 1983	Oct 1984	Mar 1985
Would agree to its being built	19	16	17	14	14	15
Would not oppose though would feel anxious about it	25	24	29	27	27	25
Would oppose it	34	42	37	42	44	48
Would not feel anything	12	11	10	13	11	9
Don't know	10	6	7	4	5	3

The most significant shift as measured by this question was the increasing opposition to the building of a local power station: rising from one in three in 1976 to one in two in 1985. Opposition to the idea in the March study was greatest among Labour supporters (64 per cent), Liberals (60 per cent) and the middle-aged (57 per cent of those aged 35–44).

In 1980, a third question on the perceived safety of nuclear power stations was added to the trends. Since then, slightly over 60 per cent of the public have seen power stations as either fairly safe or very safe, while around a third have said they thought they were not very safe or actually dangerous. A fourth question was included from January 1984 onwards on the disposal of nuclear waste: whether burying long-term radioactive waste at sea or deep underground was a risk worth taking. Two in five felt that it was a risk worth taking, but one in two thought otherwise.

Finally, in March, two further questions were introduced which had previously been asked in the Eurobarometer surveys. Two in three of the public thought that the danger one would have most reason to worry about was radioactive leaks while the power station was working. Dangers associated with the storage of radioactive waste came second on the list (mentioned by 43 per cent), followed by those resulting from an explosion at the power station (36 per cent). When asked how such a thing would happen, 44 per cent thought it would be through human error, 16 per cent blamed a technical breakdown and 33 per cent thought it would be due to a combination of the two.

In June, Gallup took part in a nine-country study of its Swedish equivalent, SIFO, on the public acceptance of nuclear power. In all the countries involved — the USA, Japan, Britain, France, West Germany, Switzerland, the Netherlands, Sweden and Finland — there was widespread expectation that the demand for electricity would increase. In Britain, 74 per cent thought that the total usage of electricity would increase, 17 per cent thought it would stay the same and 6 per cent felt that it would decrease.

Despite varying experiences of nuclear energy (dating back almost 30 years) and varying degrees of dependency on nuclear electricity, the public's view on the future of this form of energy were somewhat uniform, with one exception, that its use would increase in the years to come. Majorities — ranging from 52 per cent in West Germany to 75 per cent in Switzerland — felt that nuclear generation of energy would increase in the future. In the one exception — Sweden — the country's Parliament had already decided that no further reactor construction would take place. There, 33 per cent thought that the nuclear generation of energy would increase while 54 per cent thought its level would stay the same — reflecting the Parliament's decision. On balance, the nine countries were in favour of the nuclear generation of electricity, yet there were significant differences in attitude, with the British, for example, being evenly divided on the subject.

Table 4.6: General Attitude to Nuclear Power

Q. Are you personally in favour of or opposed to the nuclear
   generation of electricity?

	In favour	Opposed	Don't know
France	64	27	9
West Germany	45	35	18
Sweden	45	37	18
Switzerland	45	47	8
Finland	42	39	19
USA	40	44	16
Britain	38	37	25
Japan	37	24	39
Netherlands	37	46	17

The survey revealed that only in the US and the Netherlands did
the opponents significantly outnumber the proponents. In Finland,
Switzerland and Britain, the balance between those in favour and
those opposed was a very even one. In the remaining four
countries, there was a significantly larger proportion of the adult
population in favour of nuclear energy than opposed to it. In
Britain, there was a distinct gender gap in the replies to the question, with a majority of men in favour and a plurality of women
opposed. Other demographic analyses tended to show non-manual
workers or better educated people (aged 17 or over) more in
favour than opposed.

Mention has already been made of two major causes of public
concern relating to nuclear energy: safety and safe disposal of the
waste. Two questions were therefore asked which dealt with these
topics, the first on general safety.

Table 4.7: Safety of Nuclear Plants

Q. Are you optimistic or pessimistic about our ability to run
   nuclear generating plants without serious accidents?

	Optimistic	Pessimistic	Don't know
France	62	30	8
Sweden	57	28	15
USA	55	35	11
Finland	53	36	12
Britain	47	41	12

Table 4.7 continued

West Germany	46	34	19
Switzerland	43	49	8
Netherlands	42	43	16
Japan	27	44	29

Among the nine publics questioned, the Japanese were profoundly pessimistic, both about operating risks and about the ability to dispose of the waste from nuclear generating plants. This was felt to be in keeping with the strong element of powerless fatalism which is part of Japanese culture.

Nowhere did the question of nuclear waste from power stations give rise to a balance of optimism over pessimism. In Sweden, however, the pessimists did not outnumber the optimists to any significant degree.

Table 4.8: Safe Disposal of Nuclear Waste

Q. Are you optimistic or pessimistic about our ability to dispose of waste from nuclear power plants in an acceptable way?

	Optimistic	Pessimistic	Don't know
Sweden	40	43	16
USA	39	52	9
Finland	36	54	10
West Germany	34	46	20
France	32	56	12
Britain	30	59	11
Switzerland	27	66	7
Netherlands	23	65	13
Japan	15	60	25

Again, in Britain and the other countries, women were more profoundly pessimistic about operating safety and safe waste disposal than men. The self-employed in every country were the most optimistic group in the general public, both about operating safety and about the safe handling of nuclear waste.

In September, Gallup were commissioned by PBA Communications to pose a number of statements using a five-point 'agree-disagree' scale. Again, a significant degree of anxiety was expressed by the general public in the replies to the question. Most people felt that existing methods of nuclear waste disposal were temporary and unsatisfactory, and that they were being kept in the dark by both the government and the nuclear authorities.

Table 4.9: Disposal of Radioactive Nuclear Waste

Q. I am going to read out a series of things that people have said about nuclear power stations and the radioactive waste that they produce. Given that large amounts of radioactive nuclear waste already in existence have to be disposed of somewhere, irrespective of the future waste generated, would you tell me to what extent you agree/disagree with the following statements:

	Agree strongly	Agree	Neither agree nor disagree	Disagree	Disagree strongly
The public ought to be given more information on how radioactive waste generated by nuclear power stations is being disposed of at present	43	43	6	6	1
The disposal of radioactive nuclear waste is one of the biggest problems associated with nuclear energy	31	54	9	5	0
We need a separate public body, independent of government and the nuclear industry to oversee the safe disposal of radioactive nuclear waste	24	57	9	9	1
We should not keep radioactive nuclear waste on the UK mainland	21	47	14	15	3
No more nuclear power should be generated until a safer system of disposing of the radioactive nuclear waste is found	17	37	17	26	2

Table 4.9 continued

Using proven existing North Sea Oil technology to drill 10,000 feet down into the sea bed and putting nuclear waste into steel and concrete lined bore holes would be a safer system of disposal than other methods used at present	13	58	19	7	2
It is better to dispose of radioactive nuclear waste out at sea rather than on the UK mainland	6	47	23	19	4
The benefits of having nuclear energy outweigh any problems	4	(30)	26	(31)	8
One existing system of disposing of nuclear waste — dumping drums into the sea off our coast — is perfectly satisfactory	1	11	11	51	25
Another existing system of disposing of nuclear waste — burying it in trenches about 3 metres deep on the UK mainland — is perfectly satisfactory	1	9	14	51	26

(Note: The figures for the 'don't knows', amounting to no more than 1 per cent, have not been shown in the table)

The one in two (54 per cent) of the general public agreeing with the fifth item — on a halt to nuclear power generation — encapsulates much of the data discussed earlier.

The second attitude battery consisted of a number of statements concerning British Nuclear Fuels Limited and the Central Electricity Generating Board.

Table 4.10: Attitudes towards BNFL and CEGB

Q. At the moment the government both controls and runs nuclear power stations and their waste disposal system through its nationalised industries, mainly British Nuclear

Fuels Limited (BNFL) and the Central Electricity Generating Board (CEGB). Would you tell me to what extent you agree/disagree with the following statements:

	Agree strongly	Agree	Neither agree nor disagree	Disagree	Disagree strongly
BNFL should be more accountable to the public on how radioactive nuclear waste is disposed of	23	62	9	5	0
BNFL should use the latest proven advanced technology for disposing of radioactive nuclear waste	20	65	13	1	0
We need a separate independent body to check that BNFL use the most proven advanced technology available for safe disposal of radioactive nuclear waste	17	62	11	7	1
Large UK civil engineering and oil companies (like Costain, Shell, McAlpine, BP) should be used by BNFL to develop new radioactive nuclear waste disposal systems	8	62	20	7	1
Large UK civil engineering and oil companies (like Costain, Shell, McAlpine, BP) would be suitable in helping BNFL and the CEGB develop more efficient radioactive waste disposal systems	7	61	23	6	1
The control of radioactive nuclear waste systems is best left under the exclusive control of the BNFL and the CEGB	2	27	24	37	8

Large UK civil engineering and oil companies (like Costain, Shell, McAlpine, BP) could be relied upon

Table 4.10 continued

to control and run systems for radioactive waste disposal, under contract from the BNFL	2	41	30	21	4
BNFL do a good job in keeping the public informed on how radioactive nuclear waste is currently being disposed of	1	13	17	52	15

Note: The figures for the 'don't knows', amounting to no more than 2 per cent, have not been shown in the table.

Shortly after the publication of this study, BNFL were on the point of launching a million-pound press advertising campaign in order to improve their image. These various studies suggest that they have still a lot to do, and that only time will tell how successful they have been in their aims.

In September 1984, 41 per cent of the public thought it quite likely that within the next ten years there would be a serious accident at a British nuclear power station; and by November 1985 the figure had remained fairly static, at 43 per cent. Then, 31 per cent thought a serious accident was not very likely and 14 per cent though it was not at all likely. Women and those aged between 35 and 44 were the most pessimistic about the future as far as this issue was concerned.

5 Law and Order

Crime and Violence

Even before September, when a number of people were killed in riots, there was public concern about a growing incidence of crime and violence. The violence in Brussels at the European Cup Final in May, where almost 40 people died, appeared symptomatic of present-day behaviour. In September, 10 per cent thought Britain was a violent country, 38 per cent a fairly violent country, 41 per cent not a particularly violent country and 10 per cent not a violent country at all. However, the vast majority (88 per cent) of the public felt that there was more violence in contemporary Britain than five years ago, while one in three were afraid of being the victim of a violent crime.

Table 5.1: Fear of Being a Victim

Q. How much do you fear actually being the victim of a violent crime?

	General public	Men	Women	18–34	65+
Fear a great deal	15	9	20	10	28
Fear quite a lot	16	12	21	14	18
Fear slightly	33	32	33	39	27
Do not fear at all	35	46	24	36	26
Don't know	1	1	2	2	1

The public were even more pessimistic about the future. Almost two in three (63 per cent) felt that it was at least fairly likely that in the next few years people would begin to take the law into their own hands. Around one in four (23 per cent) thought this was not very likely and 9 per cent thought it not at all likely. Yet, for once, members of the public were not disassociating themselves from the deed: 59 per cent said that it was at least fairly likely that they would take the law into their own hands if threatened, while 18 per cent thought this was not very likely and 16 per cent not at all likely.

In early November, Gallup asked the public about a number of predictions for problems that Britain might face in the future, some of which may be found in other chapters. Two dealt with crime or terrorism.

Table 5.2: A Violent Decade

Q. I am going to read out some predictions about problems that Britain might face. For each one, please say how likely/unlikely you think it is to come true in Britain within the next ten years:

Acts of political terrorism in Britain will become common events.

Riots and civil disturbances in our cities will become common events.

| | Political terrorism | | Riots | |
	Sept 1984	Nov 1985	Sept 1984	Nov 1985
Very likely	18	22	20	32
Quite likely	39	47	45	49
Not very likely	30	23	24	15
Not at all likely	11	5	8	2
Don't know	3	3	3	2

Thus, within the space of just over a year, concern about both these problems had risen: from 57 per cent to 69 per cent in the case of political terrorism, and from 65 per cent to 81 per cent in that of riots and civil disturbances.

Just over one in three of the public in April felt unsafe walking alone in their neighbourhood after dark, with the proportion rising to over one in two in the case of women and to two in three senior citizens — a similar pattern to that found in Table 5.1.

As might be expected, fear of being out alone after dark was higher in metropolitan areas such as London than in rural areas.

People were also asked whether they were aware of various local police schemes. Around one in four (23 per cent) were aware of the existence of the special constabulary and of the neighbour-

Table 5.3: Fear of the Neighbourhood

Q. *Thinking about yourself, how safe do you feel walking alone in your neighbourhood (local area) after dark?*

	Very safe	Quite safe	Not very safe	Not at all safe
General public	23	40	20	16
Men	38	45	13	4
Women	9	36	27	27
16–24	33	40	19	7
25–34	31	44	13	12
35–44	29	33	23	15
45–64	15	47	18	16
65+	6	32	30	33

hood watch scheme (22 per cent). Awareness of the property-marking scheme was somewhat lower at 12 per cent, and awareness of the victim support scheme was lower still, at 7 per cent. Awareness of all four schemes, however, was lowest among the very people who were most fearful: women, the elderly and Londoners.

In a separate study conducted in late April, preventative measures aimed at reducing crime were thought to be more helpful than attempts made at dealing with the possible social causes:

Table 5.4: Reducing Crime

Q. *I'm going to read you a list of things that some people think might help reduce crime. For each of them, would you tell me if you think it would help a lot, help a little or not make any real difference?*

	Help a lot	Help a little	Make no difference	Don't know
Putting more police on foot patrol and fewer in squad cars	67	21	11	1
More neighbourhood anti-crime patrols	51	29	17	4
The death penalty	50	15	29	6

Table 5.4 continued

More drug rehabilitation programmes	49	27	15	9
Better schools	48	22	25	5
More job-training programmes for young people	44	23	30	3

A number of significant differences in the perceived efficacy of the various proposals emerged from the detailed analysis of the question. Women, for example, were more likely than men to see more police on foot, more job-training programmes and more drug rehabilitation programmes as being helpful. There was also a generation gap, with senior citizens being more hopeful about the effects of more foot police, more anti-crime patrols, more job training programmes and the death penalty. They were least hopeful about better schools helping to reduce the crime rate. There were also political differences, with Conservatives being the proponents of the return of the death penalty and Labour supporters opting more for better schools and more drug rehabilitation programmes.

Gallup has also been asking for more than a decade a question on what people thought were the causes behind the rise in crime and violence. Not only do the trends date back to 1973, but the question was asked on two occasions during 1985, once before the riots and once after, as can be seen in the table below:

Table 5.5: Causes of Crime and Violence

Q. There has been a great deal of concern in this country over the increase in crime and violence. Here is a list of possible causes — obviously some are more important than others. I'd like you to go down the list and say, for each one, whether you think it is a very important cause of crime and violence, fairly important, or of little importance? (The figures shown are the proportions saying 'very important')

	Sept 1973	Mar 1976	July 1981	Mar 1985	Oct 1985
General breakdown in respect for authority, law and order	61	65	68	62	67
Use of drugs	48	41	30	60	67
Laws too lenient and not letting the police do their job	60	58	60	52	55
Bad example set by parents	50	51	60	46	50
Level of unemployment	—	—	66	65	49
Lack of discipline in schools	—	—	52	52	49
Conflict between whites and blacks	16	14	32	22	42
Poverty and poor housing	30	29	44	47	38
Coverage of riots and crime on TV news	32	29	47	28	31
Violence in TV entertainment	40	37	36	30	27
Coverage of riots and crime in newspapers	26	22	42	21	26
Youthful rebellion	27	27	40	28	26
Cinemas showing films with violence and sex	39	33	30	27	24
The troubles in Ireland	31	32	33	22	18

On each of the five occasions the question was asked, the proportion saying a general breakdown in respect for authority, law and order was a very important cause of the increase in crime and violence tended to be at the top of the list in ranking order. In 1985, particularly in the October study, the use of drugs surged to a high place on the table, in marked contrast to its position in 1981. Unemployment as a cause of crime and violence was seen to be significantly less important after the 1985 riots than it had been earlier. In fact, compared to 1981, almost all of the possible causes showed declines in perceived importance, with two exceptions. The first of these, the use of drugs, has already been mentioned. The second was the increased perception of a conflict between whites and blacks in Britain, mentioned by 32 per cent in 1981, falling to 22 per cent in March 1985 but then bouncing back to an even higher 42 per cent.

Race Relations

That the public saw the disturbances as at least partially racial is
reflected in the replies to questions about race relations in Britain,
asked at around the same time. Eight in ten, for example, saw
Britain's future as one of racial tension, compared with six in ten
just eight years previously.

Table 5.6: Racial Tensions: Britain's Future

Q. How do you see the future shape of the United Kingdom?

	1977	1985
As a peaceful multiracial society	15	6
As a multiracial society with tensions	38	53
As a society where different groups live separately but in harmony	16	6
As a society where different groups live separately but with tension	22	30
Don't know	9	4

An increased majority, therefore, saw Britain's future as a
multiracial society, but more people were expecting tensions,
whether in a multiracial situation or a ghettos situation.

Two in three (68 per cent) of the public in the same survey
thought that the feeling between white people and coloured people
was getting worse in Britain. This was the highest level for this
reply in more than 25 years of asking the question. Only 7 per cent
thought that things were getting better. Despite this pessimism, 67
per cent said they thought of non-white people born in Britain as
being British, though 28 per cent did not.

When asked which of various groups they would not like to have as
neighbours, the two emerging with significant increases had racial
overtones:

Table 5.7: Undesirable Neighbours

*Q. On this card are listed various groups of people. Can you
please sort out any that you would not like to have as
neighbours?*

	1982	1985
Heavy drinkers	49	45
People with a criminal record	42	44
Left-wing extremists	35	38
Emotionally unstable people	34	35
Right-wing extremists	29	31
Members of minority religious sects or cults	25	28
Immigrants, foreign workers	15	21
People of a different race	11	17
People with large families	13	16
Students	9	10
Unmarried mothers	5	8
Don't know	14	13

Compared with 1982, both immigrants and people of a different race have gone up by six points. No other group had gone up by more than three points.

The Police

A previous table (Table 5.4) included some data on attitudes towards changes in the police forces made with the aim of combating crime, and the same section dealt with public awareness of various local police schemes. A number of other studies were conducted throughout the year to measure the public's attitudes towards other aspects of the police force. In the first week of January, for example, people were asked whether they had reported a crime or accident to the police in the previous two years, or gone to them for help or advice. Just over one in three (38 per cent) of the general public said they had. Younger adults were more likely than average to have come into contact with the police in this way, as were Conservatives and middle-class people. The vast majority (78 per cent) of those who had contacted the police found them helpful, though 20 per cent thought they were not helpful. Age also had an influence in the replies to this question: just under one in two of those aged under 45 said they had found police 'very helpful', with the proportion increasing to almost two in three among those aged 45 or over.

One in five (18 per cent) of the general public had been stopped or asked questions by the police about an alleged offence in the past two years. Among the under-35s, almost one in three (31 per cent) had been stopped or asked questions, compared with only 7 per cent of people aged 65 or over. Two in three (68 per cent) of those who had been stopped or asked questions by the police found them polite, but 28 per cent thought they were not polite. When the questions were asked in July of a sample of 15- and 16-year-olds still at school, 31 per cent said they had been stopped or asked questions by the police; of these, 47 per cent said the police had been polite while 51 per cent thought they had not been polite.

People — the general public and school children — were also asked whether they had been really pleased or really annoyed with a police officer in the past two years. As the table shows, while annoyance with the police varied with age, being pleased with them did not:

Table 5.8: Being Pleased or Annoyed with the Police

Q. During the past two years, have you ever been really pleased about the way a police officer behaved towards you (or someone you know), or about the way the police handled the matter in which you were involved?

Q. During the past two years, have you ever been really annoyed about the way a police officer behaved towards you (or someone you know), or about the way the police handled the matter in which you were involved?

	Pleased	Annoyed
General public	34	20
18–34	35	28
35–44	35	19
45–64	33	16
65+	34	7
School children	28	38

Analysis by party supported also showed significant differences. While 39 per cent of Conservatives had had reason to be pleased with a police officer, 15 per cent had been annoyed with one in the past two years. The figures among Labour supporters were 32 per cent and 27 per cent respectively. When asked how satisfied, in general, they were with the way the police in Britain did their job, 76 per cent of the public said they were satisfied, 12 per cent were not satisfied, and the remainder were undecided. However, the public were less impressed by the police at a local level. In April, just over one in two (58 per cent) said that the local police had been at least 'quite successful' in dealing with crime, and 31 per cent thought they had not been successful. It also appeared that news about the local police was having a negative effect on the public. Altogether, 9 per cent had seen, heard or read something about the police in the previous month that had changed their opinion of the local police. Among these people, 21 per cent said it had made them more favourable towards the police while 78 per cent had become less favourable.

Then, in October, people were asked what they thought the *police* considered their three most important activities to be and what they themselves considered were the most important things for the police to do. The replies to these two questions were very similar, suggesting public sympathy with perceived police priorities, and the top seven items were as shown in the following table:

Table 5.9: Police Priorities

Q. Here is a list of things which the police do. Please read the list and tell me which of these activities, as you see it, are considered the three most important by the police themselves?

Q. And which do you consider to be the three most important things for the police to do?

	Public's view police priorities	Public's priorities
Fighting drug abuse	55	61
Fighting violent crime	50	54
Fighting organised crime	34	31
Measures against disturbances at major events such as football matches	33	29
Fighting terrorists	23	23
Preventive measures against crime	23	27
Fighting juvenile crime	18	22

Although the figures for the public as a whole were very similar on the two questions, there were a number of differences by political affiliation. Labour supporters, for example, put a lesser priority on controlling disturbances and riots than they felt the police did but gave a greater priority to fighting drug abuse than they thought the police did. Alliance supporters also thought the police gave a higher priority to controlling disturbances than they did. Gallup then asked whether the police should have the power to do certain things, and the replies were as follows:

Table 5.10: Police Powers

Q. Now I would like to ask you some questions about the powers of the police. Do you think the police should or should not have the power to do the following things?

	Should	Should not	Don't know
Use plastic bullets, water cannon and tear gas to disperse potentially violent demonstrators	74	19	6
Fingerprint everyone in an area where a serious crime has been committed	62	34	4
Stop and search anyone they think is suspicious	58	38	5
Question suspects before they have been allowed to consult a lawyer	36	57	7
Detain suspects for more than 24 hours without charging them	30	60	10
Have access to files containing information on citizens who don't have a criminal record	17	79	4
Tap telephones and record private conversations	14	80	6

Analysis by political leaning showed Conservatives as being more likely to approve of each of the ideas by an average of 10 points above the general public; and conversely, Labour supporters were below the national average by around eight points. Taking their normal middle line, Alliance supporters matched very closely the views of the general public. There was also a significant gender gap on the question of 'global' fingerprinting: two in three (68 per cent) women thought the police should have such powers, compared with 55 per cent of men.

Finally, with the recent rioting in mind, people were asked a question about the police handling of the situations:

Table 5.11: Police Handling of Demonstrations

Q. What is your opinion of police actions when they deal with mass demonstrations?

	General public	Con	Lab	Lib/ SDP
The police are too lenient	40	54	27	42
The police actions are appropriate	32	37	24	37
The police sometimes go too far	19	5	35	15
The police normally act in a brutal manner	4	1	8	1
Don't know	5	2	7	5

As expected from the earlier results, Conservatives were more supportive of the police, with a majority thinking that they are too lenient with demonstrators. Again, there was a gender gap, with more men (44 per cent) sharing this view than women (36 per cent).

In November, as part of a longer list of potential problems, people were asked how likely or unlikely they thought it was that in the next decade 'the police in our cities will find it impossible to protect our safety on the streets'. This was a repeat of a question asked in September 1984, when one-half of the public thought such an event was at least quite likely. In November, the figure had risen to 55 per cent, 18 per cent saying 'very likely' and 37 per cent 'quite likely'. Just over one in four (28 per cent) thought it not very likely and 13 per cent not at all likely. Concern about the future effectiveness of the police was greatest among Labour and Alliance supporters.

In mid-December, Gallup returned to the subject in a special study carried out in Birmingham, Coventry and Wolverhampton for the *Wolverhampton Express and Star*. Two of the questions were repeats from the January national study and showed very similar results. Twenty per cent, for example, of the West Midlands sample said that they had been really annoyed with a police officer over the past two years — exactly the same proportion as in the earlier, national sample. More (29 per cent) said that they had been pleased with a police officer over the past two years, compared with 34 per cent among the general public in January. The replies to the 'annoyance' question showed two significant trends: Labour supporters and younger people tended to be the groups annoyed with the police. There was no significant political differences on the 'pleased' question, but young adults were less likely to express pleasure with the police.

The overwhelming majority of the Midlands public was for the use of plastic bullets, water cannon and tear gas, but against the carrying of firearms by the police.

Table 5.12: Arms for the Police

Q. Now I would like to ask you some questions about the powers of the police. Do you think the police should or should not have the power to do the following things?

	General public	Con	Lab	Lib/ SDP
a) Carry firearms at all times, like America and some Continental countries				
Should	23	25	25	17
Should not	73	72	72	79
Don't know	4	3	3	4
b) Use plastic bullets to disperse potentially violent demonstrations				
Should	63	76	53	58
Should not	32	20	43	36
Don't know	5	3	5	7
c) Use water cannon and tear gas to disperse potentially violent demonstrations				
Should	75	83	66	75
Should not	20	13	30	20
Don't know	5	4	5	5

As can be seen in the above table, supporters of the major parties were in agreement on not arming the police but were less so on the use of plastic bullets, water cannons etc. There was also a generation gap in the replies to the three questions, with senior citizens more likely than average to support each of the three proposals. However, there were some doubts as to the possible effects of using plastic bullets, water cannon and tear gas: one in three (30 per cent) of the public felt that equipping the police with riot weapons would harm the police's relations with law-abiding citizens, though 52 per cent did not think it would and 14 per cent thought it would make no difference. Labour supporters (39 per cent) and young adults aged under 25 (37 per cent) were most inclined to see harm being done to the police–public relationship. One in three (32 per cent) also thought the use of such weapons would lead to an increase of violence against the police or on the streets generally. Slightly more (42 per cent) thought there would be a decline in the violence, and 17 per cent thought it would have no effect. Again, Labour supporters and young adults expressed most concern with more seeing violence increase than seeing it decrease.

The question eliciting the strongest response was that of whether a warning should always be given before plastic bullets were used. Ninety-two per cent of Midlanders thought that this should be done. The public were less certain, however, on the matter of who should make the decision about buying the equipment. One in three (35 per cent) thought the police themselves should decide, 30 per cent thought the decision should be left to the Home Office and 30 per cent opted for its being made by the police authority on the local council. Conservatives tended to favour the police deciding and Labour supporters were more for the local council police authority, while Alliance supporters were evenly decided between the three. The public was also evenly split on the retention of a directly elected police authority to oversee the operation of the police. Just over two in five (45 per cent) wanted this, while 42 per cent thought the police should be directly responsible to the government via the Home Secretary. There were significant differences in the replies to this question by party preference. A majority (55 per cent) of Conservatives said the Home Office should be in control, 53 per cent of Labour supporters wanted a directly elected body, and Alliance supporters reflected the public's overall view.

Two in three (64 per cent) of the public thought that a paramilitary-style 'mobile reserve force' should be established to back up the police in extreme riot situations, with 31 per cent disagreeing. Majorities in all parties and across all age groups supported the idea, though Labour supporters, men and the under-35s were less enthusiastic. The recruitment of more coloured police officers was thought to be of potential help in dealing with policing problems in areas of high ethnic populations. Three in four (75 per cent) of the public, and never less than 69 per cent in any subgroup thought that it would be a help, while 20 per cent took the opposite view. Finally, the vast majority (85 per cent) of people in the three West Midlands cities wanted more police officers on foot patrol. This compared with 4 per cent wanting more officers in cars and 10 per cent wanting things left as they were. Although one in four of the under-25s wanted more officers in cars or no changes, 75 per cent wanted more 'beat bobbies'.

Violence on Television

Four of the items in Table 5.5 dealt with the media in some way, and although they were all in the bottom half of the table, one in three members of the public thought that the coverage of riots and crime on television news was a very significant cause of the increase in crime and violence. One in four also attached blame to violence in television entertainments, and both items had been even higher in the past. To look in more detail at the public's attitudes towards violence on television, a study was conducted in late October on both entertainment programmes and news programmes.

One in two (49 per cent) of the public said that TV entertainment shows nowadays were worse than they were five years ago, and 27 per cent thought they were better. Senior citizens were the most critical of television on this question. When asked why they thought the programmes had deteriorated, 38 per cent said there were too many repeats, 32 per cent felt standards were generally lower and 27 per cent felt there was too much violence in the programmes. This compared with 8 per cent saying there was too much sex in the programmes.

Although 72 per cent of the public watched TV entertainment shows which had violent scenes in them, 47 per cent preferred to watch shows which rarely showed violence. Just under one in ten (7 per cent) preferred shows which sometimes contained violence, 42 per cent said it didn't matter to them and 4 per cent were undecided. The vast majority (70 per cent) of senior citizens (aged 65 or over) preferred programmes where violence was rare.

People were then asked whether they agreed or disagreed with various statements about TV entertainment shows. Care should be taken in reading the statements, as sometimes double negatives are involved:

Table 5.13: Attitudes Towards TV Violence

Q. *Now I am going to mention things people sometimes say about TV entertainment shows. Please tell me whether you tend to agree or disagree with each.*

	Agree	Disagree	Don't know
Television shows with violent scenes should only be shown after 10pm so most young children won't see them	85	11	4
TV entertainment shows should be realistic	67	27	6
Violent scenes are sometimes necessary to tell a good story in a TV show	65	32	4
Most adults see violent scenes on TV shows as simply entertainment and *not* as an accurate reflection of what happens to most people in real life	64	25	11
There is too much violence on TV entertainment shows	60	35	5
A law against violence being shown on TV shows is *not* necessary	58	31	11
Television networks put violent scenes in many of their entertainment shows because that's what people want to see	48	42	10
There is too much sex on TV entertainment shows	47	45	8
Most TV shows which deal with crime do *not* make criminals look like heroes	45	43	12
TV cartoon shows for children contain very *few* violent scenes	39	39	21
Most young children see violent scenes on TV shows as simply entertainment and *not* as an accurate reflection of what happens to most people in real life	38	50	12
TV entertainment shows are too critical of traditional values	36	41	23
Violence on TV shows does *not* encourage violence among adults who watch it	30	59	11
TV entertainment shows promote a better society	20	62	18
Violence on TV shows does *not* encourage violence among children who watch it	19	70	11

While the public were critical of violence in television pro-grammes, people accepted that some violence was sometimes necessary to help tell the story and that television entertainment should be realistic. Historically, one of the main criticisms of tele-vision has been about its effect on children, and it is on this issue that the study showed some of the greatest public criticism. Almost nine in ten, for example, wanted TV violence put back until after 10pm, at a time when most young children would not be (or should not be) watching, and 70 per cent felt that TV violence encouraged violence in child viewers. Similarly, one in two of the public were of the opinion that children cannot differentiate between violence as TV entertainment and its reflection of real-life situations.

As might be expected, there were a number of significant differ-ences in the views of men and women, and by age. Men, for example, were more likely to agree that violent scenes were sometimes necessary, that a law against TV violence was not necessary, that violence is in TV programmes through public demand, that violence did not have an effect on adult viewers, and that crime shows did not make heroes of criminals. Women, on the other hand, were more likely to agree that there was too much of both sex and violence on television. Analysis by age showed sharp differences of opinion on most of the statements, though there were a few on which there was almost universal agreement. However, the issues on which the generations diverged most were as follows:

'too much sex on TV': two in three young adults disagreed with this proposition, while three in four senior citizens agreed;
'too much violence on TV': just over one in two young adults disagreed, against four in five senior citizens agreeing;
'most adults recognise TV violence as entertainment, not real life': three in four under-35s agreed, the figure dropping to one in two among the 65-plus age group.

One in three (37 per cent) of the general public, including 56 per cent of senior citizens and one in two women, said that vio-lence on television bothered them. Some were affected more deeply: 15 per cent of the public overall, and 30 per cent of those aged 65 or over, were bothered a great deal by TV violence. Even more — 61 per cent of the public and 81 per cent of senior citizens felt that violence in television shows was harmful to society. One in four and one in two of these samples thought that TV violence was *very* harmful.

When asked to think about television news rather than entertainment programmes, 45 per cent thought the news programmes gave too much attention to stories of violent crimes, 10 per cent felt that not enough attention was given and 42 per cent said the treatment was about right. Again, senior citizens were more critical of TV news than were younger adults. The public was evenly divided on the question of whether or not TV news reporting exaggerated the amount of violence in Britain. While 45 per cent thought that TV news reporting did exaggerate the level of violence, 48 per cent disagreed. Perhaps surprisingly, there was no generation gap on this question; yet women had differing views to men. A majority (53 per cent) of men said there was exaggeration in TV news, while 54 per cent of women said there was not.

Finally, people were asked whether they agreed or disagreed with four statements about TV news programmes:

Table 5.14: Attitudes to TV News

Q. Now I am going to mention some things people sometimes say about TV news programmes. Please tell me whether you tend to agree or disagree with each.

	Agree	Disagree	Don't know
TV news stories about violence have made Britons more fearful than they were in the days before there was television	79	15	6
TV news stories should run more stories about good news and fewer stories about violence	65	27	8
TV news is just as interested in exploring the causes of violence as it is in reporting violent acts	58	30	12
TV news runs lots of crime stores because that's what people are interested in hearing about	47	45	9

Again, there was a gender gap in the replies to this question, with women tending to be more likely to agree with the first three statements and men more likely to agree with the fourth. The generations were most apart on the issue of more 'good news' stories in TV news. Just over half (53 per cent) of young adults agreed with this proposition, but the proportion rose to 79 per cent among senior citizens.

Social Workers

Another manifestation of Britain's violent society was the increasing abuse of children, a number of horrific cases coming to light in 1985. Part of the public anger about such cases was directed against social workers who were criticised for their handling of the families. In August, Gallup repeated a study first conducted in April 1981 on public attitudes towards social workers. People were shown a list of occupations and asked which of them were of most value to the community and which of the least value. As in 1981, doctors and policemen occupied the first two places as the valued professions. Teachers were in third place from fifth in 1981 — perhaps as a result of their increased public visibility during their pay dispute. Social workers dropped in public esteem in terms of their value to the community: the proportion seeing them as of least value rose from 7 per cent in 1981 to 13 per cent in 1985.

One in three (31 per cent) of the general public — 29 per cent in the earlier study — said that they had come into contact with a social worker (other than socially). When asked whether they had read or heard anything recently about social workers that had changed their attitude towards them, 45 per cent said yes, something had happened to make them less favourable towards social workers, while 7 per cent replied that they were more favourable. In 1981, the figures had been 27 per cent and 9 per cent respectively. The vast majority (81 per cent) who had become less favourable towards social workers cited child abuse cases as the reason for their change in attitude.

Despite the public concern about the handling of problem families by social workers, it had had little effect on the public's view of what they should be doing.

Table 5.15: The Job of Social Workers

Q. Do you think that social workers as part of their job should:

	1981	1985
Visit disabled people to investigate their needs	76	69
Help poor people get their rights	64	64
Help people with emotional problems	54	48
Look after old people in old people's homes	40	45
Decide whether a child should go into a children's home	41	42
Control and supervise disruptive teenagers	32	37
Decide on compulsory admissions of mentally disturbed people to hospital	24	20
Campaign for a zebra crossing on a busy road	16	17
None of these, don't know	3	4

Thus, the proportion who saw part of the social workers' job as deciding whether or not a child should go into a children's home remained static over the four years. Yet a further question, on the specific issue of child abuse, revealed significant shifts of opinion since 1981:

Table 5.16: Social Workers Not Ready Enough to Safeguard Children

Q. When a child is judged to be in danger of being physically or emotionally damaged by its parents, do you think social workers are too ready to remove a child from their own home, not ready enough, or is the situation about right?

	1981	1985
Too ready	8	7
Not ready enough	39	55
About right	31	24
Don't know	21	15

Women, people aged between 35 and 44 and those from the working classes were particularly critical of social workers on this question.

Finally, people were asked which of a number of phrases they would use to describe social workers. Top of the list was 'caring people in a difficult job': 43 per cent in the 1985 study and 48 per cent in 1981. This was followed by 'there to help individuals find their own solutions to their practical or emotional problems' — down from 41 per cent to 26 per cent — and 'there to ensure people get their rights — another drop, from 24 per cent to 19 per cent. Another positive description that showed a decline was 'there to encourage local people to find ways of helping their neighbours in need by voluntary actions': 22 per cent in 1981, but 12 per cent in 1985. Alternatively, the use of negative descriptions was more widespread. The number of people agreeing with 'soft-hearted do-gooders', for example, doubled from 7 per cent in 1981 to 14 per cent in 1985. Similarly, those agreeing with 'a sop to society's conscience' rose from 6 per cent to 8 per cent, while mentions of 'long-haired revolutionaries' went from 2 per cent to 5 per cent.

Justice

Mention has been made elsewhere of the acquittal of Clive Ponting on a charge under the Official Secrets Act. In February, therefore, Gallup asked a number of questions about British justice, the first dealing with its fairness and its efficiency.

Table 5.17: British Justice Efficient but Unfair

Q. Do you think our system of law and justice is or is not:

	1976	1985
Efficient		
Is	45	51
Is not	45	45
Don't know	10	4
Fair to everyone		
Is	37	34
Is not	54	62
Don't know	10	4

The passage of time — and, perhaps, the Ponting case — appears to have made a slight difference to the public's view of the judicial system, with slightly more seeing it as efficient yet not fair to everyone. It was on the latter question that analysis by party supporters showed the biggest differences. Just over one in two (52 per cent) of Conservatives, for example, thought the system was not fair, but the proportion rose to 57 per cent among Liberals, to 68 per cent of Alliance supporters and to 72 per cent among Labour supporters.

A bigger shift occurred among the general public on two questions concerning the impartiality of the courts and the issue of whether judges were influenced by the government. Both showed sharp shifts compared with a survey in 1969, so that one in two felt the courts favoured the rich and almost as many thought government influence was brought to bear on the judges.

Table 5.18: Biased Courts

Q. *In your opinion, do the courts in this country dispense justice impartially or do they favour the rich and influential?*

	1969	1985
Impartial	54	42
Favour the rich	35	50
Don't know	12	9

A majority of Conservatives said the courts were impartial in the way they dispensed justice, but a majority of both Labour and Alliance supporters said they favoured the rich and influential.

Table 5.19: Nobbling the Judges

Q. *Do you think that the judges are in any way influenced by the government in power at the time, or are they completely independent?*

	1969	1985
Are influenced	19	43
Independent	67	46
Don't know	13	11

Again, a majority of Conservatives thought that judges were independent of the government and a majority of Labour supporters took the opposite view, that judges were influenced by the government. Alliance supporters were almost evenly divided on this question. Finally, people were asked whether the main duty of civil servants was to the state or to the government of the day. A majority (55 per cent) of the general public — including majorities of supporters of all the parties — thought that the state should take priority over the government with civil servants, while 34 per cent said that civil servants' main duty was to the government.

6 International Affairs

Terrorism

The year saw a number of spectacular hijacks by terrorists, involving both airliners and an ocean liner, plus continuing problems in the Middle East, particularly in Lebanon. In late June, therefore, Gallup repeated a series of questions on terrorism first asked seven years before. The vast majority (91 per cent) of the public thought that terrorism was a very serious problem for the world, and 48 per cent felt that it was also a serious problem for Britain. In 1978 the figures had been somewhat lower, at 85 per cent and 30 per cent respectively. There did appear to be a generation gap in the replies about the problem of terrorism in Britain: while 42 per cent of the under-35s felt that it was a very serious problem, many more aged 65 or over — 60 per cent — held this view. People were also asked to what degree various causes were contributing to terrorism. The following table shows the proportion of the public who thought that each item was a major cause:

Table 6.1: The Causes of Terrorism

Q. Let me read to you what some people have said are causes of the terrorism that is taking place around the world these days. For each, please tell me if you feel that this is a major cause of terrorism, a minor cause or hardly a cause at all.

	1978	1985
Terrorism is growing in the world because the countries in the world have been too soft in dealing with terrorists	75	72
Acts of terrorism receive so much coverage in the news that this encourages terrorists to further acts of terror	60	69
Terrorism has been the weapon used by radicals who feel the system is totally unjust	44	56
Racial and religious minorities feel their cause can only be brought to attention through terror acts	42	56

Table 6.1 continued

As in Germany, young radicals feel they can draw attention to their cause only by committing acts of violence	42	52
Professional terrorists are trained by Palestinian Arabs in Lebanon	39	48
A modern, complex industrial society makes it easy for a small number of terrorists to commit acts of violence	34	41
Professional terrorists are trained by President Gaddafi of Libya	18	39

Table 6.2: Dealing with Terrorism

Q. Now let me ask you about some solutions that have been proposed as ways of dealing with terrorism. For each, tell me if you favour or oppose that solution. (Proportions are shown for those favouring the proposal.)

	1978	1985
Every country should develop special teams of commandos who are experts at capturing terrorists while saving the lives of hostages	85	89
All those caught committing acts of terror should be convicted and given the death penalty	71	71
All airline services should be cut off to and from any country which allows terrorists to use that country as a base of training or operations, or which gives refuge to terrorists or lets them go free	67	76
A special world force should be organised which would operate in any country of the world and which would investigate terrorist groups, arrest them, and put their leaders and members to death	66	63
Countries should refuse to make concessions to terrorists, such as paying ransoms or freeing other terrorists from prison, even if this means people who are kidnapped or held hostage end up being killed by the terrorists	65	50

The public's reaction to acts of terrorism was to take a tough line, with seven in ten supporting the death penalty for terrorists.

It is apparent from the table that support for one possible solution — namely, the idea of not negotiating with terrorists on behalf of hostages — had decreased, while support for an airline boycott of countries thought to be aiding the terrorists had increased in favour since 1978. As one might expect, Conservatives showed more support for both of these proposals than did the public as a whole.

The United States

Though America in recent years has gained the image of a somewhat impotent giant, the *Achille Lauro* affair gave it an opportunity to flex its muscles, as it plucked from the air the plane carrying the hijackers from Egypt to Tunisia. Despite the hardline attitudes taken by the British public towards terrorists in general, neither the United States nor President Reagan gained much in public esteem in Britain. For example, the proportion who had either very great or considerable confidence in the ability of the United States to deal wisely with current world problems rose from 23 per cent in late September to 28 per cent a month later. This latter figure, as can be seen from the following table, was only a few points above the annual average for the last three years:

Table 6.3: Lack of Confidence in America

Q. How much confidence do you have in the ability of the United States to deal wisely with present world problems: a great deal, a considerable amount, little or very little? (Annual averages — figures in brackets indicate number of surveys conducted each year.)

	A great deal, a considerable amount	Little	Very little, none at all
1985 (4)	24	28	41
1984 (5)	23	25	47
1983 (6)	23	26	45
1982 (5)	27	27	40
1981 (3)	30	25	36
1980 (4)	33	25	32
1979 (4)	28	25	36

Table 6.3 continued

1978 (2)	36	23	28
1977 (2)	48	22	22
1976 (1)	33	27	26
1975 (6)	30	26	31
1974 (7)	33	24	31
1973 (7)	28	26	32
1972 (6)	30	25	31
1970 (2)	29	28	27

In reply to a subsidiary question, around one in three of the British public said that their confidence in America's ability had gone down lately, and one in ten said that it had gone up. The former figure was one that proved consistent throughout the year, though the proportion having increasing confidence in the United States after the *Achille Lauro* incident was up on the year's average.

In contrast to his predecessors, President Reagan has yet to impress the British people. In the five years since he took office, Mr Reagan has consistently had more people saying he was not proving to be a good president than saying he was. Even in late October, the critics outnumbered his supporters by 47 per cent to 43 per cent. However, there does appear to be a long-term improvement in the British public's rating of President Reagan, from a low point in 1982:

Table 6.4: Rating of Presidents Carter and Reagan

Q. Do you think Mr ... is or is not proving to be a good president of the United States? (Annual averages — figures in brackets indicate number of surveys conducted each year.)

	Is	Is not	Don't know
Reagan			
1985 (4)	40	48	13
1984 (4)	32	55	13
1983 (6)	29	59	13
1982 (5)	27	58	15
1981 (2)	30	34	37
Carter			
1980 (3)	50	35	16
1979 (4)	38	44	18
1978 (2)	45	33	23
1977 (2)	61	11	29

Again, it seemed that almost regardless of what President Reagan did or did not do in 1985, around one in four of the British public said their impression of him had gone down, and less than one in ten said their impression had improved.

Yet, in the spirit of the Atlantic Alliance, the public tended to see the two countries drawing closer together rather than growing farther apart. Averaged across the year, without much variation, just over 40 per cent saw the relationship becoming closer, while one in four saw the two nations drifting apart. This is in sharp contrast to the period when the United States involved itself in the affairs of Grenada. In 1983, more than one in two thought the relationship was strained and only one in five felt that it was becoming closer.

The World Powers

On the whole, the British public disapproved of America's role in the world, disapproved even more strongly of Russia's role, and was undecided — perhaps through lack of information — about China. Throughout 1985, around one in three approved of the role the United States was playing in world affairs and around one in two disapproved. This was similar to the pattern found in 1983 and in 1984; but disapproval was less prevalent a decade or so ago. When asked about the roles of Russia and China in world affairs, the proportion approving of Russia's role was half that approving of America's, with a concomitant increase in both those disapproving and in the 'undecideds'. On the question of China's world role, the 'undecideds' was the largest group: around one in two of the public neither approved nor disapproved. Yet among those who gave an opinion, those approving outnumbered those disapproving.

Despite this general disapproval of the role of the major powers in world affairs, the public was relatively optimistic about the prospects for world peace in the next decade or so. In November, only 4 per cent thought it very likely that there would be a world war involving Britain and Europe, and 11 per cent thought it quite likely. However, the vast majority of people thought that a world war in the next decade or so was either not very likely (39 per cent) or not at all likely (40 per cent). Labour supporters and Liberals were the most concerned, with 18 per cent and 17 per cent respectively thinking a world war at least quite likely.

Although the public thought that the November meeting in

Geneva between President Reagan and President Gorbachev had achieved something, a significant minority saw the meeting as a wasted opportunity and were pessimistic about future meetings achieving anything.

Table 6.5: Reaction to Reagan–Gorbachev Geneva Meeting

Q. Do you think that anything worth while was achieved at the recent meeting between Mr Reagan and Mr Gorbachev in Geneva, or was it a wasted opportunity?

	Public	Con	Lab	Lib/SDP
Something was achieved	50	57	46	51
Wasted opportunity	27	21	32	27
They could have achieved more	13	10	13	15
Don't know	11	13	9	7

A majority (57 per cent) of the public thought that it was at least somewhat likely that something would come from future meetings between the two leaders, but 36 per cent thought that it was either not very likely or not at all likely. Again, Conservatives tended to be the most optimistic about such meetings: two in three (66 per cent) said it was very likely or somewhat likely, compared with 62 per cent of Alliance supporters and 48 per cent of Labour supporters taking the same view.

One obvious area in which nothing was achieved was that of arms agreements, and perhaps the public's favourable attitude towards the Geneva meeting was mainly to do with the friendly relations between the two leaders and their decision to meet again in the future. However, the meeting made no impact on the public's attitude towards both American and Soviet attempts to reach agreement on the controlling of nuclear weapons.

Table 6.6: Criticism of Arms Control Agreements

Q. Do you think the United States has done everything it reasonably could to try to reach agreements with the Soviet Union about controlling nuclear weapons, or should the United States do more?

Q. *Do you think the Soviet Union has done everything it reasonably could to try to reach agreements with the United States about controlling nuclear weapons, or should the Soviet Union do more?*

| | United States | | | Soviet Union | | |
	Has	Should do more	Don't know	Has	Should do more	Don't know
Jan	18	75	7	8	83	9
June	19	72	9	9	80	10
Sept	18	75	7	7	84	10
Oct	20	70	10	11	76	13
Nov	18	73	9	10	79	11

As can be seen, the November study, conducted after the meeting in Geneva, showed a similar pattern of replies for both countries compared with the earlier studies. Conservatives tended to be twice as likely as Labour supporters and Alliance supporters to think that the United States had done everything it reasonably could; while Conservatives and Labour supporters tended to take a similar view of the Soviet Union's attempts, with Alliance supporters slightly more critical of Russia.

'Star Wars'

A few years ago, President Reagan started a project known officially as the Strategic Defence Initiative (SDI) but which has since become popularly known as 'Star Wars', despite great efforts to play down the aggressive connotations of such a name and to emphasise the defensive uses of the project. At the beginning of the year, Gallup asked a number of questions to measure the public's awareness of and attitudes towards the 'Star Wars' project. In spite of the potential confusion with cinematic sci-fi ideas and some colourful media coverage, the public was relatively accurate in its knowledge of SDI, with 41 per cent saying that the idea was to find a way of defending against a nuclear attack. A further one in four (28 per cent) said that it was to shoot down enemy satellites in space. When told that the idea behind SDI was to find a way to shoot down enemy missiles before they hit their targets, 43 per cent of the public thought that it would never be possible to defend against a nuclear attack by such means, though almost as many (39 per cent) thought it would. While the public as a whole were almost evenly divided on this question, one in two (49 per cent) Conservatives thought the idea could work and 37 per cent felt that it would not. Labour supporters took the opposing view, with 32 per cent saying the idea was possible and 48 per cent thinking otherwise.

A majority (58 per cent) of the British public thought that the weapons were being developed mainly to defend America, though 23 per cent felt that they were being developed to defend both America and Western Europe, and 5 per cent thought they were mainly for the defence of Western Europe. The public was more evenly split on the effects of the SDI project on world peace: almost as many thought they made war more certain as thought the weapons made war less certain. Again, Conservatives and Labour supporters held diametrically opposed views:

Table 6.7: SDI and Chances of War

Q. Do you think that such weapons make war more certain or less certain?

	Total	Con	Lab
More certain	35	21	51
Less certain	37	56	24
No difference	14	15	10
Don't know	14	9	15

The public were similarly divided on the question of the banning of space weapons as a negotiating ploy in talks with Russia on the wider problem of arms control. Just over one in three (37 per cent) felt that the West should agree to ban space weapons in talks with the Russians so as to avoid a dangerous arms race; but 37 per cent thought that banning space weapons would mean the West forfeiting a technological advantage and that, anyway, the Russians might cheat. A final question found majorities of the British public wanting space to be weapons-free, sceptical of America's reaction to a hostile Europe about the weapons and concerned about an accelerating arms race.

Table 6.8: Attitudes towards SDI

Q. President Reagan has said America will develop weapons in space able to destroy an enemy's nuclear missiles after they have been fired. I am going to read out some things people have said about this plan. For each, tell me if you agree strongly, tend to agree, tend to disagree, or disagree strongly:

	Agree strongly	Tend to agree	Tend to disagree	Disagree strongly	Don't know
The United States will go ahead and develop weapons in space even if the European countries oppose the idea					
	56	28	3	2	12
Space should be kept free of all weapons					
	52	23	10	6	10
The Russians will try to match or get around any American weapons in space, leading to a new arms race					
	50	28	4	3	16
The United States should agree new defence policies with its European allies before agreeing to anything with the Russians					
	45	31	5	3	16
If the United States goes ahead with its plans to put weapons in space, Britain's own nuclear weapons will lose their value entirely					
	26	26	16	11	21
To develop these weapons in space, the United States will have to borrow money that would otherwise go to help new industries in Europe					
	19	26	16	16	24
President Reagan put forward this plan mainly to get the Russians to negotiate about other things					
	14	30	18	12	26
As far as the Russians are concerned, disagreements between the United States and its European allies about nuclear weapons would be a better outcome than an agreement to control nuclear weapons					
	13	29	16	10	33
President Reagan's so-called 'Star Wars' plan can never be made to work					
	13	17	23	17	31
By providing a defence against Russian missiles, American weapons in space would make us all safer					
	12	20	21	27	20
The threat to blow up Russian cities is a surer way to prevent Russia from starting a war than having new weapons in space					
	10	15	18	35	22

The statement that produced the most significant political differences was the penultimate one, about the new weapons making us safer. One in two (49 per cent) Conservatives agreed with the statement, while 36 per cent disagreed. Among Labour supporters, 27 per cent agreed and 55 per cent disagreed.

The topic was returned to in April and yet again in August, using a slightly revised set of questions with some additions. Little had changed in the replies to the preliminary questions, though slightly fewer people recognised 'Star Wars' as either a way of defending against a nuclear attack or as a way of shooting down enemy satellites in space. The combined figure of 69 per cent in January dropped to 63 per cent in April and then to 58 per cent in August. The public were also less sanguine about the chances of the weapons ever working successfully.

A new question asked about government expenditure on such weaponry, and a majority (52 per cent) of the public were against any money being spent. One in three (32 per cent) supported the idea of more being spent on defence, 3 per cent wanted more to be spent on offensive weapons, and 9 per cent said spend more on both. A continuing reason for the West in general, and Britain in particular, not to relax its defences has been a deep distrust of Russian intentions. Almost 40 years ago, within a few years of its being an ally in the war against Germany and Japan, Russia was seen to be a country with world domination in mind. In April and August, one in four thought Russia could generally be trusted to keep to its agreements on nuclear arms, but three in five thought otherwise. Finally, a question was asked on the subject of Britain's involvement in the research should it be given the opportunity of co-operating with America. In April one in two (48 per cent), rising in August to 56 per cent, felt that Britain should take part in the research, given the opportunity. Just over one in three (39 per cent) in April and 35 per cent in August took the opposite view.

The questions were repeated in early November after Anglo–US discussions about British participation in SDI research. The pattern of replies was very similar to that found in August, with a few exceptions. Slightly more people, for example, thought that the 'Star Wars' project made war less certain (35 per cent) than thought it made war more certain (28 per cent). The figures in August were 32 per cent and 36 per cent respectively. Similarly, fewer people in November than in August thought that the West should agree to ban space weapons in talks with the Russians, while slightly more thought to do so would mean the West forfeiting a technological advantage.

In November, a further question was also added on the subject of trust in America to provide a comparison with the 'trust in Russia' question. The replies to these two questions in November were as follows:

Table 6.9: Trust in Russia/United States

Q. Do you think the Russians can generally be trusted to keep to their agreements on nuclear arms or not?

Q. Do you think that the United States can generally be trusted to keep to its agreements on nuclear arms or not?

	Russia	United States
Can be trusted	22	30
Cannot be trusted	64	56
Don't know	14	14

Analysis by party affiliation showed even larger differences in trust for the two nations. While 40 per cent of Conservatives thought the United States could be trusted, 17 per cent thought Russia could be. Among Labour supporters, the figures were 32 per cent and 29 per cent respectively, and among Alliance supporters 23 per cent and 22 per cent respectively.

Nuclear Weapons

Mention has already been made in Chapter 2 of other results, with particular relevance to Labour's defence policy. At the end of September, Gallup asked a number of questions for the Campaign for Nuclear Disarmament. The public were almost evenly divided on the issue of a British defence policy based on the possible use of nuclear weapons. While 40 per cent supported such a policy, slightly more (46 per cent) opposed it. Note that the question asked about the possible use of nuclear weapons, not about the mere retention of such weapons. The public was more definite in its views on buying the Trident submarine-launched nuclear missile system 'at a cost of £11 billion'. Two in three (64 per cent) thought that Trident should not be bought at this price, though 22 per cent felt that it should. The final question was a repeat of a question asked in June about government expenditure, and the results were very similar. Briefly, they showed majorities of the general public thinking that the government was not spending enough on the National Health Service (80 per cent), on education and schools (78 per cent), on old-age pensions (71 per cent), or on roads (50 per cent), while 53 per cent felt that too much was being spent on armaments and defence.

At about the same time, a single question was asked for the SDP on the subject of the Trident missile programme. Here, a plurality approved of cancelling the programme but maintaining a minimal nuclear deterrent:

Table 6.10: The Trident Programme

Q. *Would you approve or disapprove of the following policy for Britain's defence?*
   We should cancel the Trident submarine missile programme but retain a minimal nuclear deterrent.

	Total	Con	Lab	Lib/SDP
Approve	45	37	49	51
Disapprove	39	48	32	34
Don't know	16	14	19	15

Analysis by age revealed nothing of the normal generation gap associated with this topic, but there were differences between the sexes on the question. Slightly fewer men (43 per cent) approved than disapproved (48 per cent), while among women the figures were 46 per cent and 31 per cent respectively.

In early October, two other questions were asked for Policy Research Associates, one dealing with Britain's nuclear deterrent and the other with cruise missiles. Basically, the replies showed that if the Soviet Union is brought into the question, majorities supported Britain's retention of its own nuclear weapons and the retention of cruise missiles:

Table 6.11: Britain's Nuclear Deterrent

Q. Do you think that Britain should or should not continue
to possess nuclear weapons as long as the Soviet Union
has them?

	Total	Con	Lab	Lib/SDP
Should	68	83	49	73
Should not	26	12	44	23
Don't know	6	5	8	4

Again, there were no significant differences in the replies by age,
neither was there a gender gap:

Table 6.12: Cruise Missiles

Q. Do you think that Britain should or should not remove
cruise missiles from this country, whether or not the
Soviet Union dismantles its SS–20 nuclear missiles?

	Total	Con	Lab	Lib/SDP
Should	35	24	46	37
Should not	52	65	39	53
Don't know	12	11	14	10

Apart from the obvious differences between supporters of the
three 'parties', there was a slight tendency for the under-45s to be
more in favour of removing cruise missiles than those aged 45 and
over.

Further questions were asked in early November for the
Foundation for Defence Studies, dealing not only with attitudes
but also with the public's knowledge of defence matters. The first
of these dealt with the subject of which military alliance had more
conventional forces deployed in Europe. Almost one in three (30
per cent) thought that the Warsaw Pact had more, 23 per cent said
NATO had more, 4 per cent said the two had equal amounts, but
the largest single proportion (43 per cent) said they did not know.

Conservatives and Alliance supporters tended to see the
Warsaw Pact as the stronger, while Labour supporters saw NATO
as being ahead. Although the public were almost evenly divided in
its perception of who had more forces, they saw the two sides quite

differently in terms of the balance of power. Among those saying NATO had more forces, less than one in two said that it was by 'a lot more', compared with two in three making the same judgement about the Warsaw Pact's advantage. Similarly, the Warsaw Pact was thought to have deployed, and to still have in place, more medium-range nuclear missiles in Europe over the past ten years: just under one in three (29 per cent) said the Warsaw Pact, compared with 21 per cent thinking it was NATO. Again, the largest single proportion (47 per cent) were unable to answer the question, while 4 per cent thought the two alliances were equal. Also, as with the second question, people were inclined to see the Warsaw Pact as 'a lot more' ahead and NATO as only 'a little more'.

The public were more certain, though still divided, when it came to the history of American nuclear missiles in Britain. Two in five (42 per cent) of the public thought that the statement 'Before the arrival of US cruise missiles in Britain in 1983, there were no significant numbers of American nuclear weapons in Britain' was false, 31 per cent thought it was true, and 27 per cent were undecided. Young people and Labour supporters tended to think the statement was true, while Conservatives, Alliance supporters and middle-aged people thought it was false.

Three questions were then asked to test the public's knowledge of the cost to Britain of a nuclear defence policy. More than two in five (44 per cent) of the public, for example, were unable to estimate what proportion of Soviet nuclear weapons Britain's nuclear weapons represented. Among those who could answer the question, 21 per cent was the biggest group, thinking that Britain's strength was less than 5 per cent of the Soviet Union's. Around one in ten each thought that it was between 5 and 9 per cent and 10 and 19 per cent, while six per cent each thought that it was 20–29 per cent or 30 per cent or more. Again, around two in five (38 per cent) could not say what percentage of Britain's annual defence budget was spent on the nuclear force or what percentage of the GNP was taken up by Britain's defence spending (43 per cent). Those of the public who did give an answer gave a wide range of replies: 4 per cent, for example, thought that less than 5 per cent of the defence budget was spent on nuclear forces, while 11 per cent thought it was more than one-half. Similarly, when estimating what proportion of the gross national product was taken up by defence spending, 13 per cent said 10 per cent or less while 10 per cent said over 30 per cent.

Despite the special relationship between Britain and America, and the usual mistrust of Russia, the United States was seen as as much of a threat to peace in Europe as Russia was:

Table 6.13: Threats to Peace in Europe

Q. Which superpower do you believe poses the greater threat to peace in Europe: the United States or the Soviet Union?

	Total	Con	Lab	Lib/SDP
United States	32	22	40	33
Soviet Union	33	41	26	33
Both equally	28	30	25	28
Don't know	7	7	8	6

Although only one in three of the public saw the Soviet Union as the greatest threat to peace in Europe, two in three (68 per cent) felt that Britain should keep an up-to-date nuclear deterrent as long as the Soviet Union continued to possess nuclear weapons. Nine in ten (88 per cent) Conservatives shared this view, as did 69 per cent of Alliance supporters and a narrow majority (52 per cent) of Labour supporters. It is hardly surprising, therefore, that 88 per cent of the general public thought that before we entered into any arms control agreements with the Soviet Union there should always be a reliable method of checking that both sides were not cheating on the conditions of such agreements.

Again, the public were not entirely one-sided in their attitude to arms control negotiations which have taken place since 1960: one in seven thought the East had been the more constructive, while one in three thought the West had.

Table 6.14: The Most Constructive Side in Arms Control

Q. Which side do you think has been the more constructive in arms control negotiations over the last 25 years: the East or the West?

	Total	Con	Lab	Lib/SDP
East	14	10	21	10
West	36	43	31	35
Neither	25	25	21	28
Don't know	26	21	27	27

The public, however, had little idea as to how many arms control and disarmament agreements have been signed between the East and the West in the last 25 years. Almost one in two (47 per cent) were unable to answer the question, and those who did so ranged from less than five (14 per cent of the public) to sixteen or more (10 per cent of the public).

A majority (52 per cent) of the public felt that a country which reduces its defences is more likely to be attacked than less likely to be, though there were some significant differences by political persuasion:

Table 6.15: Reduce Defences and Be Attacked

Q. *Do you believe that a country which reduces its defences:*

	Total	Con	Lab	Lib/SDP
Is less likely to be attacked because it poses no military threat to others	27	14	38	27
Is more likely to be attacked because it is less able to defend itself	52	71	37	52
Don't know	21	15	25	21

An extension of the concept of non-nuclear defence is the idea of 'nuclear-free zones'. Three in four (76 per cent) of the public saw such areas as having no effect on whether or not the areas were attacked, 8 per cent thought it made an attack more likely and 8 per cent less likely.

In early December, the final questions for the year on this topic were asked on behalf of CND. These questions showed an overwhelming opposition to being first country to use nuclear weapons in a war — and to belonging to an alliance which would do so. This latter result was in contradiction to the public's earlier support for Britain to remain a member of NATO, and reflects the public's lack of knowledge — or its misinformation — on defence topics. In the third of three questions, the public wanted the British Government to work towards dismantling both NATO and the Warsaw Pact.

Three in four (75 per cent) of the general public thought that

NATO should not use nuclear weapons first in a war and 14 per cent thought it should. Support for first use of nuclear weapons was highest among Conservatives (20 per cent). Earlier surveys showed a substantial majority of the public supporting Britain's continued membership of NATO; yet in the study for CND 60 per cent thought Britain should not belong to an alliance with a policy of using nuclear weapons first, and 26 per cent thought it should. Majorities in all sectors of the public shared this view, though there were some significant differences in the replies. Just over one in three (35 per cent) Conservatives, for example, thought that Britain should belong to an alliance prepared to be first to use nuclear weapons. This compared to 26 per cent of Alliance supporters and 16 per cent of Labour supporters. Not quite one in two (46 per cent) of the general public thought that the British Government should 'aim to get both NATO and the Warsaw Pact dismantled', while fewer (33 per cent) took the opposite view and 21 per cent were undecided. It was on this question that the party supporters were most at odds, even among the Alliance. Conservatives, for example, were on balance opposed to the idea by a margin of 36 per cent saying we should aim for such a dismantling, against 42 per cent saying we should not. On the other hand, a majority (58 per cent) of Labour supporters were for the dismantling and 24 per cent were opposed. Alliance supporters overall were similarly divided: 48 per cent and 34 per cent respectively. However, the two sections of the Alliance were not unified on this question. While 39 per cent of Liberals supported the idea, 51 per cent of SDP or Alliance supporters did so. There was more agreement on the proportions in opposition: 31 per cent and 34 per cent respectively.

The United Nations

In October, the United Nations celebrated 40 years in the field of international diplomacy, though in the eyes of many throughout the world it had failed to live up to the heady expectations of the post-war period. In only two countries of an 18-country survey conducted in the spring did a majority of the public think the United Nations was doing a good job. In nine of the countries, the critics outnumbered the proponents:

Table 6.16: A Disappointing United Nations

Q. In general, do you feel the United Nations is doing a good
   job or a poor job in trying to solve the problems it has had
   to face?

	A good job	A poor job	No opinion
Netherlands	66	23	12
Philippines	64	15	21
Switzerland	49	24	27
Australia	49	34	17
USA	38	44	18
Canada	36	39	26
Belgium	34	17	49
Argentina	32	32	36
Greece	31	36	33
Brazil	27	23	50
Great Britain	26	47	27
West Germany	25	31	44
Uruguay	25	49	27
Turkey	22	43	35
Portugal	17	14	69
Japan	16	28	56
South Africa	13	65	22

Not surprisingly, in South Africa, one of the two non-member
countries surveyed, two in three thought the United Nations had
made a poor job of trying to solve the problems it has had to face.
The other non-member, Switzerland, can be found at the opposite
end of the table, with one in two of its inhabitants supporting the
UN in its endeavours.

In June, Gallup returned to the topic in Britain with a number
of other questions about the organisation. There were still more
people critical of the UN (42 per cent) than thought it was doing a
good job (33 per cent) in answer to the basic 'performance'
question. However, in a different survey also carried out that month
the overwhelming majority (71 per cent) of the British public
felt that the world would be worse off without the United
Nations and only 12 per cent saw things in the world being better if
the UN did not exist. On the question of which of two aims the
United Nations was doing best at, 36 per cent said it was helping
poor countries and 19 per cent said it was keeping the peace. (This
was a week after Lebanese Shia Muslim gunmen had seized a
TWA Boeing 727 jet on a scheduled flight from Athens to Rome;
when 15 people had been killed by gunmen in San Salvador; when

the Air India Boeing 727 had crashed off the coast of Ireland, said to be blown up; and when a bomb had exploded in a Japanese airport.) Just under one in ten (8 per cent) thought the UN was doing well at both jobs, but twice as many (17 per cent) said they were doing neither job well.

Next we have an example of the 'context effect'. After being asked the previous question on helping poor countries or keeping the peace, people were asked the basic 'performance' question. The results were significantly different from those obtained from the earlier question, where no other questions about the UN preceded it. One in two said the United Nations was doing a good job, while 34 per cent said it was doing a poor job. Prompting, so to speak, with an idea of what the function of the United Nations was, obviously helped to boost the public's attitude towards the organisation. Finally, people were asked whether the Third World, developing countries had too much influence within the United Nations. While one in three (31 per cent) thought they did, 48 per cent disagreed. The detailed demographic analyses showed some interesting differences of opinion. Slightly more Conservatives, for example, thought the Third World countries had too much influence in the UN than thought they did not. On the other hand, majorities of both Labour and Alliance supporters felt that the developing countries did not have too much influence. There was also a generation gap, with increasing age tending to be accompanied by the feeling that the Third World countries were too influential.

The Falklands Factor

Almost three years after the event, the sinking of the Argentine ship *General Belgrano* returned to haunt the government. On February 11, Clive Ponting, an assistant secretary in the Ministry of Defence, was acquitted of breaching the Official Secrets Act by leaking documents about the sinking to Labour MP Tam Dalyell. A fortnight later, 94 per cent of the public said they had heard or read something 'recently' about the *General Belgrano*.

These people were then asked two further questions, previously asked in September 1984 when the story broke. Over the intervening months, the government appears to have won the argument about the sinking of the *Belgrano*. Gallup asked: 'From what you know about the incident, do you think the government was right or wrong to order the sinking of the *Belgrano*?' Just over one in two (57 per cent) thought the government's course was right, while 28 per cent thought that it was wrong. This compared with 49 per cent and 31 per cent respectively in September. Naturally enough, the vast majority (81 per cent) of Conservatives supported the government's line, as did a majority of Alliance supporters. Almost one in two Labour supporters thought the government had been wrong to order the sinking, though one in three felt it had been right. The public were less likely to think that Mrs Thatcher had told (or had been able to tell) the whole truth about the *Belgrano* affair. One in five thought she had, but three times as many (62 per cent) felt that she had not. Even Conservatives were divided on this question, with 43 per cent supporting Mrs Thatcher and 37 per cent saying she had not told the whole truth.

The Channel Link

The idea of a more convenient way of crossing the English Channel has intrigued the British and her European neighbours for almost 200 years — and resurfaced in 1985. Although a majority of the British public favoured the idea of a Channel link, they were less enthusiastic about it than they had been in the early 1960s. In the 20 or so years since the 'Swinging Sixties', opposition to the idea of a link with France proved to have doubled:

Table 6.17: Support for a Channel Link

Q. Should Britain support the idea of building a Channel tunnel or bridge between Britain and France?

	1963	1985
Should	69	53
Should not	17	32
Don't know	14	15

Support was highest among men, people aged between 35 and 44 and (surprise, surprise!) recent cross-Channel travellers. Women tended to be less enthusiastic about the link, and people aged 65 or over were evenly divided on the subject. It was also people in the south-east who were most opposed, with 47 per cent saying Britain should support the idea but 39 per cent that we should not. Why did people like the idea — or, perhaps of more importance — why did they oppose it? Among the supporters, one reason stood out: that it would make the Channel crossing easier or quicker. Just over one in two (58 per cent) gave this reason. Four other reasons were mentioned by around one in ten of those in favour: a Channel link would improve import potential (12 per cent), would improve Anglo-French relations (12 per cent), would make cross-Channel trips cheaper (10 per cent), and perhaps would create more jobs (9 per cent).

Those opposed to the link gave a greater variety of reasons as to why the idea should not be pursued. Top of the list came the cost — 'a waste of money' — cited by one in four of this group. This was followed by the 'island' syndrome — 'like being on an island' — mentioned by 20 per cent, and by the feeling that an additional link was superfluous (19 per cent). Perhaps remembering one of Napoleon's wishes — to invade Britain in 1805 — and Hitler's more recent attempts, 16 per cent thought the link was a bad idea because it made an invasion that much easier. A further 12 per cent were concerned about the potential for spreading diseases such as rabies, while 10 per cent were worried about other unwelcome visitors — immigrants. Finally, 10 per cent took a Francophobic stance, confessing that they did not like the French or that they were not friends of ours.

Despite the decline in the popularity of the link since 1963, the public remained solidly behind the idea of a 'Chunnel' rather than a bridge. One in two (51 per cent) preferred a tunnel, 10 per cent a bridge, and 16 per cent a combination of the two. In 1963, the figures were 41 per cent, 14 per cent and 20 per cent respectively. The idea of a tunnel was more popular with men than with women: while 63 per cent of men opted for a tunnel and 6 per cent for a bridge, for women the figures were 41 per cent and 15 per cent respectively. Again, those living in the south-east corner of England took a slightly different view. For example, this group included a higher-than-average number of 'don't knows' (27 per cent) and a lower-than-average number (44 per cent) in favour of a tunnel.

The Common Market

To some degree the public's less than wholehearted support for a
Channel link, and some of the reasons why they were against the
idea, were symptomatic of Britain's attitude towards the Common
Market. In January, more of the public felt that Britain's membership was a bad thing (39 per cent) than a good thing (32 per cent)
— even after what was officially over a decade in Europe! There
was also the chance that, given the opportunity, the British public
would vote to leave the Community.

Table 6.18: Britain's Membership of the Common Market

*Q. If there were to be a referendum tomorrow on the
question of Britain's membership of the Common Market,
how would you vote: to stay in or to leave?*

	Total	Con	Lab	Lib/SDP
Stay in	43	62	27	42
Leave	45	30	60	50
Wouldn't vote	4	3	5	3
Don't know	8	5	8	5

In July 1984, the public had been even more hostile towards the
Market, with 47 per cent saying they would have voted to leave
and 37 per cent to stay. It was therefore hardly surprising that in
1985 36 per cent of the public said they would be relieved to be
told that the Common Market had been scrapped and 35 per cent
said they would be indifferent to the news, while only 23 per cent
said they would be very sorry. No doubt the initiators of the idea
of the European Economic Community would be distressed by this
lack of enthusiasm on the part of the British public, but perhaps
even more so by the 72 per cent who saw the Community as a
divided body.

The public, as well as taking a generally negative view of the
Common Market, were critical of the government's policy in dealing with that institution. Almost one in two (46 per cent) thought
that the government was not being tough enough, 32 per cent felt
that the policy was about right, and 8 per cent thought that they
were being too tough. This criticism was as true among Conservatives as it was among Labour or Alliance supporters. Finally,

Gallup asked a number of questions about the member-countries of the Community; for example, France (47 per cent) and West Germany (23 per cent) were thought to be the most influential countries, though 11 per cent thought all the countries were equally influential. These two were also expected to be the most influential in five years' time, 29 per cent mentioning West Germany and 26 per cent mentioning France. However, on the subject of which country had the strongest economy, West Germany dominated the replies with 56 per cent, and also topped the list with 41 per cent as the country expected to have the strongest economy in five years' time. No other country achieved double figures in answer to either question.

Eurobarometer

In the spring, Gallup once again took part in the regular Euro-barometer series of surveys sponsored by Brussels, along with its colleagues in the other EEC countries. In addition to the regular questions on satisfaction with life and the way democracy works, people in the ten countries were also asked about five major issues:

a people's Europe;
the relative benefits of Community membership so far;
the accession of Spain and Portugal;
the plan for European political union;
awareness of the European Parliament and attitudes towards it following the 1984 elections.

There were some signs of a slight rise in the level of satisfaction with life in some countries: Denmark, Germany, Italy and Luxembourg. It had remained stable in France, the Netherlands and the United Kingdom, but had dropped in Belgium and Ireland.

As for the way democracy worked, 72 per cent in Italy were dissatisfied, as they had been twelve years earlier; Italy was the only country in the Spring study to have a majority dissatisfied. On balance, the Community was slightly more satisfied with how democracy worked than dissatisfied. In the United Kingdom, for example, 51 per cent were satisfied and 43 per cent dissatisfied, closely matching the Community average. In 1973, the figures for Great Britain (Ulster excluded) were 44 per cent and 54 per cent

Table 6.19: Satisfaction with Life

Q. On the whole, are you very satisfied, fairly satisfied, not very satisfied, or not at all satisfied with the life you lead?

	Belgium	Denmark	West Germany	France	Ireland	Italy	Luxembourg	Holland	UK	Greece
September 1973										
Very satisfied	43	51	17	15	53	8	40	41	33	NA
Fairly satisfied	49	44	65	62	39	57	49	52	52	
Not very satisfied	6	4	15	17	6	27	9	5	11	
Not at all satisfied	2	1	2	5	2	7	2	1	3	
March/April 1985										
Very satisfied	26	63	24	13	31	15	39	40	33	19
Fairly satisfied	58	32	60	63	50	52	53	50	54	48
Not very satisfied	13	3	14	18	12	23	7	6	9	22
Not at all satisfied	2	1	2	5	6	9	1	2	4	11

respectively. Three topical issues were examined which related to specific measures designed to strengthen the Community's identity and to boost its public image. The first of these was the abolition of administrative checks and formalities at borders. This was welcomed overall by six in ten Europeans, but there were significant differences between countries. Two in three people in the United Kingdom, for example, were against the idea, as were 56 per cent of the Danes and 48 per cent of the Irish — the publics who tend to be most anti-European. The creation of a European legal area whereby criminals fleeing from one member-state to another would automatically be handed over to the home authorities was even more popular, with 87 per cent of the Community and 91 per cent in the United Kingdom being in favour of the idea. Analysis of this question using a left-right scale showed not only that those placing themselves on the left of the scale were less enthusiastic about the idea but that they had become less so since the late 1970s. The third item dealt with the idea of the possible creation of a European currency. Around one in three (32 per cent) of the Community's adults were in favour of national currencies being replaced by a European currency and slightly more (38 per cent) were opposed. In the United Kingdom, the figures were 12 per cent and 64 per cent respectively: very much a thumbs-down from the British. Six Europeans in ten and one in two in the United Kingdom were in favour of extending the idea so that national currencies and a European currency could be used concurrently.

The optimistic messages put across by the media following the agreement on Spanish and Portuguese accession appears to have increased support slightly both for the principle of European unification and for the Community. For the first time since autumn 1978, there were more positive replies than negative ones to a question on the trend in understanding between Community countries. On the other hand, one in two saw no change in the understanding.

General attitudes towards Community membership had changed little in the short term, though larger shifts had occurred over the longer period. Denmark and the United Kingdom remained the two countries least enamoured of their membership.

Thus, while the United Kingdom became slightly less hostile to the Community over the twelve-year period, Denmark became distinctly more hostile.

Table 6.20: General Attitude towards Community Membership

Q. Generally speaking, do you think that … (your country's) membership of the European Economic Community (Common Market) is a good thing, a bad thing, or neither a good thing nor a bad thing?

	Belgium	Denmark	West Germany	France	Ireland	Italy	Luxembourg	Holland	UK	Greece
September 1973										
A good thing	57	42	63	61	56	69	67	63	31	NA
Neither good nor bad	19	19	22	22	21	15	22	20	22	
Bad thing	5	30	4	5	15	2	3	4	34	
Don't know	19	9	11	12	8	14	8	13	13	
March/April 1985										
A good thing	64	29	54	68	53	72	83	77	37	45
Neither good nor bad	24	27	30	21	21	18	10	11	28	26
Bad thing	6	31	7	6	20	4	3	5	30	17
Don't know	6	13	9	5	6	6	4	7	5	12

On the question of the enlargement of the Community with the accession of Spain and Portugal, six in ten Europeans welcomed the prospect. This proportion ranged from around four in ten in Denmark and the United Kingdom to three in four in Luxembourg. In the United Kingdom, Ireland, Denmark and Greece, three in ten or more of the general public had yet to make up their minds about the membership of Spain and Portugal. The European public still appeared to know little about the idea of a plan for European political union, with four in ten — including 55 per cent in the United Kingdom — being either indifferent or undecided. Among those who did express an opinion, the supporters of the plan outnumbered the opponents by three to one. The replies differed considerably from country to country: in seven of the ten there was a majority in favour; only in Denmark was there a majority against; in the United Kingdom the public were almost evenly balanced. The survey also showed that two-thirds of those in favour of a European union believed that if the member-states were unable to agree on the idea those countries which did agree should go ahead alone. Even among opponents of the plan, one in five would not object to it proceeding without waiting for the countries which did not agree. Generally speaking, the countries whose participation was judged essential if the union was to have any meaning were Germany and France, followed by the United Kingdom and Italy.

With a view to the next elections for the European Parliament in June 1989, a decision was made to monitor trends in public opinions and attitudes on a regular basis between elections. One of the questions dealt with awareness of the European Parliament: whether or not the general public had heard anything about it recently. Roughly six in ten Europeans said they had, with one-third saying they had gained a generally favourable impression, a further third saying they had gained a generally unfavourable impression and the remainder giving either a neutral reply or no reply at all. That the European Parliament had an image problem there can be no doubt: even among those who regarded Community membership as a good thing, one in four had a generally unfavourable impression of the European Parliament. Similarly, 12 per cent overall regarded the role currently played by the European Parliament within the EEC as very important, 40 per cent regarded it as important, 28 per cent saw it as not being very important and 6 per cent not important at all. The countries which were most positive on this issue were Ireland, Italy and France, and the least positive ones the Netherlands and West Germany. The final question in the series on the Parliament was concerned with the role that people would like to see it play. By and large, the replies were positive: 56 per cent of Europeans said they were in favour of it having a more important role. This view was held by majorities in all the member-states with the sole exception of Denmark.

The Écu

In March and April, as part of the regular Eurobarometer survey, a study was commissioned on Europeans and the *écu* (European common unit of currency) by the Banque Bruxelles Lambert of Brussels, the Crédit Agricole (Cégéspar/Titres) of Paris and the Cassa di Risparmio Delle Provincie Lombardo of Milan. The public were far more aware of financial and monetary developments than might have been thought. The papers, radio and television provide news about the stock exchange and changes in the exchange rate of the dollar. Coverage may be superficial, yet it reaches many people: only three in ten Europeans received no such news whatsoever. Europeans are also fond of travel: almost half of them had spent some time abroad in the last three years and had therefore had an opportunity to become familiar with foreign currencies. Since this was particularly true of young people, familiarity with other currencies is bound to increase in years to come.

The public also saw a link between the health of the national currency and everyday life. Respondents were quite prepared to pronounce on the strength of the national currency. A high proportion of Germans, and an even higher proportion of the Dutch, were convinced that their currency was sound. In contrast, the British and above all the Italians thought that their national currency was in poor shape. One in three (32 per cent) were in favour of the idea of the national currency being replaced by a European currency, and slightly more (38 per cent) were against it. Although the balance was against, there was a substantial minority in favour of this radical proposal. What is more, the most educated and influential sectors of the population clearly supported a replacement of the national currency by a European currency. These findings reflect the reactions of Europeans as a whole. Yet attitudes varied considerably from country to country: in Belgium,

Luxembourg, France, and particularly Italy, most people were pre-
pared to accept replacement of the national currency by a
European currency; while in the Netherlands, Germany and
Britain most people rejected the idea.

The idea of a European currency existing side by side with
national currencies was supported by six in ten Europeans (59 per
cent), with less than two in ten (18 per cent) against. The most
enthusiastic supporters were to be found in France, Italy, and
Luxembourg (three-quarters of the public), while support in Germany and Britain was somewhat less than enthusiastic. On the
whole, however, the idea was accepted; thus it can be said that
public opinion in the Community favoured the idea of a European
currency.

By contrast, the *écu* which has been with us for several years
now, still had a very low profile: familiarity with it varied considerably from one country to another. In this respect, the countries of
Europe broke down into three groups:

> Luxembourg, Belgium and France (where more than six in ten
> had heard of the *écu*);
> Germany, Italy and the Netherlands (where three in ten had
> heard of it);
> Great Britain, where only one in ten had heard of it.

It is clear that this situation was not due to what psychologists call
'selective perception', that is to say where only the predisposed
were receptive to information: in point of fact, only 42 per cent of
those who supported the idea of a European currency had actually
heard of the *écu*. There was, however, a serious information gap in
Germany, Italy and the Netherlands — and a very serious one in
Britain. (It must be said that Germany is known to be hostile to the
écu.) Most Europeans who had heard of the *écu* were convinced
that its existence was important and that it could be an effective
means of helping Community countries to agree on a common
economic policy. It goes without saying that the most ardent supporters of the Community were those who were most confident
about the future of the *écu*; yet not even the opponents of the
Community questioned the existence of the *écu*. With the information it now has, the public attaches more importance to the
economic and symbolic role of the *écu* than to the day-to-day
material advantages its use could bring.

The Anglo-Irish Agreement

In mid-November, after many months of discussion, Mrs Thatcher and Dr Fitzgerald signed a consultative document about Northern Ireland. The agreement was warmly received in Britain but gained the condemnation of both Dr Paisley in Ulster and Mr Haughey in the Irish Republic. The attitudes of the general public in Britain and in the Republic are shown in the following table:

Table 6.21: Support for the Anglo-Irish Agreement

Q. Mrs Thatcher and Dr Fitzgerald, the Irish leader, signed an Anglo-Irish agreement on Friday 15th November. From what you know of the Anglo-Irish agreement, are you personally in favour of, or opposed to, that agreement?

	Total	Britain Con	Lab	Lib/SDP
In favour	41	50	28	46
Opposed	16	13	22	18
Don't know	43	37	50	35

	Total	Irish Republic Fine Gael	Lab	Fianna Fail
In favour	57	80	64	42
Opposed	19	4	15	30
Don't know	25	16	21	28

In Britain, therefore, despite the support given to the agreement by Mr Kinnock, his party's supporters were less committed to the idea. However, their opposition may have been more to do with the fact that the agreement originated from Mrs Thatcher rather than with opposition to the agreement itself. Similarly, Mr Haughey's criticism of the agreement was not reflected in the views of Fianna Fail supporters in the Republic. In so far as the British results are concerned, the number of those who are 'undecided' is remarkably similar to the number who expressed 'no opinion' when, on the eve of the Second World War, Gallup asked a constitutional question about Ireland. In February 1938, the people of Britain were asked: 'Would you like to see Northern and Southern Ireland under one constitution?' Around one in four (28 per cent) were in favour, 26 per cent were opposed to the idea, and the largest proportion (46 per cent) had 'no opinion'.

South Africa

In March, on the twenty-fifth anniversary of the Sharpeville massacre, further bloodshed occurred when South African police opened fire on a crowd on its way to a funeral of victims of earlier unrest. Ninety per cent of the public were aware of the latest incidents, compared with 94 per cent 25 years earlier at the time of the Sharpeville killings. The British public's reaction to the two incidents, separated as they were by the passing of more than two decades, was very similar.

Table 6.22: Britain's Attitude towards Apartheid

Q. What, in your opinion, should be Britain's attitude to the South African Government's policy of apartheid (racial segregation)?

	March 1960	March 1985
The South African Government are right in their racial policy and we should support them	7	3
South African affairs are nothing to do with us and we should not become involved	12	12
The South African Government's policy is wrong but we should leave them to sort it out themselves	22	17
The South African Government's policy is wrong and we should be outspoken in our criticism	30	37
We should refuse to have anything to do with the South African Government until they change their racial policy	20	23
Don't know	9	9

Analysis by political allegiance showed Labour and Alliance supporters as more inclined than Conservatives to either criticise or boycott South Africa. There was also a generation gap, with younger adults wanting Britain to take a more definite line against South Africa's apartheid policy. Although the public's view of

what Britain should do had hardly changed over two decades, significant shifts had occurred in its view of what the actions of South
African whites should be.

Table 6.23: South African Whites' Attitude towards Coloured Population

Q. What do you think should be the attitude of the whites in South Africa towards the coloured native population?

	Oct 1965	March 1985
Equal political rights and social equality	42	72
Equal political rights but separate social development	18	12
Both political and social development separate	19	6
Don't know	21	10

The 1965 question had been slightly different, relating to the 'attitude of Europeans in Rhodesia and South Africa', and is therefore
not strictly comparable; yet the differences in the replies are almost
certainly a function of a change in attitude rather than of a change
in the wording of the question. Majorities among the supporters of
all parties and in all the demographic groups analysed felt that the
coloured native population in South Africa should have equal
rights and social equality. In late October, following the Commonwealth Conference, Gallup returned to the subject. On balance —
by a margin of two to one — people disapproved of the government's policy towards South Africa, though a substantial minority
had yet to make up their minds. While 23 per cent approved of the
Government's policy, 45 per cent disapproved, and 32 per cent
were undecided. Even among Conservatives, only 43 per cent
approved and one in four (27 per cent) disapproved. When asked
why they approved, 21 per cent of the public doing so said
sanctions would harm Britain, 15 per cent thought sanctions would
make no difference and 10 per cent thought it would harm the
South African blacks. A further 13 per cent felt that it was nothing
to do with Britain and that we should not get involved. On the
other hand, 29 per cent of those disapproving said we should sup-

port or instigate sanctions, and 22 per cent thought we should at least do something, if not impose sanctions. Almost one in four said that they disapproved because they were against apartheid.

When asked how tough the Government's policy had been, 42 per cent said that it had not been tough enough, 7 per cent felt that it had been too tough, and 28 per cent felt it had been about right. Although one in two Conservatives thought the government had got its policy right, one in four thought this was not tough enough. On the specific question of applying economic sanctions against South Africa, the public was almost evenly divided. While 44 per cent thought we should apply sanctions, 36 per cent thought not, and 20 per cent were undecided. Further questions shed light on why the British public was not more behind the idea of sanctions, and to some degree reflects an acceptance of Mrs Thatcher's line.

While 30 per cent, for example, felt that sanctions would lead to a relaxation in South Africa's apartheid policy, 41 per cent thought otherwise. Similarly, 28 per cent thought the sanctions would do more harm to South Africa, but 30 per cent felt they would do more harm to Britain, and 20 per cent saw both countries being equally damaged. Finally, a majority (55 per cent) thought that sanctions would cause more hardships to the coloured native population of South Africa, though 23 per cent thought that they would not. While the subject of sanctions against South Africa was on their minds, people were asked their attitudes to boycotting goods from other countries. The replies showed a mixture of jingoism, patriotism and anti-European sentiments. Of the four countries asked about, Argentina came top, with 31 per cent approving of a boycott of her products. Japan, with 25 per cent approving, was followed by France (22 per cent) and Russia (21 per cent). One in two disapproved of a boycott of goods from the Argentine, and around three in five disapproved in relation to the other three countries. Analysis by age showed a flat approval pattern on the issue of boycotting Argentinian goods, but increasing approval with increasing age in relation to Japan, France and Russia.

The following month further questions were asked which to some degree confirmed the October results. Just over one in two (56 per cent) of the public said they were following the events in South Africa at least fairly closely, and 42 per cent not very closely. As in October, 43 per cent thought that Britain had put too little pressure on South Africa to reform its system of racial segregation, 12 per cent thought too much pressure had been applied, and 26 per cent said this had been about right. By a margin of almost three to one, Conservatives, too, said that too little pressure had been applied. The replies to two further questions showed by how much the British Government, particularly Mrs Thatcher, was out of touch with the British public on the subject of its actions against South Africa.

Table 6.24: Sympathies in the South African Situation

Q. *In the South African situation, are your sympathies more with the black population or more with the white South African Government?*

Q. *And would you say Mrs Thatcher's sympathies are more with the black population or more with the white South African Government?*

	Self	Mrs Thatcher
More with black population	55	6
More with white government	14	57
Both equally	13	8
Neither	6	5
Don't know	12	24

Although a plurality (39 per cent) of Conservatives said they sympathised more with the black population in South Africa, the proportion was significantly below that among both Alliance and Labour supporters (70 per cent and 63 per cent respectively). One in five (21 per cent) Conservatives sympathised with the white South African Government. Even this was in sharp contrast with their views of where Mrs Thatcher's sympathies lay. Eleven per cent of Conservatives thought Mrs Thatcher sympathised with the black population, but 42 per cent with the South African Government.

Finally, people were asked which of two statements was more important: giving South African blacks more freedom even if this meant weakening the country's stability and loosening its ties with the West or maintaining South Africa as a stable Western ally even if that meant delaying giving the country's blacks more freedom. Just under one in two (48 per cent) of the public opted for the first statement, and one in three (34 per cent) for the second. Again, there were party differences. One in two Conservatives were for maintaining South Africa as an ally, while one in three were for giving South African blacks more freedom. The position was reversed among both Labour and Alliance supporters, with majorities actually favouring the first option.

7   Social and Other Non-political Issues

The Church of England

At the turn of the year, Gallup conducted a survey for the Church Society to assess aspects of current belief and attitudes among the laity, clergy and bishops in the Church of England. A unique feature of the survey was that comparable questions were asked of these diverse groups. Clearly, the fact that the questionnaire had to be understood by the man in the street imposed certain limitations on the theological sophistication which could be introduced into the questionnaire. The final responsibility for the questionnaire topics and wording lay with Gallup, who consulted a wide range of clergymen within the Church of England and other churches as well as religious correspondents of national newspapers, editors and others.

In the case of the laity, interviews were made with both churchgoers and non-churchgoers of all religious denominations in personal interviews with a nationally representative sample of 983 adults in Great Britain in October 1984. The clergy were interviewed by means of a self-completion postal survey sent to a random sample of 1,000 Church of England clergymen whose addresses were taken from *Crockford's Clerical Directory*. Fifty-three per cent of the clergy responded, divided between 413 full-time clergy and 117 retired clergy. The true response rate was closer to 60 per cent because a number of the clergy had died or moved away since the address lists were collated and Gallup was satisfied that this was a representative survey of clergymen in terms of the age and educational profiles of the respondents.

The questionnaire was also sent to the 42 diocesan bishops, 61 suffragan bishops and 42 assistant bishops of England and Wales. While 19 assistant bishops and 18 suffragan bishops replied to the questionnaire, only six diocesan bishops replied, giving a total of 43 bishops in the survey. The reason for the lower rate of response from the bishops compared with that of the clergy was the following advice, given to them at November's Synod meeting: 'It is morally open to them [the Bishops] to decline to answer the questions asked rather than to assist an exercise which, in the end, may well mislead the general public about the religious beliefs and attitudes of Church people.' Gallup regretted this response to the questionnaire on the part of the bishops. The low response rate (30 per cent) meant that the results of the bishops' survey must be treated with caution, particularly since so few diocesan bishops took part in the survey.

Majorities of the public (83 per cent), bishops (84 per cent) and full-time clergy (57 per cent) wanted the Queen to continue as supreme Governor of the Church of England, but only a minority of the public (23 per cent), bishops (33 per cent) and full-time clergy (19 per cent) thought that Parliament should continue to have the final say in the decisions relating to the Church of England. In doctrinal matters, the majority of Church of England churchgoers (53 per cent), bishops (67 per cent) and full-time clergy (68 per cent) believed that it was a historical fact that Christ was born of a virgin, but almost a third (31 per cent) of Church of England members who had attended a service in the last month believed the Virgin Birth to be a legend. Among Roman Catholic church attenders in the last month, 81 per cent believed in the Virgin Birth; but Nonconformists were equally divided between believing it to be either a historical fact or a legend. The majority of the public (55 per cent) were satisfied with the current leadership of the Church by Archbishop Runcie, and the proportion rose to 75 per cent among Church of England members who had attended a service in the last month, to 77 per cent among the bishops and to 72 per cent among the full-time clergy.

The survey revealed strong support for the Church of England continuing to run its own schools, with 66 per cent of the public in favour and only 23 per cent against. Among the bishops support was overwhelming, with 98 per cent in favour, and amongst the clergy it was 86 per cent. Among regular Church of England attenders support was very high, at 81 per cent, and there was also strong support from Roman Catholic monthly church attenders: 82 per cent in favour of the Church of England continuing to run its schools. It was not surprising, then, that a mere 15 per cent of the public were in favour of the Church of England handing over any of its schools to adherents of non-Christian faiths: all groups were distinctly against this.

The survey examined some of the other doctrinal areas which were currently under discussion. The results showed that in general the bishops and full-time clergy were fairly orthodox in their beliefs, but that among practising Church of England members there was a considerable diversity of beliefs, particularly when compared to a similar group of Roman Catholics. For example, with regard to the Resurrection, whereas 84 per cent of all bishops and 77 per cent of clergy believed that Jesus had been raised bodily from the dead three days after his crucifixion, only 52 per cent of Church of England members who had attended a church service in the last month believed in the bodily resurrection. A large group of them (31 per cent) believed that Jesus was not raised bodily from the dead but made his personality and presence known to his disciples in a spiritual, as opposed to a bodily, way. Among a similar group of Roman Catholics, 72 per cent believed in the bodily resurrection.

With regard to the gospel miracles, the greatest proportion of Church of England members who had attended a service in the last month (45 per cent) believed that the gospel miracles were the gospel writers' interpretations and only a minority (31 per cent) believed that they were historical facts. Among a corresponding group of Roman Catholics, 52 per cent believed that they were historical facts, and the proportion rose to 62 per cent among full-time Church of England clergy and to 70 per cent of full-time bishops. Nevertheless, 21 per cent of bishops and 32 per cent of full-time clergy believed that the miracles were gospel writers' interpretations. Ironically for the study, more Catholics (42 per cent) than Church of England members (26 per cent) or Nonconformists (30 per cent) believed that the Bible was of divine authority and that its teachings were absolutely reliable. The greatest proportion of bishops (63 per cent), full-time clergy (47 per cent) and regular Church of England attenders (57 per cent) believed the Bible to be mostly of divine authority but that some of it was unreliable. In the national population, almost a third (30 per cent) believed the Bible to be mostly a collection of stories and fables. Given these views about the Bible, it was interesting to note that a majority of the general public (65 per cent) still thought the Church would survive even if the idea that the Bible was of divine authority was rejected.

A majority (55 per cent) of regular Church of England members believed that a person who had been divorced and whose former partner was still alive should be allowed to be remarried in church; only 29 per cent of regular members believed that such a person should not be allowed to be remarried. Even among regular Catholics, only 50 per cent believed that a divorcee should not be allowed to be remarried in church. Among bishops the majority (56 per cent) were against remarriage, but among the clergy only a minority (44 per cent) were against remarriage. Clearly, public opinion was divided in the Church of England and to a lesser extent in the Roman Catholic Church on the issue of divorce.

There was less division on attitudes towards homosexuality. Almost two in three bishops and full-time clergy (61 per cent) agreed that 'the Church can never approve of homosexual acts', as did 56 per cent of regular Church of England members. Just over a quarter of full-time clergy (26 per cent) and more than a third of regular Church of England members (35 per cent) disagreed that 'the Church can never approve of homosexual acts'. While 56 per cent of Roman Catholics who had attended a service in the last month thought the Church could never approve of homosexual acts, 29 per cent disagreed with this. The majority of bishops (56 per cent) and full-time clergy (75 per cent) were against allowing clergymen to be Free-masons, but the regular Church of England members were much more tolerant, with the largest proportion (41 per cent) saying they should be allowed to be Freemasons and a smaller proportion (34 per cent) against. Both Nonconformists and Roman Catholics were against clergymen being Freemasons.

Two in three (69 per cent) of the public thought that the Church should not take sides in political issues, and this rose to 75 per cent among Church of England members who had attended a service in the last month. In contrast, a majority (67 per cent) of bishops and full-time clergy (59 per cent) thought the Church should take sides in political issues, and obviously there was a divergence of views between the laity and clergy on these issues. The survey revealed that only 22 per cent thought the Church should become involved in the miners' strike but a much greater proportion thought the Church should become involved in the question of unemployment (38 per cent) and nuclear weapons (36 per cent). Clearly, there was a thin dividing line between what the general public regarded as the Church's rightful concern for major social and moral issues and what could be seen as undue meddling in political issues.

The vast majority (81 per cent) of regular Church of England members were in favour of the negotiations between the Church of England and the Roman Catholic Church on unity. The proportion rose to 89 per cent among full-time clergy and to 98 per cent among the bishops. Additional questions asked of the bishops and clergy only revealed that the greatest proportion of them thought the Church of England and Roman Catholic Churches would unite over the next few years, compared to 23 per cent thinking they would unite with the Nonconformist Churches over the next few years. A small proportion of bishops (12 per cent) thought all three Church groupings would unite over the next few years. The vast majority (81 per cent) of bishops were in favour of the Church of England remaining the established Church within England. But there was less support for this among the full-time clergy, with 57 per cent in favour and 30 per cent against. An overwhelming majority (93 per cent) of bishops agreed with the ARCIC Commission that the Pope should become the Universal Primate, but there was less support for this among the full-time clergy (56 per cent), with almost one-third (32 per cent) disagreeing and the remaining 12 per cent not sure.

Great dissatisfaction was expressed among bishops and full-time clergymen with the current system of Synodical government in the Church of England. Only 25 per cent of bishops and 36 per cent of full-time clergy were in favour of it, although there was more support among Church of England members who had attended a service in the last month (48 per cent). Despite this dissatisfaction, the study found that the bishops and clergy were not in favour of direct elections from parishes, although this idea was more warmly received by the laity.

In late March, a sample of Anglicans were asked further questions about the Church of England. A majority (52 per cent) said that they were satisfied with the leadership of the Archbishop of Canterbury, while 19 per cent expressed some dissatisfaction. The proportion not particularly satisfied with the Archbishop rose to 34 per cent of elderly Anglicans. As a group, Anglicans were critical of the part played by the bishops in the past few years: almost one in three (31 per cent) thought the bishops had helped people to accept the Church of England, but slightly more (39 per cent) thought they had not helped. Again, criticism came particularly from elderly people and from churchgoers in the past month.

A majority (58 per cent) of Anglicans thought that the Church should keep out of political matters, but 35 per cent said it should express its views on day-to-day social and political matters. Among those Anglicans who had attended church at least once a month, more thought the Church should express its views than thought it should refrain from doing so. Around one in eight (13 per cent) said that recent controversial comments by prominent people in the Church of England had made them feel more favourable towards the Church, while 25 per cent said it had made them less favourable, and the remainder (62 per cent) had either been unaffected or had not heard enough to say. One in three of the larger groups affected — those who had become less favourable to the Church — cited comments by the Bishop of Durham, specifically on the miners' strike, and one in two expressed dislike of the Church's involvement in non-Church issues.

Anglicans were then asked what impact comments on five specific issues had had on their attitude towards the Church, and in the main the issues appear to have had little effect:

Table 7.1: Controversies within the Church

Q. For each of the following topics discussed recently, would you tell me whether they have made you feel more or less favourable to the Church?

	More	Less	No effect	Don't know
Poverty in inner-city areas	29	10	39	22
Nuclear disarmament	20	19	43	18
The miners' strike	15	28	44	13
The Resurrection of Christ	10	9	50	31
The Virgin Birth	5	13	50	32

On four of the five issues, there was a tendency for the proportion being critical to increase with age. The exception was on the question of nuclear disarmament, where the various age groups reflected the national average to a greater degree.

Most Anglicans (57 per cent) thought the Church of England had the right balance in its religious teachings, but 8 per cent felt it was too liberal and 18 per cent that it was not liberal enough. Another controversial issue had been that of personal prayer. Three in four (74 per cent) Anglicans said they believed in personal prayer, rising to 86 per cent of those aged 65 or over, and to 94 per cent of those going to church at least once a month. Around one in five (18 per cent) said they didn't believe in personal prayer; this included 29 per cent of young Anglicans and 30 per cent of those never attending church. Finally, the vast majority (82 per cent) of Anglicans thought the Church should accept women as priests. Even at its lowest point, 74 per cent of elderly Anglicans accepted the idea of women priests.

Religious Beliefs

A month later, in a study of religious beliefs among the general public, 20 per cent said that they attended religious services at least once a month. Around one in four said that they went a few times a year or almost never (23 per cent each), while one in three (34 per cent) never attended religious services. Among the people who considered themselves to be very religious — 8 per cent of the general public — 61 per cent said they attended religious services almost every week or more often. Three in four regular churchgoers (at least once a month) said that they had attended religious services at least that often five years ago, while one in five said they had not.

The change in religious attitudes can be seen in the replies to a further question, where almost one in two of the public said they followed childhood religious rules but one in three said they had developed their own personal rules. Analysis by age showed a distinct generation gap:

Table 7.2: Childhood versus Adult Religious Rules

Q. Would you say you pretty much follow the religious rules you learned as a child from your church or synagogue, or have you developed your own set of personal religious rules now that you are an adult?

	Childhood	Personal set	Not religious now	Don't know
General public	47	37	14	3
16–24	24	42	26	9
25–34	35	45	17	3
35–44	44	40	15	1
45–64	60	31	7	2
65+	68	26	5	0

A similar generation gap was apparent in the replies to a question on how religious people felt they were. There was also a gender gap, though to a much lesser degree. While 40 per cent of men said they were not religious at all, 28 per cent of women gave themselves the same rating.

Table 7.3: Religiosity

Q. Would you say you are very religious, somewhat religious or not religious at all?

	Very religious	Somewhat religious	Not religious	Don't know
General public	8	56	34	2
16–24	2	42	52	3
25–34	7	49	43	1
35–44	8	52	38	3
45–64	9	67	23	2
65+	14	69	17	0

All but the 'don't knows' were then asked whether they had felt the same way five years before. The vast majority (86 per cent) said that they had, though the proportion was only 65 per cent among young adults, rising to 95 per cent among senior citizens.

Sunday Trading

In spite of the passing of almost 30 years, a typical Sunday in Britain remains to a large degree very similar to how it was in 1958. Watching television then was the most popular activity and still is, though the proportion doing so has substantially increased.

Table 7.4: Sunday Activities

Q. Please tell me whether you did any of these things last Sunday?

	May 1958	Nov 1985
Watched television	51	81
Listened to the radio	47	48
Went for a walk or a drive in a car	41	36
Visited or entertained friends	28	32
Read a book	21	28
Worked in the garden	28	15
Went to church	12	14
Went to work	8	10
Played football, etc.	6	5
Went to the cinema	6	1

It should be borne in mind that the apparent decline in popularity in going for a walk or drive or working in the garden is probably less a function of the passage of time than of the season in which the questioning took place: the early replies (in May) and the more recent ones (in November) will reflect to some degree the different types of activity preferred at different times of year. And as might be expected, there were a number of generational differences in the replies to this question. Listening to the radio, for example, tended to be more popular among younger adults aged under 35, while watching television scored highest among senior citizens. Visiting or entertaining friends or going for a walk were also more popular with the younger generation. Alternatively, churchgoing, working in the garden and reading a book increased with age.

In recent years there has been an increase in Sunday trading, in contravention of the law, to highlight anomalies in the Acts relating to shopping on a Sunday and to bring about a change in the law. Though a majority of the public overall thought the change would be a good idea, a majority of senior citizens took the opposite view.

Table 7.5: Attitudes to Sunday Trading

Q. *The government is intending to scrap all restrictions on shop opening hours and introduce Sunday trading. Do you think this is a good idea or a bad idea?*

	A good idea	A bad idea	Don't know
General public	52	39	9
18–34	61	32	7
35–44	58	35	7
45–64	51	35	13
65+	33	58	9

For once, Conservatives and Labour supporters agreed on something, with 58 per cent of both groups thinking such a change would be a good idea. Social Democrats were marginally in favour, and Liberals were marginally opposed. Three main reasons emerged for wanting freer Sunday trading: that it would be convenient, for working people in particular (45 per cent); that the law *should* be changed (24 per cent); and that people would like to be able to shop more as a family on Sundays (23 per cent). Among those people opposed to the idea, two in three (64 per cent) thought that six days were enough and that Sunday should be a day of rest, 25 per cent thought that a seventh day would be unfair to shopkeepers and their staff, and 13 per cent said Sunday should be kept as a religious day.

The public, although in favour of Sunday trading, saw that it could have its advantages and disadvantages: for example, 41 per cent thought that the plans would lead to an increase in prices, 50 per cent thought there would be no change, and 4 per cent saw prices actually dropping. A majority (57 per cent) also thought that the small local corner shop would be harmed by the advent of wider Sunday trading, 34 per cent thought it would make no difference, and 5 per cent thought it would help the smaller shops. Alternatively, 51 per cent thought that it would lead to more people being employed, with only 3 per cent thinking it would mean more unemployed and 41 per cent that it would have no effect.

The Sexual Revolution

The so-called 'sexual revolution' was dealt with as part of a full-scale study conducted for Southern Television (detailed in Chapter 8). A few months earlier, other questions had been asked on the topic. The replies to the first of these showed both a distinct gender gap and a generation gap.

Table 7.6: Agreement with the Sexual Revolution

Q. In the late 1960s and 1970s, attitudes towards sexual activity began to get somewhat freer. Some people called it 'the sexual revolution'. Would you say you agree with most of the changes that resulted from the sexual revolution or not?

	Agree	Disagree	Some of them	Don't know
General public	32	41	16	11
Men	40	34	16	10
Women	25	47	15	12
16–24	51	18	14	16

Table 7.6 continued

25–34	48	19	21	12
35–44	28	46	18	8
45–64	22	56	14	8
65+	11	65	11	13

It goes without saying that a majority (55 per cent) of people who attended church services at least once a week disagreed with most of the changes that had resulted from the sexual revolution, as did 64 per cent of those who considered themselves very religious.

Despite the level of agreement, even partially, with the changing sexual attitudes in the 1960s and 1970s, the majority (72 per cent) of people felt that they had been pretty much on the sidelines during the sexual revolution. Around one in eight (13 per cent) thought that they had taken some part in it, including almost one in four of those aged between 25 and 44.

Two in five (41 per cent) of the public overall, possibly influenced by the mood of the times, said that their own personal attitudes towards sexual behaviour had become more liberal in the last five years, though 18 per cent said they had become more conservative. Of the remainder, 33 per cent had not changed their views, 2 per cent were 'middle of the road', and 6 per cent were undecided. As might be expected, there was a generation gap in the replies to this question, but not so great as in the previous two. Among the under-25s, 46 per cent said that they had become more liberal, while 12 per cent had become more conservative. Among those aged 65 or over, the figures were 30 per cent and 23 per cent respectively.

Birth Control

In January and again in June, despite the judgement against Mrs Victoria Gillick, a majority of the general public thought that doctors should not be allowed to prescribe the contraceptive pill to under-age girls without first informing their parents.

Again, the young and their elders disagreed on this question. While those aged between 16 and 24 were almost evenly divided in their replies, senior citizens supported Mrs Gillick's position by a ratio of more than five to one. When asked why they took the view

Table 7.7: Contraceptive Advice to Under-Age Girls

Q. Do you think that doctors should or should not be allowed to prescribe the contraceptive pill to girls under 16 without telling their parents first?

	Jan	June
Should	33	38
Should not	57	55
Don't know	9	7

they did, 42 per cent of those thinking doctors should be allowed to prescribe the pill without first informing the girl's parents said that it was because this would stop or prevent unwanted pregnancies. Just over one in five (22 per cent) said that parents didn't always understand or would not be agreeable. Of those opposed to doctors being given the freedom to prescribe in this way, 34 per cent took the view that the parents should know, 20 per cent said the girls were still the responsibility of their parents and 18 per cent thought the girls were too young to make a decision.

Those who thought a doctor should not be obliged to consult the parents first or who were undecided on the matter were then asked whether or not the parents should have the right to know that their daughter had been prescribed the pill. Almost one in two (47 per cent) said they should have the right, but 36 per cent took the opposite view.

On the wider issue of whether or not contraceptive advice should be available to young unmarried people, the overwhelming majority (86 per cent) of the public thought it should. Ten years earlier, slightly fewer (74 per cent) had shared the same view. Among young adults (aged under 25) 97 per cent thought the advice should be available, compared with 60 per cent of those aged 65 or over. Just over one in two (56 per cent) of the general public thought that commercials for family planning and contraception should be shown on television, while 35 per cent thought they should not. In 1975, the pattern of replies was almost the same: 54 per cent and 35 per cent respectively. Again, seven in ten young adults in 1985 thought TV commercials for family planning should be shown, while around one in three senior citizens shared this view.

Etiquette

Chivalry was not dead in Britain in April, at least not in the minds of the public. Three in four (78 per cent) of the public and even more men (85 per cent) thought that men should usually open doors for women. Younger adults, however, were less inclined to be chivalrous, with 68 per cent of the under-35s saying men should open doors for women. Sexual equality was very much in evidence in the replies to a question on who should pay for the meal when a single woman invites a single man out for dinner. One in five said the man should pay, while 24 per cent said the woman should do so; but the largest proportion thought they should split the cost between them. Men were more likely to say the man should pay, while women tended to think the women should.

In addition to driving on the left, the British public were just as definite on the subject of placing the fork to the left of the plate when setting the table for dinner. Just over eight in ten (83 per cent) of the public said they did so, while 6 per cent said they put it on the right, 9 per cent confessed to not having thought about it and 2 per cent were undecided. Men and younger adults were more inclined to say they had not given the subject a thought. Yet the public was evenly divided on the question of who should go through a door first when one person trying to go out a door at the same time that another is trying to come in. Just over one in four (27 per cent) said it should be the person going out, 28 per cent said the person coming in, and 38 per cent said it didn't make much difference either way. There was a slight gender gap on this question, though not a particularly significant one: men were slightly more in favour of the person coming in, while women tended to favour the person going out.

Around one in eight (13 per cent) of the general public said that they or someone else in their family had read a book on etiquette in the last few years or so. The under-25s were the least likely to have done so (7 per cent), while the 35–44 age group, at 17 per cent, were most likely to have done so. This lack of acquaintance with etiquette books might explain why the public viewed the manners of most British people as at best in need of some improvement or as pretty sloppy. One in four thought British manners were generally okay, but 36 per cent thought they could do with some improvement and 39 per cent thought them pretty sloppy. Again, the young and not-so-young disagreed. While 34 per cent of the under-25s thought the manners of most British people were generally okay and 29 per cent said they were sloppy, the replies were 13 per cent and 55 per cent respectively for those aged 65 or over.

The Decline of Civilisation?

In spite of the advances made in medicine and education since the war, and the relative affluence of present-day living, the public are becoming less satisfied with the state of the British people and with the human race at large, especially at the spiritual level.

Table 7.8: The British People and the Human Race

Q. *Do you think that the ... are/is getting better or worse from the point of view of ...?*

	British people		Human race	
	Dec 1949	Jan 1985	Dec 1949	Jan 1985
Health				
Better	51	45	65	44
Worse	20	36	17	40
Same	18	11	8	8
Don't know	11	8	10	8
Intelligence				
Better	42	37	54	46
Worse	20	28	18	20
Same	24	25	16	24
Don't know	14	10	12	11
Moral conduct				
Better	10	5	12	7
Worse	58	72	50	62
Same	18	17	24	21
Don't know	14	6	14	10
Inner happiness				
Better	15	10	15	10
Worse	38	53	44	48
Same	21	22	19	24
Don't know	26	15	22	18

Each of the four items showed a significant perceived decline since the war, with one in four thinking that the intelligence of the British public was deteriorating. It is perhaps a cause for concern that on three of the items Britain appears to be doing slightly worse than the world as a whole. Only on the question of health (probably with the drought crisis in central Africa in mind) does the world at large score lower.

Party politics had an effect on people's perceptions of how the British public was doing. Whereas Conservatives, for example, by a margin of two to one, thought that health in Britain was improving, Labour supporters felt that on balance it was declining. On the other hand, Labour supporters took a slightly more optimistic view on the subject of intelligence in Britain.

Alcohol

Although drunkenness ranks fairly low down on the public's list of social problems compared with others such as drugs, bad housing and violence, around two in five saw it as a very serious social problem in Britain. The problem is, of course, not confined to Britain alone; for that reason in June and July three questions on alcoholic consumption were asked around the world.

Table 7.9: Alcohol

Q. Do you have occasion to use alcoholic beverages such as spirits, wine or beer, or are you a total abstainer?

Q. Do you sometimes drink more than you should?

Q. Has drinking ever been a cause of trouble in your family?

	Ever drink	Overindulgers	Family trouble
Greece	89	30	11
Sweden	86	16	10
Netherlands	84	12	9
Britain	83	30	10
Iceland	82	35	32
Norway	82	27	14
Switzerland	80	NA	15
Mexico	78	20	12
Canada	77	26	17
Colombia	77	14	14
South Korea	76	39	20
Australia	76	29	18
Finland	74	23	13

Argentina	72	6	13
West Germany	71	21	9
Belgium	69	14	11
Japan	69	34	14
Southern Ireland	68	35	14
USA	67	32	21
Uruguay	67	9	9
Brazil	60	14	25
Philippines	56	11	25
Israel	44	6	2

As can be seen from the table above, Britain ranked fourth of the 23 countries in terms of the proportion consuming alcohol in one form or another, joint sixth on the question of occasional over-indulgence, but joint eighteenth on the question of drink as a cause of trouble within the family. Greece topped the table as far as the proportion of consumers was concerned, but South Korea, closely followed by Iceland, Southern Ireland and Japan, had the highest percentage of self-confessed overindulgers. Iceland also led the other countries — by a significant margin — when it came to alcohol being a family problem. In Britain, alcohol consumption was greater among men (89 per cent) than among women (78 per cent), and tended to decline with increasing age. Whereas 91 per cent of young adults aged from 16 to 24 said they drank alcohol, the proportion fell to 70 per cent among senior citizens. Analysis of the overindulgers showed a similar pattern, with 40 per cent of men saying they sometimes drank more than they should, compared with 20 per cent of women. Also, one in two of the 'impetuous young' confessed to overindulging sometimes, compared with a mere 5 per cent of senior citizens. Given a national average of only 10 per cent ever having drink as a cause of trouble in their family, the pattern of replies was much flatter than for the previous two questions. However, for those aged between 25 and 34, the proportion was almost twice the national average.

The State of Britain

When asked in April how things were going in Britain compared with five years earlier, and how well Britain would be doing in five years' time, the public saw a decline that showed little sign of being reduced.

Table 7.10: Britain's Decline

Q. *I would now like to ask you a few questions on how things are going in Britain. On a scale of one to ten — if one were the worst possible situation and ten were the best possible situation — what number would you give to the way things are going in Britain at the present time?*

Q. *Where would you say Britain was five years ago? Remember, one is the worst possible situation and ten is the best possible situation.*

Q. *And, just as your best guess, how would you rate Britain five years from now?*

	5 years ago	Today	5 years' time
10	2	1	2
9	2	0	4
8	13	4	11
7	15	10	11
6	17	13	8
5	18	26	14
4	12	15	8
3	6	10	8
2	4	5	8
1	4	11	12
Don't know	8	5	14
Average	5.4	4.5	4.7

Conservatives, not unexpectedly, took a more optimistic view of Britain's future: from an average of 5.4 for five years ago to 5.6 today and to 6.3 in five years' time. In the case of Labour supporters, on the other hand, the averages went from 5.3 to 3.6 and to 3.6 respectively. Young adults (aged under 35) were similarly pessimistic, producing averages of 5.5, 4.5 and 4.6 respectively.

Patriotism

At the same time, in April, patriotism also appeared to be on the wane compared with five years previously as far as the public were concerned. Two in three (65 per cent) felt that Britons had less pride than five years earlier, 12 per cent thought people had more pride, and 16 per cent thought things had not changed. The decline was also thought to have occurred on a personal level, though not to the same degree as in the general public.

Table 7.11: Decline in Pride

Q. *Would you say that you yourself have more or less pride in this country than you did five years ago?*

	General public	Con	Lab	Lib/SDP
More	17	33	9	14
Less	41	18	54	48
Same	39	47	32	37
Don't know	3	2	5	1

In spite of this, just over one in three described themselves as strongly patriotic:

Table 7.12: Level of Patriotism

Q. *Do you consider yourself strongly patriotic, somewhat patriotic, or not very patriotic at all?*

	Strongly	Somewhat	Not very
General public	38	38	23
Conservative	51	39	10
Labour	27	38	34
Liberal/SDP	43	35	20
18–34	18	42	38
35–44	37	39	22
45–64	53	32	15
65+	53	37	8

Men were more likely than women to consider themselves strongly patriotic (43 per cent and 33 per cent respectively). This feeling of patriotism, however, did not translate itself into owning a national flag. Sixteen per cent said they owned a union flag or a national flag, with only 8 per cent of Labour supporters saying they did so.

Finally, Gallup asked people if they would support Britain even if it did something they disagreed with. Just under one in two (48 per cent) said they would support the country and 36 per cent said they would not. Conservatives, by a ratio of 57 per cent to 26 per cent, were the most supportive politically, beaten only marginally in patriotism by senior citizens (60 per cent and 24 per cent respectively).

Education

At the beginning of the year, before schools had become involved in the long-running teachers' dispute, Gallup asked a number of questions about satisfaction with the education system and about subjects that should be part of the curriculum. The first of these showed a feeling on the part of the public of declining education standards, declining standards of achievement and declining standards of discipline.

Table 7.13: Educational Standards

Q. *Thinking back over the last few years, in your opinion, have standards of achievement at schools gone up, gone down or remained about the same?*

Q. *Over the last few years, in your opinion, have standards of discipline at schools gone up, gone down or remained about the same?*

Q. *And over the last few years, in your opinion, have educational standards gone up, gone down or remained the same?*

	Achievement	Discipline	Educational
Gone up	16	3	16
Gone down	46	69	45
Same	21	19	25
Don't know	17	9	15

There was clear evidence of a generation gap in the replies to these questions. For example, on the matter of discipline, the proportion believing standards of discipline to be falling was 58 per cent among those aged under 25 but rose to 71 per cent among those aged 65 or over.

On the question of the curriculum, the public continued to be firm believers in a good grounding in the 'three Rs'. They also wanted more emphasis given to science and to foreign languages.

Table 7.14: The School Curriculum

Q. I am going to read you a list of some subjects currently taught in schools. For each of these subjects could you tell me whether they should be given more emphasis and attention in schools, less emphasis, about the same as occurs now, or should not be taught at all?

	More	Same	Less; not at all
Reading	76	19	0
Maths	71	24	1
English	70	27	1
Science	61	31	3
Foreign languages	54	33	7
Political studies	36	35	21
Anti-racism studies	35	27	27
Peace studies	34	26	27
Sex education	31	44	18
Multicultural studies	33	34	17
Religious studies	28	49	18
Anti-sexism studies	18	27	37

Note: For reasons of space the replies for 'less' or 'not at all' have been combined and the 'don't knows' have been omitted.

Again, a generation gap was clearly shown when people were asked to judge the above list of subjects. Religious education registered the widest gap of all, with only 21 per cent of the under-25s wanting more emphasis compared with 57 per cent of senior citizens speaking up for more RE. When it came to sex education, political studies, anit-sexism and anti-racism studies, the relationship was reversed, with younger people demanding more attention while the older group opted for less emphasis. But the other eight subjects showed, in varying degrees, a generation gap that proved older people to be keener supporters of the subjects than younger adults. Take, for example, sex education: of the under-25s, a total of 43 per cent felt that the subject should receive greater emphasis from teachers, while 13 per cent of the over-65s felt that way. There were also some 'gender gaps' to note in the study. In science, for example, far more men (71 per cent) than women (54 per cent) thought it should be given greater emphasis.

Teachers

In mid-April, Gallup started to measure public reaction to the teachers' dispute, using two questions. The first dealt with where people's sympathies lay, with the local authorities or with the teachers, and the second with whether or not the teachers should get the pay increase they were asking for. Throughout the dispute, those siding with the teachers ranged between 42 and 49 per cent, while support for the local authorities tended to be lower, at 26–35 per cent. From the outset, a majority of the public (ranging from 50 per cent up to 61 per cent) felt that the teachers should be paid the increase. The proportion against ranged from 28 to 37 per cent.

In May, two other questions were added as the teachers stepped up their actions. Again, the public's attitude hardly changed. Although there was a slight increase in the proportion approving of the teachers' methods, starting at 26 per cent and peaking at 34 per cent, a majority (57–65 per cent) consistently disapproved. Also, around one in two (47–55 per cent) felt that at the end of the dispute the individual teacher would be neither better nor worse off. On balance, though, slightly more (20–29 per cent) thought teachers would be better off than worse off (12–17 per cent).

In November, Gallup repeated a study from June 1984 and some questions from an even earlier survey, one that took place in April 1959. Parents were asked what were their main concerns or worries about their children's schooling; and in the November study the teachers' strike topped the list (mentioned by 21 per cent) followed by the concern that they would be properly educated (13 per cent). A further 10 per cent cited a drop in educational standards, and 9 per cent were worried by a lack of facilities. The teachers' dispute may have had one good effect on the parent-teacher relationship: in November, 36 per cent said they had spoken to a teacher about their child's progress in the last four weeks, compared to 23 per cent in June 1984.

When Britain's spending on education was compared with that of Germany, the USA and Russia, Britain came bottom of the list with 10 per cent. When allowance was made for the different sizes of the four countries, Germany mentioned by 28 per cent, was thought to be spending the most in this area, followed by the USA with 22 per cent and Russia with 13 per cent. There was also an increasing feeling among the general public that we were not giving enough attention to education. In 1959, 59 per cent thought we were, but the figure dropped to a mere 19 per cent in the November study.

Table 7.15: Declining Attention to Education

Q. Do you think that we in Britain are or are not giving enough attention to education?

	April 1959	June 1984	Nov 1985
Giving enough attention	59	26	19
Not enough attention	34	69	75
Don't know	7	5	6

Both in the short term and the longer term, two trends appear to be arising in the public's attitudes towards teachers as opposed to the educational system itself. The most significant of these was the increase in the proportion thinking that teachers were among those who had proved unable to make the top grades at university. At the same time, the public had less admiration for teachers as a group.

Table 7.16: Attitudes Towards Teachers

Q. Considering schoolteachers as a group, which of these statements most nearly expresses your views about them?

	April 1959	June 1984	Nov 1985
They are overworked	18	16	17
They don't work as hard as they might	20	24	24
They do a reasonable day's work	58	57	56
They are overpaid	8	6	6
They are underpaid	25	27	35
Their pay is reasonable	51	55	51
They get too long holidays	53	45	45
They need the holidays they get	42	47	47
They should not have to attend to all the extra duties like school meals	47	44	46
The extra duties shoudl be regarded as part of their job	43	52	50
I admire them very much	18	9	9
I admire them	34	34	31
They're all right	40	44	46
I didn't think much of them	4	10	12

242   *Social and Other Non-political Issues*

Table 7.16 continued

People who take up teaching are:			
among the best and cleverest at the universities;	31	18	17
unable to make the top grade at the universities	24	42	46
People who take up teaching:			
are looking for an easy job;	7	5	6
do so because they want to do a worthwhile job;	58	63	62
think it's as good as any other job	28	27	27

The public's view of teachers, therefore, was that they did a reasonable day's work, that their pay was reasonable (though perhaps lower than it should be) and that they had taken up teaching because they saw it as a worthwhile job. Yet the public were evenly divided on the subject of teachers' holidays and on the question of whether school meals should be accepted as extra duties or as part of the job. The November survey also included another two questions on educational standards, both of which revealed the public's increasing negativity on the subject.

Table 7.17: Declining Standards

Q. On the whole, would you say that children today are getting a better education than your generation did, or not?

	April 1959	June 1984	Nov 1985
Are getting a better education	71	45	42
Are getting about the same education	11	14	14
Are not getting as good an education	16	34	41
Don't know	2	7	4

The generations disagreed in their answers to this question: 29 per cent of those aged between 18 and 34 thought today's children were getting a better education than their generation did, with the figure rising to 55 per cent among senior citizens aged 65 or over. Finally, Gallup asked parents whether they were satisfied or dissatisfied with the education their children were getting. In 1959, 82 per cent were satisfied, with the number falling to 61 per cent in 1984 and dropping even further, to 52 per cent, in 1985.

AIDS

Even before the untimely death of the film star Rock Hudson from AIDS (Acquired Immune Deficiency Syndrome), the media had already taken up the disease, under such headlines as 'the gay plague'. By the time Gallup had carried out its first study in Britain, in March, 97 per cent of the public had become aware of the disease. Even at the lowest point, among people aged 65 or over, 93 per cent had either heard or read something recently about AIDS.

Those who were aware were then asked a number of questions about the disease. The first of these dealt with concern about the possibility of it spreading, and 62 per cent said it was a matter of great concern, with a further 30 per cent saying it was of some concern. When asked who were most at risk from AIDS, 66 per cent mentioned homosexuals and 24 per cent mentioned blood donors or blood recipients. Awareness of how the disease spread was also fairly accurate. Around one in three said they thought it was through sexual intercourse (37 per cent) without being more specific, while 36 per cent said through blood transfusions and 30 per cent through homosexual activities. People were then prompted by being shown a list of possible ways in which the disease spread, and here the top four items were homosexual activities (84 per cent), blood transfusions (82 per cent), sexual intercourse (70 per cent) and infected needles (49 per cent).

Because of the link with homosexuality and with the trans-mission of the disease through blood, people were asked if they would approve or disapprove if all male blood donors were to be asked if they were practising homosexuals. The vast majority (92 per cent) said they would approve and 6 per cent disapproved. Similarly, nine in ten thought there was then no cure for AIDS, though 2 per cent thought there was. People were less sure about the mortality rate: one in four (24 per cent) thought that everybody who caught the disease died from it, 39 per cent said that most did, and 26 per cent said that some did. Finally, 51 per cent felt that the news-papers had been too sensational in their coverage of the disease, though almost as many (43 per cent) disagreed.

The topic was returned to in September, repeating some of the questions from the March study and adding some previously asked in the United States. When asked whether there were any new public health problems that especially concerned them, 14 per cent of the public mentioned AIDS. No other problem was mentioned by more than 1 per cent, though 12 per cent were concerned about government cuts and their effect on the health service. On a specific question about the spread of the disease, similar results were obtained to those in March when the question was first asked. Two in three (65 per cent) expressed great concern and 27 per cent some concern. Personal concern, however, had not reached panic level in Britain or in the United States.

Table 7.18: Worries about Contracting AIDS

Q. How worried are you that you or someone you know will get AIDS?

	Britain	United States
Very worried	15	14
A little worried	20	27
Not very worried	31	27
Not at all worried	33	31
Don't know	2	1

Concern about AIDS was also less widespread in America than in Britain, as was reflected in the replies given to a question on the possibility of the disease reaching epidemic proportions. In Britain, 19 per cent felt that this was very likely and 31 per cent thought that it was somewhat likely; while in the United States the figures were 27 per cent and 35 per cent respectively. The British public's pessimism about the mortality rates involved in AIDS remained at a similarly high level to that found in March. Two in three (66 per cent) thought that all or most people who caught the disease died from it, and 92 per cent said that there was no cure for it at present. Replies to a question on the acceptance of homosexuals by society showed yet again that Britain was more tolerant than the United States.

Finally, people were asked whether they had any homosexual friends or acquaintances. The figures were 16 per cent in Britain and 22 per cent in the United States. In Britain, the proportion with homosexual friends or acquaintances was above average

Table 7.19: Homosexuals in Society

Q. *Do you think homosexuals as a group are becoming more accepted or less accepted by society?*

	Britain	United States
More accepted	61	53
Less accepted	24	34
No change; don't know	15	13

among women (19 per cent) and young adults aged 18–34 (26 per cent).

Despite the obvious concern about AIDS, the public were quite prepared to admit that they knew very little about the disease. In a November study only 4 per cent said they knew a great deal about AIDS, and 28 per cent a good amount. However, a large proportion (45 per cent) said they didn't know much, while 23 per cent said they knew almost nothing at all. The level of awareness where AIDS was concerned was very similar for both sexes, and — as one would expect — young adults claimed to be more aware than their elders. To test this claimed knowledge, people were asked whether the disease was more contagious or less contagious than the common cold. A majority (54 per cent) said that it was less contagious, but almost one in three (28 per cent) said that it was either more contagious (17 per cent) or about as contagious (11 per cent). Further questions also showed a disturbing lack of awareness about the disease.

Table 7.20: Shake Hands But Don't Take Blood

Q. *I'm going to read you a list. For each item please tell me if you think that it is or is not a way for someone to catch AIDS from someone who has it. If you are not sure, please tell me. Can you catch AIDS from:*

	Yes	No	Don't know
Blood transfusions	95	2	3
Intimate sexual contact	93	2	5
Sharing intravenous needles	91	3	6
Kissing	30	49	21
Using the same drinking glass	23	57	21
Being sneezed on	17	68	16
Sitting on a toilet seat	17	68	15
Shaking hands	5	88	7

If we exclude the first three items in the table, it would take exceptional circumstances for a person to contract AIDS through the five remaining ways and, assuming peole do not have these in mind, the results show a significant minority of the public to be misinformed about the disease. This was confirmed by the replies to yet another question. A majority (58 per cent) of the public felt that it was safe to associate with someone who had AIDS as long as there was no intimate physical contact, but 27 per cent thought it unsafe. Senior citizens, in particular, were concerned about this: as many (39 per cent) thought it was unsafe as thought it would be safe (38 per cent).

Cases have occurred both in Britain and the United States of children either being born with AIDS or contracting it through no fault of their own, and this had caused some concern among the parents of other children with whom they mixed at school. Gallup therefore asked a number of questions designed to measure the public's reaction to this potential problem. One in four (26 per cent), for example, were opposed to students with AIDS attending school even if health officials said there was no danger, but 61 per cent supported the idea. Similarly, 25 per cent said they would keep their children at home if they thought a child with AIDS might be at their school, though 63 per cent said they would send them to school. One in seven of the public disagreed with the idea of parents being informed should such a situation arise, possibly because they were afraid of the reaction this would cause.

Table 7.21: Attitudes towards AIDS

Q. I'm going to read a few statements. For each, please tell me if you agree, disagree, or if perhaps you have no opinion on that statement.

	Agree	Disagree	Don't know
School officials should tell parents if a child with AIDS is attending their child's school	80	14	6
If I had to receive a blood transfusion right now, I would be afraid that I might contract AIDS from someone else's blood	67	29	4
I would be willing to pay extra taxes if that money were used to find a cure for AIDS	61	28	11

The government would be spending more money on AIDS research if the disease did not mainly affect homosexual males	59	25	16
School employees found to have AIDS should be taken off the job	53	35	13
People with AIDS should be put into quarantine in special places to keep them away from the general public	28	58	15

It is perhaps a measure of the degree of public concern about AIDS that despite the relatively long history of the National Blood Transfusion Service, two in three of the public would now feel apprehensive about receiving someone else's blood. Moreover, three in five said they would be prepared to pay more in taxes in order to help combat the disease.

Homosexuals

At the same time as the March study on AIDS, but asking the questions of a different sample of people, Gallup repeated a series of trend questions on attitudes towards homosexuals to try to measure the effect, if any, of the AIDS scare. In terms of the seven questions used, dating back to 1977, there appeared to have been little change in basic attitudes, despite the perceived link between homosexuals and AIDS.

A majority (71 per cent) of the general public thought that homosexuals could be hired as sales staff but not as prison officers (67 per cent) nor as junior school teachers (66 per cent). On balance, the public were against homosexuals being clergymen or doctors, but evenly split when it came to the armed forces. Only on the last-mentioned item had there been any significant shift in opinion. In August 1977, 50 per cent thought homosexuals should be allowed in the armed forces and 36 per cent thought not. The 1985 figures were 45 per cent and 43 per cent respectively.

One other slight shift, though possibly unconnected with the publicity surrounding the AIDS problem, was the increase to 52 per cent (from 43 per cent in 1977) in the proportion of those thinking that there were more homosexuals 'today than 25 years ago'. On the other hand, the number of homosexual approaches made to males over the same period showed no such rise. One in four males (23 per cent) said that at some time, either as a child or since, they had been approached by a homosexual. In 1977, the figure had been virtually the same (24 per cent).

The public remained set in its divided view on the cause of homosexuality, though more of them opted for the idea of its being something inborn than thought it was the result of other factors:

Table 7.22: Causes of Homosexuality

Q. In your opinion, is homosexuality something a person is born with, or is it due to other factors such as upbringing or environment?

	Aug 1977	July 1979	Oct/Nov 1981	Mar 1985
Born with	31	39	37	34
Other factors	28	29	33	27
Both	21	19	17	22
Neither	3	2	1	2
Don't know	17	13	12	14

Yet the public were not so divided on three other questions. For example, two in three (69 per cent) took the view that homosexuals should not be allowed to adopt children; and this proportion had neven been below 63 per cent since 1977. In terms of religious persuasion, 74 per cent felt that a homosexual could be a good Christian. A majority (61 per cent) also thought that homosexual relations between consenting adults should be legal. One in four (27 per cent) disagreed. Over the eight-year period since 1977, there appears to be a decline in the number of 'don't knows', with a slight tendency to give a negative reply to this question.

The Modern Household

In Chapter 8, a few figures will be found on the ownership of consumer durables, comparing 1985 with the mid-1960s. As part of our ongoing 'commercial' work, however, more detailed figures are available over a shorter period on the ownership of labour-saving devices in the modern home.

Table 7.23: Ownership of Small Electrical Appliances

Q. Which, if any, of these items do you have in your home at present?

	Sept 1982	Sept 1985	Change
Electric kettle (any)	85	90	+ 5
Electric steam iron	45	40	− 5
Electric pop-up toaster	45	50	+ 5
Pressure cooker	41	43	+ 2
Electric dry iron	39	31	− 8
Electric steam spray iron	31	40	+ 9
Electric sandwich toaster	27	44	+17
Electric coffee percolator	26	28	+ 2
Electric knife	18	27	+ 9
Electric teamaker	15	12	− 3
Electric slow cooker/crockpot	13	18	+ 5
Electric deep fryer	13	22	+ 9
Electric coffeemaker	11	22	+11
Electric steak grill	8	10	+ 2
Electric tin opener	8	13	+ 5
Electric yoghurt maker	4	5	+ 1
Electric air purifier	2	6	+ 4
Electric waffle maker	2	2	0
Electric ice-cream maker	1	1	0
Electric kettle — traditional shape	—	66	—
Upright vacuum cleaner	—	63	—
Fridge	—	59	—
Combined fridge/freezer	—	41	—
Cylinder vacuum cleaner	—	41	—
Freezer	—	38	—
Electric kettle — jug shaped	—	29	—
Microwave oven	—	16	—
Dishwasher	—	6	—
Hand-held vacuum cleaner	—	4	—
Wet'n'dry vacuum cleaner	—	3	—

As can be seen, ownership of most of the items grew over the period between the two studies: particularly of sandwich toasters, coffee makers, electric knives and steam spray irons. Yet dry irons and steam irons are to be found in fewer homes today. Analysis by age shows why the ownership of dry irons has declined over the past few years: they are not fashionable. Less than one in five housewives aged under 35 have a dry iron, but two in five aged 65 or over do so.

As one would expect, younger housewives are more likely to own consumer durables than the not-so-young: housewives aged under 25 own on average eight of the listed appliances, compared with an average of six. There are, however, other examples of the effect of fashion on ownership. Almost all households have an electric kettle or vacuum cleaner, but designs of both have changed over the years. The jub-shaped kettle, for example, is owned by two in five young housewives but by only half as many housewives aged 65 or over. The 'traditional' shaped kettle (surprise, surprise!) is owned by one in two young housewives and by three in four senior citizens. Similarly, ownership of upright vacuum cleaners increased with age, while ownership of cylinders was more evenly spread and almost equalled that of uprights among the under-25s.

There were also regional differences in the 1985 summer study along north–south divisions, particularly in so far as Scotland was concerned. For example, ownership of dry irons or steam irons was lower in Scotland though the Scots were keener on the steam spray variety. Dry irons tended to be more popular in the southern half of the country. Electric deep fryers were also more popular in Scotland, as were 'traditional' shaped kettles and upright vacuum cleaners. Ownership of electric coffee percolators and coffee-makers was below the national average in the north of England, and freezers, too, were in few homes in the north or Scotland. Housewives in Scotland also appeared less interested in jug-shaped kettles or cylinder vacuum cleaners — preferring the 'traditional' models in both products.

The Elderly

In late November, as part of a Christmas exercise for Age Concern, a sample of people aged 60 or over were asked: 'What one thing at Christmas would make it a happier time for you?' The thing most often mentioned was to have their family around them — mentioned by 23 per cent overall and by 26 per cent of women in this elderly group. This was followed by either more money or fewer money problems (17 per cent), world peace (10 per cent) and good health (7 per cent). Overall, around one in five (21 per cent) said that there was nothing they required to make Christmas a happier time for them.

The Future

In the early spring, 17 members of the Gallup International chain asked a question on what the world would be like in a decade's time. In only one country did a majority think things would be better, while majorities in two thought things would get worse. Britain came tenth in the 'optimism' list.

Table 7.24: The World in Ten Years' Time

Q. Do you think for people like yourself, the world in 10 years' time will be a better place to live in than it is now, or worse place, or just about the same as it is today?

	Better	**Worse**	**Same**	**No opinion**
Uruguay	54	23	15	9
Greece	46	29	15	10
Argentina	44	27	21	8
USA	30	30	35	5
Brazil	27	48	17	8
Turkey	26	38	12	24
Switzerland	23	33	40	4
Philippines	21	29	42	8
Canada	19	35	41	4
Great Britain	18	45	31	6
Portugal	16	37	9	38
Netherlands	15	26	53	6
Belgium	15	31	37	17
Australia	14	41	38	7
South Africa (whites)	13	52	28	7
Japan	12	53	18	17
West Germany	4	31	46	19

As can be seen in the above table, in only three countries did optimists outnumber pessimists, in one country the two groups were equal, and in the remainder pessimists outnumbered optimists.

In Britain, pessimists outnumbered optimists in all groups analysed: by party affiliation, sex, age, and scoio-economic class. Optimism was highest among Conservatives (26 per cent) and the middle classes (23 per cent) and lowest among Labour supporters (11 per cent).

8   Britain 20 Years On

In June 1985, Gallup were commissioned by T.V. South to conduct a major study of contemporary attitudes with the use of as much material as possible that was comparable to the 1960s. The survey was to provide the basis for a series of Saturday night television programmes hosted by David Frost. The questionnaire contained more than 100 questions and was divided into five major sections: 'the good life', 'law and order', 'family life', 'the sexual revolution' and 'land of Hope and Glory'. The following chapter describes some of the main findings.

'The Good Life'

The Sixties are the 'Best'

Almost half of Britain (47 per cent) believed that the 1960s was the best decade, the time when British people 'never had it so good'. Among those of all ages, from 16 to 70 years, the sixties was the most popular decade — even with those who had no personal experience of it. Most enthusiasm for the sixties was found amongst those who were aged 30 to 39 and who had experienced the sixties when in their teens and twenties.

Table 8.1: The Best Decade

Q. Do you think the British people 'never had it so good ...?

In the twenties	2
In the thirties	4
In the forties	3
In the fifties	14
In the sixties	47
In the seventies	16
In the eighties	14
None of these	5
Don't know	8

The survey revealed a considerable degree of nostalgia for the six-ties period and considerable gloom about Britain's future prospects. This is demonstrated by responses to the following questions over a 20-year period:

Table 8.2: Britain's Decline

Q. *Is Britain nowadays moving towards prosperity or away from prosperity?*

	1965	1985
Towards prosperity	48	28
Away from prosperity	25	62
Don't know	27	11

It can be seen that in 1985 more than six out of ten (62 per cent) believed that Britain was moving away from prosperity compared to 25 per cent in 1965. Conservative voters were the most optimistic and Labour voters the most pessimistic. Britain was also much less confident about its relative prosperity in terms of the world economy in 1985 compared to 1965:

Table 8.3: Britain's Worsening Prospects

Q. *Compared with most other countries, do you think Britain's prospects for the future are better or worse?*

	1965	1985
Better	55	43
Worse	19	42
Don't know	26	15

It can be seen that Britain today is equally divided about whether its future prospects are better or worse, whereas in 1965 the nation was much more confident about its world economic role.

One of the reasons for this economic pessimism must be the continual effect of unemployment on economic expectation. In 1966, the most urgent problem facing the country was inflation (48 per cent), followed by housing (16 per cent). In 1985, an overwhelming 79 per cent claimed unemployment was the biggest problem, followed by cost of living (4 per cent), law and order (4 per cent) and health (2 per cent).

In spite of this, people believed that they were much better off in economic terms than their parents had been and that their own children would, by and large, be better off in economic terms than them. However, the survey revealed that people did not believe that this economic improvement would necessarily bring happiness or increased satisfaction with life — quite the opposite, in fact. The majority of people thought that their parents had been more satisfied with life and happier, and less than one in five people thought that today's children, on reaching their age, would be happier or more satisfied with life than they were. On the other hand, they did think that in future people would be better educated, better read, more widely travelled and more ambitious. Some even thought that in future people would be more idealistic, while it was generally agreed that they would be less religious.

Table 8.4: The Generation Gap

Q. *Thinking about your parents when they were your age now, do you think they were ...?*

Q. *And what about children today? Do you think when they reach your age now they will be ...?*

	Parents' generation	Future generation
More satisfied with life	55	18
Happier	40	16
More religious	39	7
Healthier	26	48
More idealistic	23	34
Better read	19	40
Economically better off	18	41
More ambitious	17	49
More educated	11	56
More widely travelled	9	67

Overall, we look back to the sixties as a period when Britain was, perhaps, in retrospect, at its post-war peak; when British industry was still an important world leader and, in addition, launched on the world the Beatles, the miniskirt and other paraphernalia associated with the period. In short, we were optimistic, confident and looking forward to a better life. In fact, people today are much better off in real terms compared to the sixties, yet they do not have the same economic confidence that the future will be bright.

As a measure of our current prosperity, it is interesting to compare ownership of household durables in 1965 and 1985:

Table 8.5: Ownership of Durables

Q. Which of the following household gadgets do you own?

	1965*	1985
Refrigerator	42	93
Vacuum cleaner	78	92
Washing machine	56	86
Telephone	25	79
Freezer	NA	72
Tumble dryer	NA	43
Microwave oven	NA	17
Dishwasher	1	6

*Source: Audits of Great Britain Ltd, Home Audit

All these gadgets have made housework easier; but then in 1965 the majority of married women were not holding down a job as they are today.

Asked which of these appliances was considered the most important in the running of a home, the washing machine was voted the favourite by a majority of women.

Table 8.6: Most Important Appliances in the Running of the Home in 1985

Q. Which one of these time-saving appliances or household gadgets, if any, is most important to you in the running of your home?

	General public	Women
Washing machine	45	51
Fridge	18	19
Telephone	15	11
Vacuum cleaner	9	10

It is interesting to note that the telephone was rated as more important than the vacuum cleaner.

Attitudes towards the Rich

The survey revealed that most people were indifferent in their feelings about rich people, with more people likely to respect or like them than envy or dislike them. Labour voters were more likely than others to be irritated by them and envy them, but the differences between the political parties were relatively small. There was also very little difference between the different social classes in their attitudes towards the rich.

Table 8.7: The Rich

Q. Which of the following, if any, describe your feelings about rich people?

Admire them	12
Respect them	15
Like them	12
Indifferent	46
Dislike them	4
Envy them	13
Irritated by them	12
None of these	17

From this survey there appeared to be little evidence of any deeply held class hatred. Perhaps one of the reasons for this was that virtually half the employees questioned (47 per cent) wanted to work for themselves or to run their own business.

Table 8.8: The New Self-Employed

Q. Do you or have you ever worked for yourself or have your own business? (All respondents working for an employer)

Yes	47
No	51
Don't know	2

Even more interesting was the type of business they would like to own, the most popular being as follows:

Table 8.9: A Nation of Shopkeepers

Q. What sort of business would this be?

	General public	Men	Women
Shop owner	21	11	35
Restaurateur/publican	13	7	22
Interior painter/decorator	6	10	0
Exterior builder	4	7	1
Artist/writer/actor	4	6	2
Hairdresser	3	1	7
Secretary	1	0	2
Insurance broker	1	2	1
Computer related	1	1	0
Chartered accountant	2	2	1
Medical doctor	1	0	3
Other professional	4	5	4
Other non-manual	7	6	8
Other manual	18	25	8

It can be seen that many more women than men wanted to be shop owners, by a ratio of three to one. Similarly, many more women wanted to run restaurants or pubs than did men, who were more interested in working in a variety of semi-skilled jobs.

The Best Years of People's Lives'

Almost without exception, people thought that the twenties was the best period of their lives — this was true for all age groups aged 20 and over — with the teens coming a close second.

Table 8.10: The Best Years of Your Life

Q. And what about you personally, which have been the best years of your life so far?

Childhood	8
Teens	24
Twenties	28
Thirties	16
Forties	8
Fifties	3
Over 60	2
No particular years	3
All years good years	7

People in the lower social classes (DE) were much more inclined to believe that their childhood years were better years than people in the upper middle classes.

The survey found that doctors, clergy and next-door neighbours were the most trustworthy, while Members of Parliament were the least trustworthy.

Table 8.11: Trust in Others

Q. Please look at this card and tell me in general which groups of people you trust most.

Q. Which group in general do you trust least?

	Trust the most	**Trust the least**
Doctors	33	2
Clergy	13	2
Next-door neighbours	13	7
Policemen	10	8
Nurses	9	0
Solicitors	5	9
Bank managers	3	1
Teachers	3	2
Your employer	2	4
Scientists	1	3
Accountants	1	2
Estate agents	0	16
MPs	0	30

One in three (33 per cent) of the population trusted doctors, but almost the same percentage (30 per cent) distrusted MPs, and estate agents were also considered untrustworthy. Next-door neighbours were a mixed blessing, being seen as both trustworthy and untrustworthy.

Attitudes towards Management and Work

The following comparisons were made between 1965 and 1985 on attitudes towards various aspects of management and work among employees:

Table 8.11: Hard At It

Q. Do you think that managers or supervisors at your place of work do or do not work hard enough?

	1965	1985
Do work hard enough	51	48
Do not work hard enough	26	42
Don't know/no answer	23	11

Q. Do you think that the 'Boss' does or does not work hard
   enough?

	1965	1985
Does work hard enough	55	59
Does not work hard enough	20	30
Don't know/no answer	25	11

Q. Do you think that people working with you do or do not
   work hard enough?

	1965	1985
Do work hard enough	66	68
Do not work hard enough	18	20
Don't know/no answer	16	12

Q. What about yourself, do you think that you work as hard as
   you might?

	1965	1985
Do work hard enough	85	81
Do not work hard enough	9	18
Don't know/no answer	6	2

It can be seen that the overwhelming majority (81 per cent)
thought that they worked hard but that they were more critical
when it came to other people: only 68 per cent believed that others
worked hard enough.

They were also likely to see themselves as taking more pride in
their work than the average worker did.

Table 8.13: Pride in Work

Q. How much pride, if any, do you personally take in the work
   that you do?

Q. And how much pride, if any, do you think people in
   general take in the work they do?

	Self	Others
A great deal	78	26
Some	18	47
Not very much	2	24
None at all	2	1
Don't know	0	2

As with previous questions on strikes, it is always 'them' who are not working hard enough, not taking pride in what they do, being too quick to down tools, and never 'us'.

Cultural Activities

After a hard week at work or in the home, what do we do for relaxation? People were asked when was the last time they had indulged in various activities, and the table shows the proportion doing so in the past twelve months:

Table 8.14: Cultural Activities

	1965	1985
Opera*	16	6
Concert of classical music	11	12
Theatre, ballet	28	28
Museum	25	44
Professional football match	21	12
Zoo	32	25
Botanical garden	19	25
Cinema	67	38
Stately home	26	24
Rock or pop concert	na	15
Disco or other dancing	na	53
Safari/large theme park	na	17
Evening class/course	na	17
Bingo	24	11

*Included 'musical' in 1965

Significant changes in leisure activities can be seen from the above table. While we appear to be attending concerts of classical music, the theatre, ballet or visiting stately homes no more frequently than we did 20 years ago, museum attendances have almost doubled. Perhaps because they tend to be free or relatively inexpensive? The decline in attendances at football matches and at cinemas, in particular, is apparent. Only one in four (22 per cent) people in their forties, for example, had been to the cinema in the last twelve months, and the figure amounted to 21 per cent of people aged 50 to 64 and to a mere 6 per cent of those aged 65 and over. Bingo, too, despite its continuing popularity, showed a declining audience, perhaps due to the plethora of newspaper bingo schemes introduced in recent years.

That times were considered as somewhat hard was shown in the replies to a question on reduced expenditure, with two in three members of the public — one in two of senior citizens — saying they were trying to cut down on something. Top of the list, particularly among the under-20s, was cutting down on sweets or chocolates (27 per cent). This was closely followed by smoking (22 per cent), holidays (19 per cent) and eating out (19 per cent).

One in four (24 per cent) of the public and one in three women were also attempting to reduce something else — their weight! This was the proportion who said that they had been on some sort of weight-reducing diet in the previous twelve months. The activity was also particularly popular — or perhaps necessary — among people in their thirties.

Religious Attitudes

The year 1985 was a year when renewed pressure emerged for a relaxation in the laws on Sunday trading. Almost two in three (63 per cent) of the general public thought that Sundays should be 'a family day', 28 per cent felt that it should be like any other day, 16 per cent thought it should be a day of worship, and 9 per cent said all commercial activity should be closed down 'as it is wrong to buy anything on a Sunday'. The proposition that Sunday should be a day of worship was particularly popular among four related groups: widowed people (36 per cent), people aged 65 or over (34 per cent), single-person households (30 per cent) and retired people (31 per cent). It was even higher (42 per cent) among people who attended religious services at least once a month. The idea that nothing should be sold on a Sunday followed similar trends though the pattern tended to be flatter. This latter group amounted to 24 per cent of the public overall, 31 per cent of women, 38 per cent of widowed people, 35 per cent of those aged 65 or over, and 32 per cent of people who had finished their full-time education at 19 or over. Around one in ten (8 per cent) of the public said they attended religious services at Christmas or Easter only, 12 per cent attended once a year, and 8 per cent less often. Almost one in two (47 per cent) said they never went to religious services. These tended to be males (59 per cent) and the under-30s (56 per cent).

Despite this lack of attendance at 'houses of God', 70 per cent said they believed in God and one in three (31 per cent) believed in the devil. Again, there was both a gender gap and a generation gap on the subject of these beliefs, as shown in the following table:

Table 8.15: Religious Beliefs

Q. Which, if any, of the following do you believe in?

	General public	16–19	65+	Men	Women
God	70	57	75	66	75
Sin	51	50	59	49	53
A soul	50	50	53	44	56
Heaven	48	38	61	41	54
Life after death	43	33	45	37	49
The devil	31	28	33	30	31
Hell	29	23	30	28	29
Astrology, the stars	22	35	18	15	28
Reincarnation	20	19	28	16	23
Transcendental meditation	9	11	10	9	9
None of these	14	27	10	18	11

It can be seen, therefore, that on the whole young adults are less likely to hold these beliefs than are senior citizens, and that women are more likely to do so than men. However, there are a number of interesting sidelights to this generalisation. The under-20s are, for example, twice as likely as the elderly group to believe in 'the stars'. Age is also a better discriminator of one's belief in God and in heaven than knowing their gender. The position is reversed when it comes to belief in a soul: here sex is a better discriminator than age.

Law and Order

Despite the riots of recent years, the public did not consider Britain to be a particularly violent country, and on balance thought it neither more nor less violent than it was 20 years ago. Slightly fewer than one in ten (7 per cent) considered Britain to be very violent, 43 per cent fairly violent, 44 per cent not particularly violent, and 6 per cent not a violent country at all. When asked whether there was more violent crime or less violent crime 20 years ago, 41 per cent said there was more in the 1960s and 45 per cent said that there was less. The remainder either said things had not changed or were undecided.

The public were great believers in self-help as a means of trying to reduce their exposure to crime. For example, three in four (73 per cent) had home contents insurance, and 60 per cent had life assurance. One in two said they had a burglar alarm or some other form of burglar-proofing in their homes, and 43 per cent said they either avoided certain places after dark or did not go out alone. This was especially true of women (64 per cent) and of senior citizens (57 per cent). Twelve per cent had either a weapon or a household item that they intended to use as a weapon — usually a stick or poker.

One in ten said that they had been the victim of a violent act in the past five years, and of these 4 per cent said the attack had been made by someone known to them. Victimisation tended to be higher among men (16 per cent) and young adults aged between 20 and 29 (18 per cent). About one in five actually feared being a victim.

Table 8.16: Fear of Personal Violence

Q. How much do you fear actually being the victim of a violent crime?

	General public	Men	Women	Council tenants	Scotland
A great deal	9	3	15	15	17
Quite a lot	13	8	18	15	22
Slightly	34	30	37	33	34
Not at all	44	59	29	37	26

Perhaps surprisingly, senior citizens scored no higher on the scale than the public at large.

When asked which violent crimes particularly worried them, attacks on children topped the list, mentioned by just over one in two of the public. Mugging, again mentioned by around one in two, was the crime that most people thought was on the increase. The top ten items were as follows:

Table 8.17: Child Abuse and Muggings a Concern

Q. Which violent crimes particularly worry you?

Q. And which particular violent crimes do you think are on the increase?

Table 8.17 continued

	Worried about	On the increase
Attacks on children	54	43
Mugging	50	55
Rape	43	37
Sexual attacks on women	37	33
Assault	30	28
Football violence	28	42
Mob violence	26	23
Housebreaking	24	35
Picket violence	17	22
Hold ups	16	17

One answer dominated the list of reasons people gave for the increase in violent crime: one in two (49 per cent) put the responsibility on unemployment, particularly among young people. The next most often-mentioned reasons were a decline in parental discipline (14 per cent) and lack of money (11 per cent). There were some significant differences in the way people perceived the problem. Conservatives, for example, were less likely to blame unemployment and more likely to blame the more traditional values associated with discipline. This was also true of senior citizens.

The frontier vigilante spirit of 'doing what a man's gotta do' was

Table 8.18: The Public Takeover of Law Enforcement

Q. How likely do you think it is that in the next few years people will begin to take the law into their own hands to reduce violent crime?

Q. If you were threatened, how likely would you be to take the law into your own hands?

	Others	Self
Very likely	28	33
Fairly likely	35	24
Not very likely	25	18
Not at all likely	9	19
Don't know	3	7

still very much alive in the Britain of 1985. Almost two in three members of the public foresaw that in the near future people would take the law into their own hands, and over one in two thought it likely that they themselves would do so if threatened. In terms of personally taking the law into their own hands, the likelihood tended to be higher among men, people in their forties and people who had left school at 15 or under.

As can be seen in other chapters of this book, crime was not the only social problem facing Britain in the eighties: unemployment, poverty and poor housing also loomed large in the public's consciousness.

Table 8.19: The Serious Social Problems

Q. Do you regard any of these as raising very serious social problems in Britain today?

	General public	16–19	65+	Con	Lab	Lib/ SDP
Hard-drug-taking	92	94	96	95	91	93
Unemployment	86	89	85	80	90	86
Mugging	81	73	88	84	79	79
Crimes of violence	78	76	82	84	74	77
Glue sniffing	76	67	82	82	74	73
Rape	73	82	85	74	75	70
Soft-drug-taking	70	60	89	77	64	70
Juvenile delinquency	65	49	72	73	58	67
Bad housing	62	58	56	53	67	64
Poverty	60	57	59	50	63	66
House breaking	58	49	73	62	54	61
Organised large-scale crimes	48	51	59	50	46	50
Drunkenness	48	42	55	48	46	48
Youth	37	25	47	37	38	40
Divorce	35	34	44	36	34	33
The elderly	32	23	40	31	36	30
Immigrants, coloured persons	31	24	40	39	24	29
Prostitution	29	46	42	28	27	27
Gambling	28	21	45	29	28	25
Homosexuality	25	17	44	31	24	18
Abortion	21	23	34	22	21	18
Heavy smoking	19	14	32	19	18	17

A number of things were immediately noticeable about these analyses. The elderly, for example, were more concerned about all items — with a few exceptions — than the public overall. There were also some problems that concerned both youngsters and senior citizens to a greater degree than average. The taking of hard drugs was one such problem, as were rape, organised large-scale crime, prostitution and abortion. Then there were a number of problems to which the two groups attached different degrees of concern — with juvenile delinquency coming as no surprise. They also disagreed about housebreaking being a problem, about young people, immigrants, gambling, homosexuality and heavy smoking. Analysis by supporters of the three main 'parties' showed a flatter picture, but there were still some differences of opinion. Conservatives, for example, put less emphasis on unemployment, bad housing and poverty but more on delinquency and drugs. On a separate question about terrorism — a more widespread problem — the public took a decidedly pessimistic view. Just under one in two (44 per cent) thought that it would be increasingly with us forever, 13 per cent thought it would eventually diminish and 38 per cent thought it would remain at about the current level.

The media came in for criticism in the study for their handling of stories relating to the level of violence in our society. One in two thought the media overestimated it, 31 per cent thought they got it right, and 14 per cent said they underestimated it. Men, people in their thirties, the upper class and the better-educated tended to be the most critical of the media.

Finally, Gallup asked a number of questions about the police and sentences to round off the law and order section. Compared with 20 years ago, we are now less likely to see the police as being efficient and more likely to see them as a corrupt, violent force.

Table 8.20: Image of the Police

Q. Which of these statements do you believe is true in the main of the British police force?

	1965	1985
They are efficient and do their job well	68	48
They are not very efficient because of the way they are organised	16	15
There are cases of corruption and violence, but they are very scattered	23	43
Cases of corruption and violence occur too often	8	17

The shifts in opinion here are quite stark, particularly on the corruption and violence dimension. The proportion saying that these things happened too often was highest among people in their thirties, Labour supporters and the better-educated.

There has also been a shift since 1965 on what the aim of court sentences should be. More people saw it as a punishment than had done so 20 years earlier.

Table 8.21: Court Sentences

Q. What should be the first concern of the courts in sentencing a criminal?

	1965	1985
To punish him for what he had done to others	44	52
To punish him to stop others following his example	25	26
To do what they can to reclaim him as a good citizen	28	18
Don't know	3	4

Table 8.22: Combating Crime

Q. How likely would you personally be to support each of the following measures to help restrict crime?

	Very likely	Fairly likely	Not very likely	Not at all likely
Harsher punishments	61	22	10	5
Capital punishment	50	16	12	19
Corporal punishment	48	23	12	14
A large police force	45	33	16	6
Neighbourhood watch schemes	36	34	18	9
More prisons	35	31	24	7
Identity cards	26	19	21	29
More probation officers	25	30	27	13
More laws	19	23	32	22

Note: The 'don't knows', amounting to no more than 5 per cent, have been ignored

It was hardly surprising, given this result, that majorities of the public supported the introduction of harsher punishments, including capital punishment, in order to combat crime. Women tended to be more in favour than men of more probation officers — and more laws — as possible measures to reduce the crime rate.

Family Life

Marriage

Almost seven out of ten (68 per cent) believed that marriage should be for life in Britain today, in spite of the fact that almost one in seven couples were on their second marriage. Even among those who were currently divorced or separated and had not remarried, a majority (53 per cent) believed that marriage should be for life. Teenagers aged between 16 and 19 and those who had been married for about seven years (the 'itch'?) were less convinced that marriage should be for life. Among this group, around one in six (15 per cent) did not believe this. Asked what was the best thing about being married, the following factors emerged: companionship, sharing, having a family, togetherness and love.

When asked about the things that most annoyed them about their partner men said that women argued and contradicted them; while women were most likely to complain — in equal proportions — that men were either untidy or too tidy, and also complained about the husband's personal habits, such as biting nails, taking socks off last when undressing or leaving them inside out, squeezing the toothpaste tube in the middle and leaving the toilet seat up.

When asked what reasons they thought could cause a breakdown in their marriage, the most frequently cited reason — given by 41 per cent of married couples — was consistent unfaithfulness, closely followed by violence (36 per cent). In addition, couples thought that if they ceased to love each other or if one or both of them fell for someone else, or if one partner became a habitual heavy drinker, these could be possible reasons for a breakdown in their marriage. Only one in three people suggested that their marriage was so stable as not to be threatened by any of these. Among the one in ten people who had been married before, the main reasons given for the breakdown of their previous marriage were that the former partner had been consistently unfaithful, that the two of them had ceased to love each other, or that the partner(s) had fallen for someone else.

The majority of people (57 per cent) believed that married couples should not stay together for the sake of the children if their marriage had broken down.

Table 8.23: Children in a Broken Home

Q. Do you believe that married couples should stay together for the sake of their children even if overall their marriage has broken down?

	General public	Men	Women	Married	Divorced/ separated
Yes, should stay together	35	45	27	33	23
No, should not	57	47	66	59	72
Don't know	8	8	7	8	4

Among the older generation, aged 65 and over, a large majority (62 per cent) were in favour of couples staying together for the sake of their children.

People were equally divided about whether to put their elderly parents in an old persons' home if they were no longer able to look after themselves (42 per cent) or to have them live with them (40 per cent). Elderly people aged 65 and over were overwhelmingly in favour of going into a home, but young people up to the age of 30 were convinced that the elderly were best looked after by their children. The reasons why an elderly persons' home was preferred was because people felt their parents would be better cared for in a home, or that it would cause too much tension if they stayed in the family. People felt it better to look after their elderly parents because their parents had looked after them in their childhood and they wanted to return that care.

Companionship also topped the list among both men and women as the good points about living with the opposite sex. The replies for women were as follows:

Table 8.24: Men's Good Points

Q. What do you think are (or would be) the good points about living with a man?

Companionship	35
Security/protection	18
Sharing things	12
He does heavy jobs/decorating	14
Sexual relationships	8
Love and tenderness	7

Among the 'sixties' generation of women, sex was much more important than for any other age group. When men were asked a similar question, the top items mentioned were as follows:

Table 8.25: Women's Good Points

Q. What do you think are (or would be) the good points about living with a woman?

Companionship	43
She does the housework, etc.	20
Sexual relationships	17
Love and tenderness	11
Sharing things	11
Family life	7
She looks after me	6

In general, women felt that men did not restrict them in terms of working outside the home, pursuing a career, meeting female friends or pursuing leisure activities. The only area in which their partner restricted them was in meeting male friends — one in three claimed this.

Both men and women thought that the ideal size of family was 2.4 children. A large majority (73 per cent) of both men and women agreed that the children of working wives suffered, at least to some extent, and the proportion was even higher (84 per cent) of those who thought that children of single parents suffered. Men and women were unanimously agreed (82 per cent) that parents these days were less strict than in their own childhood.

A large majority of women (64 per cent) thought that women these days had an easier life than their mother's generation, though 17 per cent thought that women these days had a more difficult life. The reasons why women today were thought to have an easier life was because nowadays there were many 'mod cons' to help them around the home, that women had more freedom and choice, were financially better off and more independent. Similar results were found when men compared their lives to their fathers, but men were less convinced than women. This was primarily because they had greater worries concerning employment than did women these days, felt that there were more pressures on them, and felt that men had lost power and status with the increasing independence of women.

Almost one in five married women (19 per cent) thought it would put a strain on their marriage if they earned more than their husband, whereas only 5 per cent of men thought this would result; thus women are more sensitive about earning more than men. Two in five married men claimed that they would be likely to give up their job and look after the house if they were able to manage on the wife's income alone — and 3 per cent said that this was already the case. One in three wives thought it likely that their husband would give up his job to look after the family in those circumstances.

The most important pressures on women going out to work, in the view of both men and women, is that they have to run a home as well in addition to going to work.

Table 8.26: Work Pressures on Women

Q. Which, if any, of the following put pressure on women at work?

	Men	Women
Having to run a home as well as working	46	50
Having to take days off when children are unwell	30	48
Sexual harrassment from male colleagues	22	22
Disapproval by her husband/partner	19	25
Lack of job prospects compared with men in the same position	18	29
General discrimination against women by management	18	21
A patronising attitude of male colleagues at work	17	22

The survey revealed — surprisingly — that two in five males (39 per cent) were sympathetic towards the women's movement compared to 27 per cent of women. Overall, two in three women (65 per cent) claimed they were not sympathetic towards the women's movement.

The Sexual Revolution

Sexual Equality

One in two (48 per cent) of the public felt that both sexes had equal say in their households, though men, on balance, were thought to be the decision-makers. Three in four (76 per cent) however, including 81 per cent of women, felt that women have to work harder to achieve the same as men at work. Here was a question where the normal generation gap between young adults and senior citizens did not

Table 8.27: Decision-makers in the Home

Q. Who would you say ultimately has the most say in your household?

	General public	Men	Women
The husband/man	24	30	19
The wife/woman	19	16	23
Both equal	48	46	49
Don't know	9	8	10

appear, with 67 per cent of both groups agreeing with the concept behind the question.

On the other hand, 58 per cent of the public thought that when a man invites a woman out socially he should pay for the outing regardless of what they both earn. One in five (19 per cent) thought they should share the cost regardless of what they each earned, 13 per cent felt they should share if their earnings were similar, and 6 per cent that he should pay only if he earned more than she did. Among the under-20s, as many said the cost should be shared (47 per cent) as thought he should pay (49 per cent).

When asked which of the sexes had benefited most overall in the past 20 years, a majority (51 per cent) felt that women had, 16 per cent thought that men had, and 27 per cent felt that neither sex had done any better than the other. Even 46 per cent of women felt that their sex had benefited more over the past 20 years.

Birth Control

While three in four (78 per cent) of the public approved of abortions in cases where the mother's health was at risk, only 17 per cent thought that it should be available on demand.

The study for TVS confirmed the findings of earlier Gallup studies showing support for Mrs Victoria Gillick's case against doctors prescribing the pill to under-age girls without informing their parents first. A majority (56 per cent) of the public and of both sexes felt that doctors should not be allowed to act in this way, though 38 per cent thought they should. Those people who felt that doctors *should* be able to prescribe the pill without first telling the parents were almost evenly divided on the issue of whether or not the parents of an under-age girl should have the right to know whether she had been

Table 8.28: Approval of Abortion

Q. *Do you approve or disapprove of abortion under the following circumstances? (Percentages approving.)*

	General public	Attend religious services: At least once a month	Never
Where mother's health is at risk	78	69	78
Where the pregnancy is the result of rape	74	62	79
Where the child is likely to be born handicapped	67	50	71
Where the woman is under the age of consent (16)	40	29	46
Where a married couple do not want more children	24	12	33
Available on demand	17	11	22
Under no circumstances	7	17	4

prescribed a contraceptive pill by a doctor. Almost one in three (29 per cent) of the public would consider allowing their daughter aged 15 or under to go on the pill if they thought she might be having a sexual relationship with a boyfriend. The same proportion would consider it if she was aged 16, with the figure rising to 21 per cent in the case of a daughter aged 17 or over; but 6 per cent said they would not consider it all.

Pornography

Slightly more than one in two of the public disagreed that pornography was harmless, and three in four thought that its use could trigger sexual assaults.

Table 8.29: The Use of Pornography

Q. *Do you strongly agree, agree, neither agree nor disagree, disagree or strongly disagree with the following statements?*
a) The use of pornography is harmless and has no serious effects on those who have a taste for it.
b) The use of pornography can trigger sexual assaults.

Table 8.29 continued

| | Harmless | | | Trigger assaults | | |
	General public	Men	Women	General public	Men	Women
Strongly agree	4	7	2	29	20	37
Agree	18	24	13	46	48	43
Neither agree/ disagree	16	16	16	7	9	6
Disagree	32	32	32	10	14	7
Strongly disagree	26	17	33	3	4	2
Don't know	4	4	4	5	4	5

In addition to the gender difference in the replies given to these two statements, there was a generation gap, with young adults showing less concern about the effects of pornography.

The Sexual Revolution

Despite the image of the 'Swinging Sixties' and all it involved, a majority (61 per cent) of people felt that there was more pre-marital sex now than there had been in the 1960s. The proportion holding this view rose to 78 per cent among those aged 65 and over. It was also felt that both married men and married women were more likely to have an affair now than they would have been in the 1960s. Just under one in two (45 per cent) thought this was true of married men, and slightly more (57 per cent) thought it was true of married women. Fifteen per cent of married people thought that it was possible or probable that they would have an affair while they were married. Three in four felt that it was either improbable or an impossibility.

On the whole, the public were tolerant of homosexuals though they were uncomfortable in their company. This was particularly true of men.

Table 8.30: Attitudes towards Homosexuals

Q. If you were in the company of homosexual people of the same sex as yourself, which statement would best describe your personal attitude?

	General public	Men	Women
They have rights just like everyone else, and I am comfortable in their company	30	26	34

They have rights just like everyone else, but I am not altogether comfortable in their company	52	55	49
I think they have too many rights these days	13	14	11
Don't know	5	5	5

There was also a generation gap in the replies to this question, with 40 per cent of young adults (aged 16-19) taking a more tolerant attitude towards homosexuals compared with 29 per cent of senior citizens.

Finally, Gallup asked its sample about various types of sexual behaviour, and the following table shows the proportions approving of each of them:

Table 8.31: Approval of Sexual Lifestyles

Q. Generally speaking, which of the following styles of sexual behaviour would you say you approve of?

	General public	Men	Women	16-19	65+
Platonic friendships	63	60	65	57	54
Living together before marriage	62	65	60	79	22
Living together instead of marriage	46	51	43	66	21
Celibacy	29	25	33	32	25
One-night stands	17	24	10	20	5
Open marriages	13	17	9	14	5
Bisexuality	10	11	8	16	1
Wife-swapping	5	7	3	3	1

'Land of Hope and Glory'

Britain and the World

Pride in being British was at a high level in mid-1985, with almost one in two saying they were very proud and a further 33 per cent quite proud. This was particularly true of senior citizens, Conservatives and Northerners. Yet in spite of this pride, there were few delusions of grandeur. Just over one in three wanted Britain to be a world power, while half as many more wanted Britain to follow a low-profile policy. This is a complete reversal of the 1965 findings.

Table 8.32: Pride in Being British

Q. *How proud are you to be British?*

	General public	16-19	65+	Con	Lab	Lib/ SDP	Northern England
Very proud	47	31	61	56	41	45	51
Quite proud	33	44	19	35	31	35	30
Not very proud	12	18	14	5	15	15	13
Not at all proud	4	5	3	2	7	4	3
Don't know	3	1	3	2	6	1	3

Table 8.33: Britain's World Role

Q. *Do you think it is important for this country to try to be a leading power, or would you like to see us be more like Sweden and Switzerland?*

	1965	1985
Be a world power	55	37
More like Sweden/Switzerland	26	55
Don't know	19	8

Men, more than women, and Conservatives are more likely to want Britain to try to be a world power. Yet among the better-educated group who left school at 19 or later, the world power idea is rejected by a margin of three to one.

One in three (30 per cent) of the British public took the view that British troops should be removed from Northern Ireland immediately, and another 20 per cent within five years. Just over one in three (36 per cent) said the troops should remain until a settlement was reached, and 6 per cent were against the idea of a troop withdrawal. Support for 'troops out' was highest among people in their thirties, council tenants and Labour supporters. On the other hand, men, people in the upper classes, the better-educated and Conservatives were more likely to opt for keeping British troops in Northern Ireland, at least until a settlement had been reached.

Obviously, our stereotypes of other nationalities affects international relations, so it came as no surprise to discover that we saw the Americans, for instance, as typically friendly, rich, aggressive and fun-loving. Our image of the Russian people was entirely different: hardworking, serious and inclined to be cold, with no sense of humour. And how do we see ourselves? Well, of course, we are friendly, have a sense of humour, are polite, hardworking and fun-loving. We have a slightly weaker, though negative, image of the French: cannot be trusted, rude, cultured, friendly and fun-loving. Finally, the Irish were thought to be friendly, with a sense of humour, hardworking and fun-loving. The full range of attributes can be seen in the following table:

Table 8.34: The British, Americans, Russians, French and Irish

Q. Please look at this list of characteristics and read out all those which you think apply to the British people. And what about the Americans? And the Russians? And the French? And, lastly, which of these apply to the Irish?

	British	Americans	Russians	French	Irish
Friendly	67	44	14	21	53
Sense of humour	66	27	8	13	53
Polite	46	20	16	15	21
Hardworking	42	28	43	15	39
Fun-loving	42	37	6	20	37
Can be trusted	40	11	6	8	18
Sincere	32	11	12	8	22
Peaceful	32	8	9	12	15
Serious	28	12	39	12	11
Lazy	26	11	2	15	12
Cultured	25	9	18	21	9
Aggressive	22	41	24	17	22
Rude	17	30	5	26	6
Poor	16	3	26	8	27
Cold	12	6	28	9	3
Rich	10	44	3	4	6
Cannot be trusted	8	21	24	30	14
Insincere	8	21	9	19	6
Uncultured	7	20	7	9	13
No sense of humour	5	11	28	19	4

The 'Two Nations'

Much has been made in recent years of Britain as 'Two Nations': the relatively affluent, Conservative south and the poverty-stricken, Labour north. Take away the political colours from the map, and that is very much how people see the south and north.

Table 8.35: Britain's 'Two Nations'

Q. I am now going to read you out a list of adjectives. Could you tell me all those which you think describe people living in the south of England?

Q. Now thinking about people living in the north of England, which of these adjectives best describes them?

	The south	The north
Friendly	52	74
Intelligent	48	40
Hardworking	47	63
Efficient	40	35
Intolerant	27	13
Humourless	20	7
Insincere	18	4
Poor	4	48

A number of significant differences are immediately apparent in people's perceptions of the two halves of the country. The biggest of these is on poverty, the figure for the south being only a twelfth of that mentioned for the north. People were also more likely to see northerners as friendly and hardworking. Southerners, hanging their heads in shame, were rated more highly as being intolerant, lacking in humour and insincere, but perhaps intelligent.

The concept of 'Two Nations' is not purely one of geography. One in two (52 per cent) of the public thought of British society in terms of the haves and the have-nots, though 42 per cent were dismissive of the idea. Acceptance of the divided society was highest among people aged 30-64, the unemployed and Labour supporters. Those dismissing the idea tended to be younger,and Conservatives.

The people who saw Britain so divided were then asked to which of the two groups they felt they belonged. Slightly more (42 per cent) saw themselves among the 'haves' than placed themselves among the 'have nots' (36 per cent). Analysis by social class showed people at the top end of the scale saying they were 'haves', while those at the bottom of the scale said they belonged to the 'have nots'. Similarly, home-owners, the better-educated, the self-employed, Conservatives, and people living in households with a higher-than-average family income saw themselves in the top half. The disadvantaged tended to be council tenants, unemployed, live in Scotland, or live in households with below-average family incomes.

Despite this view of a divided Britain, people thought that, on balance, the differences between the classes were no more nor less than they had been in the sixties. One in three felt there were more class differences, 34 per cent thought there were less, 27 per cent saw no changes and 6 per cent were undecided. The replies followed a very similar pattern to those indicated above. People higher up the social scale, however one chose to describe them, saw class differences becoming smaller, while those towards the bottom of the scale saw the differences becoming greater.

Finally, yet another discriminator (no pun intended!) was put to the test: race or colour.

Table 8.36: Race Relations in Britain

Q. *Would you say that, in this country, the feeling between the following groups of people living in Britain are getting better, getting worse, or remaining the same?*

	Better	Worse	The same	Don't know
White people and coloured people	30	35	30	4
British and Irish	11	36	47	6
Whites and Asians	19	41	33	7
Whites and West Indians	19	36	36	9

On the general question of the feelings between white and coloured people in Britain, the optimists tended either to come from the under-20s or to be senior citizens. The 30-49 age group tended to take a slightly more pessimistic view than did the public at large.

People were then asked how acceptable coloured people were in a number of social situations.

Table 8.37: Attitudes Towards Coloured People

*Q. Would you be pleased, not mind, or not be pleased to
have a coloured person (people) as ...?*

	Pleased	Not mind	Not pleased	Don't know
Friends	17	73	7	3
Schoolfellows for your children	9	79	7	5
Fellow workers	8	83	5	4
Your employer/ principal	5	73	17	5
Your son-in-law	4	47	41	8
Your daughter-in-law	4	47	41	8
Neighbours	3	77	17	3

Direct comparisons with a similar question asked in 1964 cannot
strictly be made, due to a change in the answer scale, but some
broad conclusions over time can be drawn. In 1964, the proportions who said they would be pleased to have coloured people in
the various social situations ranged from 2 per cent to 5 per cent,
and from 3 per cent to 10 per cent in an exact repeat in 1981. The
big shift between the two studies was a significant increase in the
proportion professing they 'would not mind': up to 76 per cent in
1981. The latest study seems to suggest that overt attitudes have
continued to decline, being replaced by the soft option. However,
it must be pointed out again that the 1985 results are not strictly
comparable with the two earlier studies.

Who were the people who answered that they 'would not be
pleased' in the 1985 study? Women, more than men, would not be
pleased to have a coloured person as a son- or daughter-in-law.
There was also a generation effect, with opposition to the idea
increasing with age. Analysis by party supported also showed
Conservatives less enamoured of the idea of having their son or
daughter marry a coloured person.

Group Influence

Gallup showed people a list of a dozen groups and asked three
questions about how much these groups were influential and
respected. The results to these questions were as follows:

Table 8.38: Group Influence and Respect

Q. Which of these groups have the greatest influence on the country's future?

Q. And who do you have most respect for in shaping the country's future?

Q. And which one do you have the least respect for in shaping the country's future?

	Greatest influence	Most respect	Least respect
Prime Minister	55	17	17
Trade unions	50	5	29
Big business in the City	47	5	4
Cabinet Ministers	34	4	2
Economists	24	3	2
Newspaper proprietors	19	0	17
Royal family	18	18	2
Civil Service	18	2	1
People like yourself	17	12	1
Churches	14	4	4
Average MP	13	4	6
House of Lords	12	2	1

Men saw big business as having the greatest influence on the country's future, while women thought the Prime Minister had the most influence. Conservatives put the trade unions top of the list, followed by the Prime Minister and big business. They also put the unions at the head of the groups with the least respect, and gave the Prime Minister as the one they most respected.

People did not rate very highly the influence they had in deciding the country's future. Only 6 per cent felt they had at least quite a lot of influence, 50 per cent said not very much and 39 per cent felt they had no influence at all. Just one group reached double figures when it came to saying it had either a great deal or quite a lot of influence: one in ten of those who attended church at least once a month felt they had that degree of influence. When asked who was mainly responsible for the economic situation, three items dominated the list: first was the Conservative government (46 per cent), closely followed by the world economic situation (43 per cent), and in third place were the trade unions (33 per cent). Needless to say, analysis by party supported showed conflicting opinions. Conservatives blamed almost equally the world economic situation and the trade unions, while Labour supporters and Alliance supporters put the government at the top of their list of culprits.

Table 8.39: More Government Spending

Q. Do you think the government is spending too much, too little, or just about the right amount on:

	Too much	Too little	About right	Don't know
Armaments and defence	57	9	28	5
Unemployment	15	54	24	7
Welfare benefits	14	48	31	7
Law and order	10	50	33	7
Roads	4	61	29	6
Old age pensions	2	67	26	5
Education and schools	2	80	15	3
National Health Service	2	83	12	2

This was a slightly longer list than that used in a previous question, but the basic conclusion was the same. The government was spending too much on defence and not enough on virtually everything else.

The Political Future

Normally Gallup asks its samples which party would win the next general election, but in the TVS survey people were asked to think even further ahead and to say which party would be in power in the year 2000. One in three (35 per cent) either could not or would not hazard a guess about the future, but one in four (26 per cent) thought the Alliance would be in power. The Conservatives (with 16 per cent) and Labour (15 per cent) were poor runners-up. Even one in five Conservatives and one in ten Labour supporters saw an Alliance government in the year 2000.

People were then asked two questions about the type of government they thought Britain would have in almost 20 years' time and which one they would actually prefer. One in three (36 per cent) thought we would still have a single-party government as now. One in four, however, thought it would be a coalition of two parties, while another 19 per cent foresaw a national government made up of members of all parties — both, presumably, with the

Alliance in mind. One in three (33 per cent) preferred the current single-party government, but almost as many (31 per cent) opted for a national government and 24 per cent for a coalition.

As well as being proud to be British, the overwhelming majority (71 per cent) thought it was very likely that, given a totally free choice, they would choose to live in Britain for the next 20 years; only 11 per cent felt it was not very likely or not at all likely. Even among the normally mobile young, three in four thought it was at least fairly likely that they would remain in Britain.

Finally, people were asked their opinions about a future world war. Roughly one in five said one was possible at the present time, or around the year 2000, or some time after; but one in five also said that a world war would never happen again. Therefore two in three, somewhat pessimistically, expect World War III to occur some time in the future.

The Twilight Years

To complete this section, a number of questions were asked about retirement and old age. The first of these dealt with financial provisions made specifically for their old age. A little over one in two (53 per cent) said they had, including 63 per cent of men and 44 per cent of women. Analysis by age showed only one in ten of the 16-19 age groups as having made provisions for their old age, with the figure rising to one in three among people in their twenties and plateauing at three in five from the age of 30 upwards. Among those people who had made provisions for their old age, an occupational pension was the most popular safeguard, mentioned by 57 per cent of the group. This was followed by a personal pension (39 per cent) and life assurance (18 per cent). Despite the continual media coverage of the 'plight of the eldery', only 15 per cent of the public said that they had any particular worries or concerns about their retirement, and one-half of these were concerned with financial matters.

The idea of remarrying after retirement due to the death of one's spouse or partner held no great appeal to the general public. One in three (31 per cent) of those with a spouse or partner thought it was at least fairly likely, but 23 per cent felt it was not very likely and 33 per cent not at all likely. As the age of the person increased, the more likely they were to dismiss the idea of remarrying late in life.

When asked to estimate what value a court would place on their life after their death, 70 per cent were unable to even make a stab at an answer. Among those who did, however, the average value was put at around £110,000. Presumably people were not thinking in financial terms, along the lines of what assets they had, but in more abstract terms of what they were worth as an individual human being. Just over one in two (58 per cent) of the public said some form of financial provision had been made for their family if they died 'tomorrow', while a little over one in three (37 per cent) had made no such provision. Naturally, men were more likely than women to have made some provision, the figures for this being 69 per cent and 48 per cent respectively. When asked what sort of provision had been made, 76 per cent mentioned life assurance, followed by a will (9 per cent), a mortgage scheme (8 per cent) and a personal pension scheme (8 per cent).

Appendices

Appendix A: How Scientific Polls are Conducted

Thirty years ago, opinion polls were a novelty to the British public. Gallup was then not the household name it is today, and the results of our polls and of those of the very few competitors we had at that time were treated with some scepticism. Nowadays we are treated with respect by the press, television and radio, the government of the day, the political parties and the bulk of the general public. Election records alone (see Appendix C) are an indication that our polls are a reliable guide to public opinion, though perfect accuracy has not been reached — and, in fact, never can be. Nor is such ideal perfection necessary or even perhaps desirable when, with the passage of events over a relatively short time, the public's view may shift according to its changed perception of the topic in question. Reliability — within a few percentage points — has in the main been achieved by Gallup and its competitors, and this reliability is the result of the interplay of two key elements: professional integrity and specialist expertise.

Professional Integrity

There are a number of professional organisations in which Gallup plays its part, for we are deeply concerned with the maintenance of professional standards. Gallup is a member of AMSO (the Association of Market Survey Organisations) to which nearly all the well-known market and social research organisations belong as companies. It has a professional code of conduct, one which is too detailed to be gone into here but which is effectively designed and used for the following purposes:

(a) To protect the general public who are informed about, or affected by, the results of our researches.

(b) To protect the privacy and the interests of those members of the public who are interviewed by us or who collaborate with us in other ways. The identity and responses of anyone approached by us are without exception totally confidential, and in due time even the records are destroyed.

(c) To ensure that the interests of clients who use our services are

285

protected, and to ensure that the profession itself remains in high repute.

AMSO, an association of research companies, is of fairly recent origin. Independent of this, the British Market Research Society, a society of individual practitioners, has a very similar code of conduct; and, beyond our shores, ESOMAR (the European Society for Opinion and Marketing Research) is a worldwide association of individuals in our profession with a similar code of conduct. It is known in the industry that these codes are not by any means window-dressing but are properly policed; and, just as in other professions, it has been necessary from time to time to invoke sanctions against those very few who have offended against the code.

Over the years, we at Gallup and our other well-known competitors have been able to build up a mood of confidence in us among important people in the media. The writers can confirm that Fleet Street editors and the producers of radio and television programmes will publicise our research without misgivings, yet would look askance at opinion poll information sent to them by unknown organisations and be unwilling to use them without first checking the credentials of such companies.

Finally, it is not generally known that Gallup, like most of its competitors, does by far the majority of its work (in Gallup's case, over 90 per cent) outside the field of opinion-polling. Using a variety of sophisticated techniques, Gallup carries out commercial, social and business research which forms the bulk of its business; the opinion polls are, in fact, merely the tip of the iceberg. An important consequence of this is that no established opinion-polling company is under any real pressure to take on opinion-polling projects of any new kind merely in order to keep up the level of the company's business: though always commercially useful, they are not commercially vital. Thus, if Gallup is unable to come to terms with a potential client about the proper way to conduct an inquiry according to its professional responsibilities, it will refuse the project — and has done so.

The Questionnaire and the Questions

In conducting a survey on a particular topic, the topic itself must be treated fairly. Awkward aspects cannot be glossed over, even if — and possibly especially if — the client has a particular point of view. The structure of the questionnaire needs careful consideration. More specifically, the sequence of questions and the topics thus raised must not be of a kind that is likely to 'contaminate' the answers to subsequent questions, for example by the introduction of such negative ideas as fears or disagreeable consequences.

The questions themselves must meet a number of criteria. They must be couched as far as possible in day-to-day language so that they are easily understood by the respondent. The nature of the question must be such that the respondent can answer fairly. Thus highly technical or scientific questions are usually inadmissible (though some questions are put in to find out the degree of awareness of knowledge of the public, and this is sometimes useful). Also, the questions must be of a balanced kind. Usually, there are a number of alternative answers that can be given, and the form of the question must be such that the respondent is not induced by the way in which the question is put to favour one answer more than another. Where alternative answers are offered, these should be clear and comprehensible. Often the respondent is shown a comprehensive list of statements or possible answers on a card. Great care is taken in ordering the statements on the card, and each list is always composed in two versions, one in reverse order, to be offered to alternate respondents. This is designed to eliminate what is known as the 'order effect'.

Sometimes a question is omitted from a survey solely on the grounds that although information is needed on the point it is impossible to construct a question which meets all the above criteria. And when questions have to be put into several languages, as regularly happens when Gallup carries out Eurobarometer surveys, a great deal of checking and cross-checking takes place to ensure that these have the same meaning in different countries with varying cultural and social backgrounds.

Interviewers

It is a matter of profound satisfaction to us that, in Britain at least, trained and accredited interviewers are able to obtain the co-operation of all but a tiny majority of the general public when conducting interviews with them. At this point it should be stated that a professional interviewer never attempts to sell anything whatsoever as part of an interview. In past years the public's confidence in interviewing was abused by unscrupulous salesmen who posed as interviewers for the purpose of gaining access to them in order to try to sell them something. Fortunately, thanks to the efforts of the Market Research Society, this practice has disappeared amongst reputable selling companies, though it still crops up now and again amongst small, disreputable ones. All professionally trained interviewers have an identity card bearing both their name and that of the company they work for, and recently this card has been modified so that it now bears the authority of the Association of Market Survey Organisations and also in some cases that of the Market Research Society.

Interviewers are properly trained initially, and from time to time briefed on new topics and forms of enquiry. They can and should carry out their jobs honestly and conscientiously. But since the whole edifice of market research and of opinion-polling relies upon the information collected, it is absolutely necessary to undertake checking operations on samples of the work. This may take place by post, by telephone, or by means of a second interview in person (in the case of Gallup, 15 per cent of interviews are checked in this way). One reason for this that comes to mind is the possibility that interviewers may be cheating. Yet cheating, though it does occur from time to time, is extremely rare. The most important reason for the checking operation — which is independently monitored by inspectors of the Market Research Society — is the information this supplies to the field manager in control of interviewers on the quality and degree of exactness required when completing the questionnaire. As for the rather more fundamental issue of honesty, this, though routinely tested, is rarely found to be in question.

Sampling

The size of the sample for opinion-polling purposes may vary according to the nature of the topic, but is very frequently of the order of a thousand cases, as is almost universally the case for the surveys in this book. In a nation of more than forty million adults, it may seem incredible that a sample consisting of a mere thousand of them can ever truly reflect the opinions of the vast bulk who have not been interviewed. Yet Gallup, for instance, using fresh samples of this size every week, consistently produces reliable information on market and social research topics. In order to achieve this the method used in constructing and selecting the sample is of crucial importance.

There are various alternative ways of producing a scientifically selected sample of individuals for surveys, and they nearly all have in common the fact that they are constructed in at least two stages. The first stage, in Gallup's case, consists of the selection of a number of sampling points which are spread throughout the country in proportion to the number of population in the twelve administrative regions, and within those according to the degree of urbanisation of districts, from the metropolitan areas down to rural ones. At each sample point chosen, the methodology can vary to some extent, and ranges from choosing voters from the electoral register, via what is known as a random walk process (for instance, interviewing at every tenth address) to Gallup's well-known and established quota method. Gallup interviewers have strict quotas which means that they must obtain, in a sample of ten people, a required number of men and women of different age groups, of different social classes and in employment or otherwise. (These quotas are interrelated.) The logic behind the different methods varies, but all of them depend either directly or indirectly upon the science of probability theory. Even to begin a logical exposition of this would require a whole book and considerable mathematical knowledge. and for that reason the subject is not gone into here.

Instead, some commonsense considerations will be put forward. For instance, sampling of the type carried out by Gallup is an integral part of modern life, and occurs in mass production in the area of quality control. Regardless of whether what is being tested is the quality of drugs or the performance of light bulbs, ammunition, car components or packaged food products, they all have in common the fact that the consumer who purchases them is protected by the use of sampling techniques designed to ensure the maintenance of levels of quality and safety. Many of the tests carried out on a small sample of such products are destructive: once a test bullet has been fired, it cannot be fired again; once a light bulb has been proved to last 500 hours it is burnt out; once the food has been chemically analysed, it is not put back in the can. Because the sampling is performed in a scientific way it is possible to infer the characteristics of the untested vast bulk of the production from the tiny sample which has been tested and often rendered unusable. This is an exact analogy of the sampling that takes place in opinion polling research. It may be argued that people are not things, but with proper questionnaire construction the answers they give, even if they are opinions, are just as factual and matters of record as anything else.

A point that is often difficult to grasp is that the accuracy of a survey depends upon the size of the sample used (among other things) but *not* upon the size of the population from which the sample is drawn. A sample of a thousand interviews in Croydon will give answers of equal accuracy to that of a sample of Great

Britain, providing the proper rules of sampling procedure are observed. The fact that one population is a hundred times or more larger than the other is irrelevant. The point is scientifically correct but intuitively difficult to accept. Intuition is wrong here, however. An analogy might be a chef preparing a soup. Providing the soup was properly prepared, stirred and blended, no matter whether he is making a small portion for himself in a tiny saucepan or catering for an entire army barracks in a great cauldron, by taking a spoonful of it — using the same size spoon, incidentally — he can taste it, and his test will be equally accurate in both cases.

Over the years Gallup has performed a number of statistical tests upon its opinion poll data leading to the conclusion that the results are substantially free of bias and show the kind of accuracy that is expected of random samples of this size. As a rule, the main results of a sample of a thousand individuals can be expected to lie within a band of ±3 per cent of the true figure. This, however, is a gross oversimplification. The results for subgroups are not as accurate as this either in theory or in practice, and the results at different levels have different kinds of accuracy. A result showing 10 per cent of the population as having a certain characteristic happens for mathematical reasons to have a smaller margin of error than another result where the percentage was 50 per cent. Over and above this, it is a matter of practical observation that nearly all the data Gallup produces, for instance, some of the series of data in this book, exhibit a higher degree of consistency than these absolute outside limits predicted by statistical theory would seem to imply. It may have something to do with the actual way in which the samples are constructed, further limiting the extent to which unrepresentative subgroups of the population can be interviewed.

Fair Reporting

It is an essential requirement of the profession that reporting of its work should be fair and full. Often limitations of space, especially in newspapers and in passing references on television and radio, place a considerable burden on the fullness of the report. Yet the report should be a fair summary of the findings, and selective reporting carried out to suit a possible sponsor's case is not acceptable. In Britain, Gallup enjoys the best possible arrangement for publication of its polls in the *Daily* and *Sunday Telegraph*: the article is written by Gallup directors, not by journalists, and published as such distinctly and separately by the *Telegraph*. Elsewhere in the newspaper, journalists can and do comment freely on Gallup findings. The reader is thus left in no doubt that the findings are as reported by Gallup, and that the interpretation which the journalists may wish to put upon these findings is an interpretation. Finally, it is good practice to indicate in every survey report the sample size, the nature of the population from which the sample is taken (such as Great Britain, the European Economic Community, etc), the type of sample, the sampling methods and the dates on which the interviewing took place. This last point can be very important. A government may suddenly announce a dramatic change in policy or some other political event may occur, and it is essential to know whether the interviewing took place before or after such an event if the views of the public are to be put in their proper perspective.

Appendix B: Diary of Events 1985

January

2	A Soviet cruise missile reported to have overflown northern Norway and crashed in Finland.
5	The National Coal Board warned that 50,000 mining jobs could be lost to deteriorating pits.
7	The Soviet-American arms talks began in Geneva.
10	The NUM voted to recommend the expulsion of the Nottinghamshire branch unless they accepted the authority of the union's national executive.
11	The pound fell to a new low of $1.1185.
14	The Bank of England imposed a minimum lending rate, for the first time since 1981. The National Coal Board claimed 38 per cent of the workforce had abandoned the strike.
18	Inflation rate dropped to 4.6 per cent in December, compared with November's 4.9 per cent.
20	Ronald Reagan inaugurated for his second term as President of the United States.
22	The government proposed cuts in future public expenditure.
23	The proceedings of the House of Lords were televised for the first time.

28   Banks raised their lending rates to 14 per cent from 12 per cent.

30   Receiver appointed to take charge of funds belonging to the National Union of Mineworkers.

31   Unemployment rose to a new high of 3,340,958.

February

4   Spain opened the frontier with Gibraltar after nearly 16 years.

11   Clive Ponting, an assistant secretary in the Ministry of Defence, was aquitted of breaching the Official Secrets Act by leaking documents about the sinking of the Argentine ship *General Belgrano*.

23   Nottinghamshire miners voted in favour of ending the overtime ban.

25   Pound fell to a new low of $1.0575.

26   2,000 schools closed in the teachers' strike.

March

3   A delegate conference of the National Union of Mineworkers voted to abandon the strike.

10   Konstantin Chernenko, President of the Soviet Union, died. Mikhail Gorbachev announced as his successor the next day.

11   National Health Service prescription charges to go up on 1 April.

12   The US–Soviet arms control negotiations began in Geneva.

19   The Chancellor of the Exchequer, Nigel Lawson, delivered his Budget.

20   High street banks cut their base lending rates as mortgage rates rose.

21   People killed and wounded in South Africa on the 25th anniversary of the Sharpeville massacre.

22   Inflation rate rose to 5.4 per cent.

27   The pound rose to $1.23.

29   Terms were agreed for admitting Spain and Portugal to the European Economic Community in 1986.

April

4   The Prime Minister began an 11-day tour of Asia.

7   The Soviet leader agreed to a summit later in the year with President Reagan.

15   The pound reached $1.2757.

18   Two Russians ordered to leave Britain for spying. Later, three other Russians were deported and three Britons expelled from Russia.

19   Inflation rose to 6.1 per cent in mid-March.

21   The National Union of Teachers called out members to support its pay claim.

May

1   President Reagan banned all trade with Nicaragua.

2   Unemployment rose to a new record for April of 3,177,200. Economic summit opened in Bonn.

3   The Social Democratic Party made substantial gains in the county council elections.

7   The government announced the intention to privatise British Gas.

14   The Nottinghamshire miners voted overwhelmingly to secede from the National Union of Mineworkers.

17   Inflation rose to 6.9 per cent, the highest for two years.

25   More than £50 million of public money was lost in the collapse of Lear Fan.

29   Thirty-eight people killed and hundreds injured in Brussels football stadium disaster.

June

3   The Secretary of State for Social Services, Normal Fowler, announced an overhaul of the Welfare State.

5   The government announced that Stansted would be developed as London's third major airport.

6   Football's governing body, FIFA, banned all English club football worldwide.

12   Spain and Portugal signed treaties of accession to the European Economic Community.

14   Gunmen seized an airliner on a scheduled flight from Athens to Rome.

15   Inflation rose to 7 per cent in May, the highest for two-and-a-half years.

23   An airliner *en route* from Toronto to Bombay blew up off
         the coast of Ireland. Two killed in bomb explosion in
         Japanese airport.

July
4   The Liberal–SDP candidate captured Brecon and Radnor
         in a by-election.
5   The pound rose to $1.32.
6   Nottinghamshire miners' leaders voted to leave the NUM
         and form their own union.
8   The United Kingdom lifted its ban on Argentine imports.
10   Explosions sank the Greenpeace flagship, *Rainbow
         Warrior*, in Auckland harbour, New Zealand.
13   Live Aid rock concert.
15   High street banks cut their base lending rates to 12 per
         cent.
17   The Government ended minimum pay rates for workers
         under 21.
29   Banks cut base lending rate to 11.5 per cent.

August
6   The Labour Party and the Trade Union Congress laid the
         foundations of a 'joint accord'.
15   Building societies announced a cut in mortgage rates to
         12.75 per cent.
22   British airliner bound for Corfu burst into flames at
         Manchester Airport.
24   A five-year-old boy accidentally shot dead by police
         during a raid.

September
2   Mrs Thatcher announced a Cabinet reshuffle.
9   President Reagan imposed a series of limited economic
         sanctions on South Africa.
10   Britain blocked joint EEC proposals to increase trade and
         cultural sanctions against South Africa.
11   The European Parliament ratified terms of EEC
         membership for Spain and Portugal.
12   Soviets ordered to leave within three weeks on spying
         allegations.
13   The USA successfully tested a weapon designed to destroy

space satellites. Inflation in August rose by 6.2 per cent.
14   British Embassy staff ordered to leave Moscow.
16   More Soviets ordered to leave London.
17   Mrs Thatcher arrived in Cairo for four day visit to Middle East.
18   More Britons expelled from Moscow.
19   Thousands killed in earthquake in Mexico City.
28   Riots in Brixton,

October
1   Violence broke out in Toxteth and Peckham.
2   Mikhail Gorbachev arrived in Paris for his first official visit to the West as Soviet leader. Rock Hudson died of the disease AIDS.
3   Unemployment rose to 3,346,198 in September.
6   Riots in Tottenham.
7   Palestinian guerrillas hijack the Italian cruise ship *Achille Lauro.*
11   Inflation in September down to 5.9 per cent.
17   British law lords ruled that doctors might prescribe the contraceptive pill to girls under 16 without their parents' consent.
18   Miners in Nottinghamshire and South Derbyshire and colliery workers in County Durham voted to amalgamate under the newly-formed Union of Democratic Mineworkers.
20   The leaders of the Commonwealth nations agreed measures to be taken against South Africa.
31   Unemployment fell to 3,276,821 in October.

November
6   Queen's speech to the new session of Parliament. Governments of 18 west European countries agreed to fund research projects under Eureka scheme.
12   Chancellor of the Exchequer, Nigel Lawson, forecast inflation below 4 per cent by the end of 1986 in his autumn financial statement.
14   High court lifted sequestration order on National Union of Mineworkers after written apologies.
15   British and Irish governments signed Anglo–Irish agreement giving the Republic the right to formal

participation in Ulster affairs. Inflation fell to 5.4 per cent in October.

20   MPs voted against televising House of Commons procedures.

21   Conclusion of Geneva summit conference between President Reagan and General Secretary Gorbachev.
Irish Parliament approved the British–Irish accord.

25   FT Index reached new closing record of 1146.9.

27   British–Irish accord approved by House of Commons. Democratic Unionist Party MPs resigned to fight by-elections in Ulster.

December

1   Archbishop of Canterbury's commission on inner cities published.

5   British Government confirmed withdrawal from UNESCO.
Labour won Tyne Bridge by-election.
November unemployment down to 3.165 million.

6   Britain signed an agreement to participate in 'Star Wars' research.

9   House of Commons voted in favour of fixed Channel link.

17   The 15 Unionist MPs in Northern Ireland resigned their seats in protest at the Anglo-Irish agreement.

27   19 people killed at Rome and Vienna airports by gunmen.

Appendix C: Gallup's Election Record 1945–1983

		Share of Votes				
Year **General elections**		**Conser-** **vative**	**Labour**	**Liberal**	**Others**	**Mean** **Error(1)**
1945	Actual	39.3	48.0	9.2	2.7	
	Gallup (2)	+ 1.7	− 1.8	+ 1.3	− 1.2	1.5
1950	Actual	43.0	46.8	9.3	0.9	
	Gallup	+ 0.5	− 1.8	+ 1.2	+ 0.1	0.9
1951	Actual	47.8	49.3	2.6	0.3	
	Gallup	+ 1.7	− 2.3	+ 0.4	+ 0.2	1.2
1955	Actual	49.3	47.3	2.8	0.6	
	Gallup	+ 1.7	+ 0.2	− 1.3	− 0.6	1.0
1959	Actual	48.8	44.6	6.0	0.6	
	Gallup	+ 0.7	+ 0.4	− 0.5	− 0.6	0.6
1964	Actual	42.9	44.8	11.4	0.9	
	Gallup	+ 1.6	+ 1.7	− 2.9	− 0.4	1.9
1966	Actual	41.5	48.8	8.6	1.1	
	Gallup	− 1.5	+ 2.2	− 0.6	− 0.1	1.1
1970	Actual	46.2	43.8	7.6	2.4	
	Gallup	− 4.2	+ 5.2	− 0.1	− 0.9	2.8
1974 (Feb)	Actual	38.1	37.2	19.3	5.4	
	Gallup	+ 1.4	+ 0.3	+ 1.2	− 2.9	1.5
1974 (Oct)	Actual	36.6	40.2	18.8	4.4	
	Gallup	− 0.6	+ 1.3	+ 0.2	− 0.9	0.8
1979	Actual	45.0	37.8	14.2	3.0	
	Gallup	− 2.0	+ 3.2	− 0.7	− 0.5	1.6
1983	Actual	43.5	28.3	26.0	2.2	
	Gallup	+ 2.0	− 1.8	0	− 0.2	1.0

Election for European Parliament

1979	Actual	50.6	33.0	13.1	3.3	
	Gallup	+ 0.4	+ 5.0	− 3.6	− 1.8	2.7

EEC Referendum

1975	Actual	*Turnout:* 64.5	'Yes'	67.5	
	Gallup	+ 0.5		+ 0.5	0.5

Notes: 1. The mean error is the average of the deviations of the final Gallup
Poll from the actual result for each party
2. Gallup final poll figures are given as deviation from the election results
for each party

Appendix D: Party Fortunes 1984–1985

Key to the Table:

Barometer	Column(s)	Notes
Voting intention	2 to 7	The answers to the question: 'If there were a general election tomorrow, which party would you support?', including the answers of the 'don't knows' to an additional question, 'Which would you be most inclined to vote for?' but excluding those who remain 'don't knows', even after the incliner question. Column 5 is a combination of people answering 'SDP' or 'Alliance'.
	7	The percentage of the total sample answering 'Don't know' to the incliner question, excluded in computing the figures shown in columns 2-6.
Government record	8	The percentage answering 'Approve' to the question: 'Do you approve or disapprove of the Government's record to date?'
Prime minister's popularity	9	The percentage answering 'Satisfied' to the question: 'Are you satisfied or dissatisfied with … as prime minister?'
Popularity of leader of the opposition	10	The percentage answering 'Good leader' to the question 'Do you think … is or is not proving a good leader of the … Party?'
Party expected to win	11 & 12	The percentages saying 'Conservative' (column 11) and 'Labour' (column 12) in response to the question: 'Irrespective of how you yourself would vote, who do you think will win the next general election?'

Voting Intention / Party to Win

Year & Month Col. 1	Con Col. 2	Lab Col. 3	Lib Col. 4	SDP Col. 5	Other Col. 6	Don't know Col. 7	Government record Col. 8	PM Col. 9	Opposition leader Col. 10	Con Col. 11	Lab Col. 12
1985 Dec	33	32½	8	24½	2	(10½)	34	39	47	47	24
Nov	35	34	10	19½	1½	(7½)	29	36	46	47	25
Oct	32	38	9	19		(9)	29	33	50	39	28
Sept	29	29½	11½	27½	2½	(9)	29	35	29	41	25
Aug	24	40	13	21	2	(8)	23	30	34	34	33
July	27½	38	12½	20	2	(6)	28	34	38	37	27
June	34½	34½	12	18	1	(7)	31	38	37	44	31
May	30½	34	12	21½	2	(8½)	28	36	38	46	26
April	34	37½	13	13½	2	(8½)	32	38	36	54	28
March	33	39½	10	15½	2	(8)	30	37	37	53	28
Feb	35	32	10½	21	1½	(9)	31	37	31	63	19
1985 Jan	39	33	9½	16	2½	(8)	33	40	36	65	16
1984 Dec	39½	31	10½	17	2	(8)	34	43	36	67	16
Nov	44½	30½	9	14½	1½	(8)	41	48	39	67	17
Oct	44½	32	6	15½	2	(9)	43	50	35	64	19
Sept	37	36	11	14½	1½	(9)	34	40	43	54	28
Aug	36	39	9½	13	2½	(8)	34	39	37	49	29
July	37½	38½	7½	14½	2	(7)	36	41	43	43	37
June	37½	38	7½	15½	1½	(8½)	36	41	43	49	31
May	38½	36½	8½	14½	2	(6)	37	41	42	50	30
April	41	36½	10	10½	2	(6½)	42	46	42	52	28
March	41	38½	9	10½	1	(8)	41	46	47	50	35
Feb	43	33½	11½	10	2	(6)	41	48	45	59	23
1984 Jan	41½	38	9½	10	1	(7)	42	49	43	58	22

INDEX